W9-CLM-750

BONE DEEP

Other Books

by CHARLES BOSWORTH JR.

Precious Victims (with DON W. WEBER)

Silent Witness (with DON W. WEBER)

Secret Lessons (with DON W. WEBER)

Every Mother's Nightmare

A Killer Among Us

Who Killed JonBenet Ramsey? (with DR. CYRIL WECHT)

BONE DEEP

UNTANGLING THE
BETSY FARIA
MURDER CASE

CHARLES BOSWORTH JR.
& JOEL J. SCHWARTZ

CITADEL PRESS
Kensington Publishing Corp.
www.kensingtonbooks.com

CITADEL PRESS BOOKS are published by

Kensington Publishing Corp.
119 West 40th Street
New York, NY 10018

All Kensington titles, imprints, and distributed lines are available at special quantity discounts for bulk purchases for sales promotions, premiums, fundraising, educational, or institutional use.

Special book excerpts or customized printings can also be created to fit specific needs. For details, write or phone the office of the Kensington sales manager: Kensington Publishing Corp., 119 West 40th Street, New York, NY 10018, attn: Sales Department; phone 1-800-221-2647.

CITADEL PRESS and the Citadel logo are Reg. U.S. Pat. & TM Off.

ISBN: 978-0-8065-4197-6

First Citadel hardcover printing: March 2022

10 9 8 7 6 5 4 3 2 1

Printed in the United States of America

Library of Congress Catalog Number: 2021948139

Electronic edition:

ISBN: 978-0-8065-4199-0 (e-book)

To my wife, Connie, and our sons, Christopher and Kyle,
whose constant support, encouragement, and love
always drive my best efforts.
—C.B.

To my wife, Mary Ann,
and my three children—Jonah, Gabriel, and Mattea—
without whom none of this would be possible.
—J.S.

CHAPTER ONE

Tuesday, December 27, 2011

Every Tuesday was game night. Six to nine o'clock. It had been that way for years for the dedicated group of friends who met at Michael "Mike" Corbin's house in O'Fallon, Missouri, a growing suburb on the northwestern edge of the St. Louis metropolitan area. They were brought together by their love of role-playing board games, where each player assumed the identity of a specific character and rolled the dice to move along the board and carry out fantasy missions of good versus evil. It was an engaging, thought-provoking, and fun way to spend some time with friends without spending a lot of money. Mike was not only the host, but also the official referee, who devised the missions and controlled the games for the players that included his longtime partner, Angelia Hulion, along with Brandon Sweeney, Marshall Bach, Richard May—and Russ Faria.

The Tuesday after Christmas, December 27, 2011, was still game night, but with a twist. Richard had to work and couldn't attend. The group couldn't really play their favorite Rolemaster game when a player was absent. That would be like trying to read a novel with one of the main characters omitted. Mike sent texts to everyone informing them of Richard's absence and offering the usual alternative: They could play a different game or they could watch a movie or two. After a text conversation among the players, they decided to show up at Mike's to enjoy whichever option was chosen.

Russ was going, and he and his wife, Betsy, texted each other several times that day to formalize their separate plans for the evening. Betsy had spent the night before at her mother's apartment and was going to the Siteman Cancer Center in nearby St. Peters at 1:30 p.m. for her regular chemotherapy session to battle the aggressive breast cancer that had spread to her liver. After that, she would go back to her mother's apartment for the evening. Russ planned a five-minute detour from his regular route home from game night to pick her up and take her home to Troy, twenty-five miles away. Their text conversations couldn't have been more normal for a modern couple, complete with abbreviations, typos, and careless punctuation.

> Betsy, 10:35 a.m.: U were supposed to get dog food. Tonight.
> Russ, 10:41 a.m.: Ya I will get it when I come in.
> Betsy, 10:41 a.m.: U got game tonight?
> Russ, 12:12 p.m.: Ya goin to game then will come get you. Will call when on way should not be too late
> Betsy, 12:13 p.m.: Ok great honey.

A few hours later, she texted a change in plans:

> Betsy, 3:46 p.m.: I got tp [toilet paper] and pam hupp wants to bring me home to bed. I need rest. wbc [white blood cell count] is low but got infusion [chemotherapy] anyway.
> Russ, 3:47 p.m.: So you coming home here
> Betsy, 3:48 p.m.: yes troy
> Russ, 3:49 p.m.: She is bri.ging [sic] you
> Betsy, 3:52 p.m.: Yes she offered and i accepted.
> Russ, 3:57 p.m.: Ok see you soon then
> Betsy, 3:57 p.m.: Ok great

Russ spent a normal day in his home office in the bare concrete of his unfinished basement working in information technology for Enterprise Leasing. He knocked off at five o'clock and started the twenty-five-mile trip southeast to game night in the early-evening darkness and late December cold. Betsy called his cell phone shortly after 5 p.m. to remind him that she was getting a ride home from

Pam Hupp. And she added that she had some news to share with him at home later.

"Good or bad?" Russ had asked his ill wife with a touch of trepidation.

"It's good," Betsy replied, "don't worry."

It was the last time he would speak to her.

He made one more call while driving to game night to let his mother know he wouldn't make the usual Tuesday family dinner at her house because he needed to run some errands on the way to game night.

Russ's red 2002 Chrysler PT Cruiser hadn't been running well, so he left it in the garage and took the blue 1999 Ford Explorer parked in the driveway next to the silver 2006 Nissan Maxima that Betsy had been driving lately. He backed the Explorer out of the driveway of the ranch house on the corner of Sumac Drive and Osage Avenue and two short blocks later turned east out of the small Waterbrooke Estates Subdivision onto rural Highway H. He cut quickly through a patch of rolling farmland to reach Route 47 in Troy, a busy road lined with fast-food restaurants and strips of stores and offices. He stopped at the Conoco service station to pump a few gallons into the gas-hog Explorer. After that, he made a quick turn south onto Missouri Highway 61, four divided lanes that connect the chain of small towns between Russ's house in Troy and Mike Corbin's mobile home in O'Fallon.

Russ stopped at a U-Gas station in Wentzville to buy a carton of cigarettes at the best price he had found anywhere. He stopped again at Greene's Country Store in Lake St. Louis and—as he promised Betsy—picked up a big bag of dog food for Sicily, their chestnut-brown chow/golden retriever mix. Then he made a final stop at the QuikTrip, or QT, station in O'Fallon to pick up two bottles of his favorite Brisk iced tea. And even after all of that, he still walked through Mike's front door in the Rolling Meadows mobile home park at six o'clock—right on time.

Mike had just started playing a DVD of what everyone would remember as the latest Conan the Barbarian movie—probably *Conan the Destroyer*. There were a few quick "How was your Christmas?"

exchanges among Mike, Angelia—known as Ange—Brandon, Marshall, and Russ, but everyone quickly settled in to watch the action on TV. When Conan had completed his path of destruction, Mike popped in another DVD of *The Road*, one of those postapocalyptic downers that soon bored the audience. About halfway down the road, everyone decided to call it a night. They said their good-byes and departed at nine o'clock into what was a light snow.

Hungry from skipping dinner, Russ drove only a few minutes before pulling into the drive-through at an Arby's Restaurant in Lake St. Louis to pick up two sandwiches he ate while drinking one of the bottles of iced tea on the drive home. His call to Betsy to let her know he was on his way went unanswered. That wasn't unusual; drained from chemotherapy, she could well be asleep already. He parked in the driveway, at what he calculated was close to 9:45 p.m., hoisted the bag of dog food over his right shoulder, and went in through the unlocked front door to the small foyer with the basement stairs on the left, the living room that opened off to the right, and the dining room and the kitchen beyond that. He dropped the dog food against the door into the garage on the left, peeled off his black Harley-Davidson leather jacket, and dropped it on the chair on the right at the entrance to the living room. He called for Betsy as he glanced into the living room still strewn with opened Christmas presents and cheery holiday decorations.

And his world exploded.

Betsy was sprawled in a contorted pose on the floor in front of the sofa with a pool of dark red, almost black, blood staining the beige carpeting under her head. As he ran to her, Russ screamed, "Betsy! Betsy!"

Betsy—a stocky five-four and 160 pounds—was lying on her right side, with the front of her body twisted downward until her left shoulder almost touched the floor. A pink flowered comforter was wrinkled underneath her. She wore a black T-shirt, blue workout pants, with orange-and-white stripes down the side of the legs, and green-and-white below-the-ankle socks. She was dressed as Russ remembered when he last saw her, and as he was used to seeing her when they relaxed at home or she visited family. Her arms were crossed in front of her and bent up at the elbows so that her hands were close to her face. As Russ dropped to the floor in front of her, he could see her face was covered in dark blood, which also was matted in her dark brown hair. There was a deep and gruesome gash across the inside of her upturned right forearm near her wrist. And then he saw it—the black handle of what appeared to be a kitchen steak knife protruding horribly from the left side of Betsy's neck, just below the jawline and above a grisly slash across her neck. There was dark, crusting blood everywhere around her head.

"Betsy! Betsy! No!" Russ heard himself screaming, over and over, as he collapsed flat on the floor near her blood-covered face. Her eyes were closed and he could see her tongue protruding between her lips. It hit him like a lightning bolt. She was already dead and gone. There was nothing he could do.

As he looked at the awful gash down to tendon and bone near her right wrist, his mind told him through the shock that she must have committed suicide. She had threatened it before—more than once. She was even hospitalized once after telling a police officer on a traffic stop that she wanted a gun to kill herself. And she once pulled a knife during an argument with Russ and threatened to harm herself. With the recent diagnosis of terminal cancer, the debilitating chemotherapy, and the constant struggle with depression, Russ's spinning mind told him she must have finally reached her breaking point.

He started to cradle her in his arms, but realized that touching anything—even the woman he loved—could create problems for the police when they tried to determine what happened. He forced himself up from the floor and started to dial 911 on his cell phone, but remembered that a 911 call should be made from a landline so police could trace it to an exact address. He staggered into the kitchen to use the phone on the wall. He dialed 911 as he collapsed weakly to the floor, knocking off his yellow baseball cap.

Dispatcher Tammy Vaughn answered at 9:40 p.m. and, after some quick preliminary questions—name, address, phone number—asked, "Russell, what's going on there?"

In a loud and nearly hysterical voice marked by constant, breathless sobs, Russ said, "I just got home from a friend's house and my wife killed herself! She's on the floor!"

"OK, Russell, I need you to calm down, honey. OK? . . . Take a couple of deep breaths. We're going to get someone on the way there, OK? What did she do?"

The sobs continued through a frenzied voice. "She's got a knife in her neck and she's slashed her arms!"

"OK, OK. Calm down, honey. Is she breathing at all?"

"No!"

"Russell, how long were you gone today?"

"I left around five. I just got back. She went to her mom's and her friend was bringing her home, so I don't know what time she got home."

"And you said that she had been depressed lately?"

"She's got cancer."

"Russell, where's the knife now?"

The pain and hysteria in his voice intensified again as the reality of his answer shocked him. "It's in . . . it's still in her!"

"It's lying right next to her?"

"No, it's in her neck!" The sobbing continued. "Oh, my God! Why would she do this to me? Why would she do this?"

"Russell, they are on the way, hon, OK? They'll be there shortly. Is there anybody else there in the house with you?"

Russ was screaming again. "No, no! There's nobody else here! . . . What am I going to do? . . . No, no, no, no, no, no!"

Vaughn continued to apply her training to try to calm the caller. "Russell, take a couple of deep breaths, OK? I don't need you hyperventilating, OK?"

"My God! What am I going to do?"

"What is her name?"

"Her name is Betsy."

"Betsy?"

"Yes! Oh, Betsy, no! Oh, my God, no!"

"Russell, do you think she's beyond help right now?"

His voice grew louder and he was sobbing again. "I think she's dead! Oh, God!"

"OK. Take a couple of deep breaths. If you need to, step outside, OK?"

Russ began to wail again. "No, no, no, no, no! I don't want you to go!"

At 9:49 p.m., while Russ was still on the phone with the dispatcher, Deputy Chris Hollingsworth from the Lincoln County Sheriff's Office (LCSO) let himself in the front door—the first of a legion of first responders about to descend on the house at 130 Sumac Drive. As soon as he saw Betsy's body, he knew this was not a suicide. This woman had been murdered. He told Russ he should leave the house to avoid contaminating the crime scene. He escorted the unsteady Russ to the front porch and steered him to one of the chairs.

Russ's head was spinning and he couldn't begin to believe what he had just seen. Why would Betsy commit suicide in the midst of her courageous and determined fight against cancer? He felt overwhelmed by grief, confusion, and panic. He wondered if he was going into shock as he began to shiver uncontrollably in the frigid December air in nothing but a T-shirt and jeans. Someone wrapped a white blanket around his shoulders and he instinctively pulled it close. Hollingsworth suggested he would be warmer in the patrol car and Russ eagerly agreed.

He chain-smoked cigarettes and struggled to concentrate as he tried to answer the deputy's questions. He told him about Betsy's cancer, her bouts of depression, the couple's activities that day, and how he had discovered her body. They had last spoken by phone about five o'clock when she was at her mother's apartment playing a board game. Her friend Pam Hupp was going to drive her home. Betsy said she had something good to talk to him about then.

Hollingsworth asked about the dog barking behind the house and Russ explained that it was unusual for Sicily to be chained up outside. She usually went out only for a quick potty break and then came right back in. The yard wasn't fenced, so she was on a chain when she was outside.

When sheriff's detectives Mike Merkel and Patrick Harney arrived and took a quick look through the house, they asked Russ to go with them to the sheriff's office to give them as much information as possible and to make a formal statement while the crime scene was being examined for evidence. Russ felt the pain of leaving Betsy crumpled on the living-room floor, but there was nothing he could do for her. She was beyond his help and his reach. He shivered under the blanket as the detectives drove him to the sheriff's office nearby in Troy.

Russ kept wondering how any of this could be real. Betsy could not be gone from him—not now and not like this. He had been preparing to lose her to cancer at some time in the not-too-distant future, but he couldn't accept her bloody death in their living room amid the Christmas decorations. None of it made sense. How could he be riding in a police car with detectives while Betsy lay dead at home? How could she have committed suicide now?

CHAPTER TWO

Russ Faria shivered again and pulled the blanket tighter around him as he sat in tiny Interview Room 2 at the LCSO. It was 10:30 p.m., barely an hour since he discovered the body of the woman he loved, the woman he struggled so hard to build a life with. He felt sick to his stomach and sensed he was slipping deeper into an emotional, mental, and physical morass. He looked it, too. A forty-one-year-old man, with disheveled, short black hair, a mustache and goatee, and a thick, stocky frame—at five-ten and 230 pounds—all wrapped up in a white blanket. His face was pale and his blank brown eyes closed or gazed toward some undefined spot across the room as he breathed heavily, almost panting.

He finally was able to form one coherent thought. "I'd like a cigarette," he said softly to Detective Mike Merkel, a slender, shaved-head detective dressed in a black SHERIFF windbreaker and khakis. Merkel went in search of a cigarette, leaving Russ alone. Russ didn't know it, but Merkel's frequent departures from the interview room over the upcoming hours would allow detectives to observe Russ's behavior when he was alone. A small, tubular "lipstick" camera hidden across the room transmitted a full view of Russ seated at the table to a monitor in another room.

They watched his first four minutes in the room as he repeatedly whispered, "No, no, no, no, no" and "Why? Why?" He buried his face in his hands and sobbed as he continued to say, "No, no, no, no, no." He turned to the table on his right, dropped his head onto his crossed arms, and began to cry, "Why? Why? Oh, God! Oh, God!" His cries soon turned into louder sobs and then anguished wails of "Oh, God! Oh, God! Oh, God!"

Merkel walked back in and said flatly, "Take a deep breath for me, Russ. Take a couple of deep breaths for me."

In his report later, Merkel would write: *It should be noted, Russell did not appear to have any moisture on his face or arms where he may have been crying.* That observation may have been factual—as well as the result of Russ wiping his eyes with the blanket—but it also may have marked the beginning of what would become an avalanche of official judgment against Russ Faria.

During the hours that followed, Merkel left Russ alone several times and watched his grief overwhelm him again and again. Once he leaned back in his chair as he repeated, "No, no, no, no, no," and then slammed his head backward into the wall several times. He seemed to be speaking to God, Merkel thought, as he said, "Oh, God, no! Why? God? Why did she do this?" Another time, Russ fell to his knees on the floor; leaning against the table, he seemed to pray with another refrain of "No, no, no, no."

Merkel returned with another cigarette for Russ and opened the interview by asking about the Farias' daily lives so he could get to know them better. Russ mustered all of his composure as he tried to provide accounts of his activities that day, the Farias' marital history, Betsy's physical and mental health, and their relationships with families and friends. Betsy's cancer and chemotherapy left her too ill to work for an insurance company, as she had for many years, and, in fact, had qualified her for disability payments from Social Security. She was still operating her part-time disc jockey service called PartyStarters for weddings or other special events and spent most weekdays at home making calls for the DJ service. She still played tennis, as often as she could manage to muster her energy, which was sapped by cancer and chemotherapy. When Russ finished his workday in his basement office, he and Betsy would have dinner together and usually watch movies before going to bed. They attended church services on Sundays and occasional activities during the week. Russ described the couple as "social butterflies" on the weekends, going out or visiting friends and family. They enjoyed riding Russ's Harley-Davidson motorcycle and had a few separate activities, such as tennis for Betsy and Tae Kwon Do lessons and game nights for Russ.

Merkel explained that the police always read Miranda rights to people they interviewed at the station. After listening to the quick recitation of his rights, Russ asked the next logical question: "Am I being arrested?" It was beginning to feel like he was. The police had put off his request to call his mother, but Merkel told him he was not under arrest and the extensive questioning was an effort to learn as much as possible about Betsy and Russ to assist the investigation.

Russ explained that neither of Betsy's two daughters from a previous relationship was living with them now. Her younger daughter, Mariah Day, seventeen, was living with Betsy's mother, Janet Meyer, in Lake St. Louis so she could graduate from the high school she was attending before the Farias moved to Troy almost two years ago. Betsy's older daughter, Leah Day, twenty-one, was staying with one of Betsy's three sisters, Julie Swaney, in nearby Creve Coeur, after a series of personal conflicts with Betsy and Russ, and also after arguing with Betsy's mother when Leah lived with her. The conflicts had led Betsy to take Leah's silver Nissan Maxima away from her the day after Thanksgiving. The girls' father, whom Betsy never married, lived in Florida with his wife and their children and rarely had contact with Leah and Mariah.

Betsy and Russ married in 2000 and the eleven years since then had not been perfect or easy, he admitted. Years ago, they engaged in frequent and loud arguments, but there had never been any violence. They separated a couple of times, including once for about a year. But they started attending the Morning Star United Methodist Church in Wentzville and the pastor was providing valuable counseling that was greatly improving their relationship. An occasional spat was nothing out of the ordinary for married couples. Coincidentally, Merkel attended the same church and offered to call the pastor to assist Russ.

"That would be great," Russ said, choking back more tears.

Merkel asked if Russ or Betsy had been involved with anyone

else during the separations. Russ said Betsy had seen a guy named Rich for a while, but he didn't know much more than that. He said he had not seen anyone else.

Russ said the worst challenge to their lives arrived in late 2009 when Betsy was diagnosed with breast cancer. She underwent a mastectomy and reconstructive surgery in 2010. The cancer was considered in remission by early 2011, but while Betsy and Russ were attending a family wedding in Rhode Island in October, her doctor called with news that the cancer had returned and spread to her liver. When they visited the doctor after returning from Rhode Island, he delivered the grim prognosis: The cancer was inoperable and Betsy likely had three to five years to live.

Betsy was disappointed, of course, but she said she had beaten cancer once and she would do it again. She even decided to keep their plans for a seven-day "survivor's cruise" to Belize, Honduras, and Cozumel with friends and family in November. She changed the theme to "a celebration of life." The group had a great time and Betsy got to swim with dolphins, an event she called one of the highlights of her life.

Russ said Betsy was a generally positive person, even during the last two years fighting cancer and enduring some medical problems with breast reconstruction. But she also was realistic. She told Russ she was making unspecified preparations for the future and for the care of her daughters after she was gone.

Did Betsy take much medication?

Russ said that, in addition to several cancer-related meds, she had been on the antidepressant/anxiety medication Celexa for at least five years. She had threatened to harm herself years ago, but that was before she was on an antidepressant. Betsy never used illegal drugs and drank alcohol sparingly. She had battled depression for years and could become depressed over events or situations.

How did Russ deal with stress?

"I just really don't have a whole lot of stress. . . . I find a lot of peace. I read my Bible. . . . The answers are all there. . . . I know that God takes care of everything."

Russ began his description of the day's events by explaining Betsy was undergoing chemotherapy at the Siteman Cancer Center in St. Peters, not far from her mother's apartment in Lake St. Louis. She usually spent nights before and after chemo sessions at her mother's to save gas and time on the longer commute between Siteman and the Farias' home in Troy, thirty-five miles away. Betsy had been staying at her mother's since Monday to await her chemo session Tuesday afternoon. They had planned for him to pick her up on his way home from game night, but she texted him that her friend Pam Hupp had offered to drive her home. Russ thought a family friend named Bobbi might have gone to chemo with Betsy that day. Bobbi lived in Texas and the Farias had bought her a plane ticket for Christmas so she could visit Janet and Betsy. Russ also remembered Betsy told him she had something good to talk to him about when they got home that evening and told him not to worry.

Russ listed the four stops he made on the way to game night and at Arby's on the way home, where he estimated his arrival at about 9:45 p.m. He talked about his four friends at game night and said nothing unusual had happened. As usual, they had smoked a little marijuana. But no one drank alcohol, not even a beer. He hadn't used his cell phone while he was there, but did get a call between 8 and 8:30 p.m. from an unknown number, which he didn't answer.

Merkel took the questioning to Russ's discovery of Betsy's body. Russ lay on the interview-room floor to demonstrate how close he got to Betsy; Merkel leaned down close to Russ and they agreed Russ had been ten to twelve inches from Betsy's face. He was still wearing the same clothes he had on when he found her body. Merkel asked if Russ noticed anything out of place in the master bedroom and Russ said he was never in any room except the living room and kitchen. He said one thing that would be noticeable in the bedroom, however, was the jewelry armoire he had given Betsy for Christmas; one of the front legs broke when he was moving it and he had propped it up against the wall.

Russ said he hadn't touched Betsy, but thought she had killed herself, "Because I saw her arms slashed."

"Both arms?"

"I don't know. I know I saw at least one. Her arm was slashed and it was slashed crossways and it was very deep . . . and I saw a knife . . ."

That image ripped open his heart again and he began to wail, "Oh, my God! Oh, Jesus Christ!" His face contorted and he began to cry and sob again. "The knife was in her neck . . ." His voice was strained and he was almost choking. ". . . and there, there was blood all over the floor."

Merkel told Russ to take a deep breath and a drink of water. Merkel moved his chair closer until his right knee was between Russ's knees. The cop said he was troubled by the lack of blood on Russ and his clothing. Russ drew a diagram on Merkel's legal notepad to show how he had approached Betsy's body from the front, where there was little or no blood except directly under her head and face. Merkel asked Russ to pull his shirt tight across his chest so he could examine it for blood spots. There were none.

Merkel said he could almost guarantee that he would have touched or embraced a loved one if he had found them like Betsy. Did Russ have a reason for not embracing Betsy?

"No, I don't. I saw that she was already gone. . . . She didn't look to be breathing and her tongue was half out of her mouth and there was blood everywhere on her face. And I knew I had to call 911 and I didn't know, at that point. . . . I thought she had killed herself. If she didn't, I knew if I touched something, it would disturb any kind of an investigation."

Merkel was surprised Russ was thinking about preserving the scene for police in the moments after finding his wife's bloody body.

"I don't know what was going through my head. I knew I had to call somebody to help. I knew she wasn't with us anymore. I knew I needed somebody to come and so I called the police. . . . I fell on the floor in the kitchen. I couldn't breathe. . . . I wanted somebody to come help me. . . . I didn't know what to do. I mean, my wife is laying on the floor dead, with a knife in her neck. I called the police. I didn't know if she had done it or somebody had done it. I didn't know."

Merkel took a break to go to the restroom and find another cigarette for Russ.

Russ sat quietly for the first two minutes, then stood abruptly and leaned his face toward the wall beside his chair, moaning, "No, no, no, no." He turned and paced across the room to lean his head against the other wall and repeated, "No, no, no, no!" He returned to the chair, wrapped himself in the blanket again, and sat still and silent, staring at nothing for long minutes before whispering more refrains of "No, no, no, no, no!" and "Why, why, why?"

Russ finally dropped his face onto his crossed arms on the table and began to ask God, "Why, why, why? Why did you take her from me?" He pounded his fist on the table. "No, no, no, no, no! This has got to be a bad dream! No, no, no, no!"

Merkel returned after a seemingly eternal thirty minutes and said the police were trying to round up more cigarettes. He said Russ couldn't go home yet because the police were still examining the house. And then he asked, "What can I do for you? I know it's probably an unfair question to ask you right now."

Russ's face clouded over again and he began to sob. "I want my family . . . my girls, my mom. I want my family. I want my baby back!"

Merkel said softly, "I know you do, Russ" as Russ began to cry loudly and covered his face with the blanket.

"Oh, God! I don't know what to do!"

"I think you're the only one who can help us with this right now. Although it's limited, I think you have the most knowledge about the last few hours of her life, as much as I hate to put it that way. The truth being what it is, it's between you and Pam, right?"

If Merkel meant to suggest Russ and Pam Hupp as a limited list of possible killers, Russ didn't catch it. He thought Merkel was talking about the people who knew the most about Betsy's final hours.

"Yeah," he said, "and there's her mom and Bobbi. She was over there playing a game. I should have gone over there and played a game with them."

Merkel nodded. "There's probably a thousand what-ifs. I can't even imagine."

CHAPTER THREE

Almost five and a half hours of interrogation by Detective Merkel were essentially replayed when Detectives Ray Floyd of the Troy Police Department and Keith Rider of the Chesterfield Police Department took over the questioning at 3:52 a.m. They introduced themselves as investigators with the Major Case Squad (MCS) of Greater St. Louis (a regional police organization that assists local police with resources and manpower) and apologized for making Russ start all over.

The questions drew some new details from the same story Russ had told Merkel. Russ and Betsy had not had any recent disagreements or arguments and, in fact, had enjoyed a great Christmas holiday. Asked if Betsy had suffered any injuries or wounds recently, Russ said he had seen Betsy on Sunday night when they had sex—"been intimate," he said discreetly to the detectives—and didn't notice anything new beyond the existing scars from her mastectomy and breast reconstruction.

Floyd asked about the last person known to see Betsy alive. "What do you know about Pam, her friend? Is there anything that would be hinky about her?"

"No, no," Russ said thoughtfully as he shook his head.

"How long have they been friends?"

"Several years. Pam came up a week or two ago to our house and they had lunch together."

He thought Pam and Betsy had met for lunch to discuss forming a nonprofit organization to collect money for people with health issues. The women had become friends when they worked for a State Farm Insurance agent years ago. Russ had met Pam's husband twice, but didn't know him well and couldn't remember his name. The Farias and the Hupps never socialized.

Detective Rider asked if Betsy had been making any plans for her inevitable death.

"No, I mean, we have life insurance. But we've always had life insurance. It's not like she got more life insurance or anything like that. She hadn't done anything differently than she normally does."

Russ said again he thought she killed herself and had been dead for some time when he found her. He didn't want to think she would kill herself, but there had been some frightening incidents in the past. Russ recounted how Betsy once pulled a knife, threatened to harm herself, and accidentally cut Russ's arm as he was taking it away from her.

What would Russ think, Floyd asked, if Betsy's death was not a suicide?

That would mean someone broke into the house and killed her, Russ said, but he had no idea who would have done such a thing. They had nothing to steal, they owed no one money and no one owed them money, and neither of them had problems with anyone.

Floyd didn't think the way Betsy died fit the pattern of a suicide.

Russ agreed, but said, again, that everyone who knew Betsy loved her. No one would want to kill her.

Asked about a will or life insurance, Russ said there was no will, but there were insurance policies totaling $300,000 or more, all naming him as primary beneficiary. There was a $50,000 policy on Betsy through his job, and there were two policies Betsy had taken out years ago for $100,000 and $150,000.

At 5:30 a.m.—after seven excruciating hours of questioning—Floyd asked Russ to write and sign a statement of his activities the night before. On an official form for the sheriff's office, Russ printed a twenty-three-line, succinct, and sparse account of Betsy's trip to chemotherapy, his hours at game night, and his discovery of her body.

Floyd asked, "Why do you think Betsy would choose this time and this day to kill herself?"

Russ choked up and began to sob. "'Cause she knew I wouldn't be home until later and she would have some time by herself."

Was there anyone who would want to hurt Betsy?

"No, everybody loved Betsy." His voice was barely above a whisper. "She was a positive soul. She always brought smiles to people. She made me smile all the time. She made me so proud. I was happy to have her in my life."

"No issues between you and Betsy right now?"

"No, we had a good weekend." Russ detailed holiday activities with both of their families on Christmas Eve, Christmas Day, and the day after Christmas. "We had a good time. She didn't act like anything was bothering her. She was really happy and we played games and . . ." His voice softened and trailed off.

"What do you think should happen to somebody if they killed Betsy?"

"If they killed Betsy, they should be put away for a very long time," Russ said with a sigh.

As the interview continued to 8:30 a.m., Floyd asked for a DNA sample. Russ agreed and Detective Merkel swirled a cotton swab inside Russ's mouth. At 9:49 a.m., Russ agreed to Floyd's request for an evidence officer to take swabs of his hands and feet.

Russ broke into more spasms of sobs and tears after the technician left and he was alone once again. He sighed heavily and repeatedly as he covered his face with his right hand or ran his hand through his hair. He was exhausted and drained. He had asked a couple of times if he could call his mother, but the detectives said he could do that later. He hadn't talked to his family or anyone but the police. He couldn't identify any feeling in his mind or body that wasn't grief and confusion and a desperate desire for this to be over.

He had no idea how much more lay ahead.

CHAPTER FOUR

Betsy Faria's death was not a suicide.

The flat statement by Detective Ray Floyd sent Russ Faria's mind into another spin of confusion. Floyd returned to Interview Room 2 at 11:20 a.m. Wednesday—almost thirteen hours after depositing Russ there—to tell him the police had concluded that Betsy did not commit suicide. Russ realized that left only one alternative: Someone murdered his wife in their home and escaped unseen. That seemed to make less sense to his fogged mind than if she committed suicide.

Floyd's next step was disturbing. He advised Russ of his Miranda rights and asked him to initial a form acknowledging he had received them and to sign a form certifying he had waived his rights. Russ did as he was asked as Floyd explained that Russ was not under arrest and was free to leave anytime. Russ felt anything but free to leave. He was feeling increasingly under suspicion in Betsy's death. Through the fog, he heard himself saying he would do anything he could to help, especially now that the police were looking for someone who murdered Betsy.

The detectives began a new series of questions. Could Betsy have had a boyfriend she was seeing on the side? No. Had Betsy been married to anyone before Russ? Yes, she had been married to Ron Carter and still maintained a friendship with him. The two men had gotten past some tension when Russ and Betsy first got together after she divorced Ron. Since then, Ron had helped Betsy with some repairs around the house. But Russ was sure Betsy was no longer attracted to Ron, and he had accepted that their marriage was over.

Floyd said he had learned the news Betsy intended to share with Russ on Tuesday night was a plan for them to move with Leah and Mariah into the first floor of her mother's former house in Lake St. Louis, while her mother and her friend Bobbi lived upstairs. The Farias would then rent out their house in Troy. Russ said he would have wanted to think about that and discuss it with everyone. He would have had to be sure that Leah and Mariah understood they had to live by the rules set by him and Betsy.

What had Russ been wearing when he was home Tuesday before he left for game night?

He had worn the same orange RHODE ISLAND T-shirt he still had on, with either a pair of black shorts with a red stripe or blue sweatpants with a white stripe; he couldn't remember which. And he would have been wearing the brown slippers he always wore when he worked in his basement office.

Then Rider asked another surprising question: Was Russ willing to take a polygraph test to prove he was "just the poor husband who had to come home and find this?"

Russ didn't hesitate. "Yeah, I mean, I've got nothing to hide. Like I said, I'm an honest person."

Floyd asked if anyone else would stand to inherit money if Betsy died.

"No, the only way they would get money with her being gone is if I was gone, too, because everybody knows that everything is in my name."

"There's been no discussion between you and Betsy and the children or her mom that some of the insurance would be shared with them upon . . . ?"

"No. I mean, she's said that, if she was to go, she would like me to give her mom some money, you know, to help her mom out. But, you know, that was always the understanding anyway."

"Are you OK with that?" Rider asked.

"Yeah. I mean, everybody kind of pitches in and helps out with her mom because she's up in years, and since she got divorced last year, she's a little bit more needy than she has been in the past. . . . I do a lot of helping out around her apartment when she needs something fixed."

Floyd said Betsy's mom seemed to think a lot of Russ and had expressed her concern for him when detectives talked to her. Russ put his right hand over his eyes and his voice choked. "She's like a mom to me, too." He continued to sob as Floyd added that Leah and Mariah had been to the police station to ask about their "dad."

Russ sobbed again as he asked how Leah and Mariah were doing.

"They're taking it as well as could be expected two days, three days after Christmas," Floyd said. "But that's why it's extremely crucial if you have any idea of where this may have come out of, anybody that maybe you could point us in the right direction so we could get on that as well. We have about fifteen guys assigned to look into this as much as we can. It's very, very important."

Rider added, "Not only have you lost your wife, those two girls have lost their mom. We can't leave any stone unturned. . . . If there's something you're holding in for pride, just let it out now, 'cause we need to know so we can get justice for you and the girls."

"No. We've got no problems with anybody. We've been really good."

Floyd asked if Betsy had made any changes to her life insurance policies or taken out new policies. "Not that I know of," Russ said.

Russ wasn't picking up on it yet, but the tone of the detectives' questions was beginning to change—and not in his favor.

CHAPTER FIVE

Elizabeth Kay Faria was stabbed so many times that the pathologist conducting her autopsy told the police he would need more time to calculate an accurate number.

Assigned to observe the autopsy at 1 p.m., Wednesday, while other detectives interrogated Russ Faria, Detective Mike Merkel asked if the number could exceed twenty-five wounds.

The pathologist nodded and said simply, "Yes."

Dr. Kamal D. Sabharwal, a forensic pathologist with the St. Louis County Medical Examiner's Office, said the number and nature of the injuries made it impossible to establish a single cause of death or a time of death. The medical examiner (ME) gave Merkel a list of the general locations of the wounds—a shocking recitation of stab wounds and slashes to the neck, face, head, arms, shoulders, chest, back, and abdomen.

Merkel rushed his report to Detectives Ray Floyd and Keith Rider: Betsy Faria was stabbed twenty-five times—and counting.

That sordid information, added to the polygraph test under way with Russ at that moment, was about to dramatically alter the tone of the Betsy Faria murder investigation and the interrogation of her husband.

By 1:55 p.m., Wednesday, the police had fed Russ lunch from McDonald's—he wasn't hungry, but he ate anyway—and had driven him to the Lake St. Louis police station, where Detective Gary

McIntyre was waiting to administer the polygraph. McIntyre read the Miranda rights to Russ for a third time and asked him to sign forms acknowledging that and confirming the polygraph was voluntary. McIntyre put a cord around Russ's chest, a blood-pressure band around his arm, and a pressure clamp on his finger—all attached to the laptop in front of the detective. McIntyre asked Russ four direct, simple questions that required a yes-or-no answer.

"Regarding whether or not you killed Betsy Faria, do you intend to tell me the truth?"

"Yes."

"Did you kill Betsy Faria?"

"No."

"Did you kill Betsy Faria with a knife?"

"No."

"Do you know for sure who killed Betsy Faria?"

"No."

And almost that quickly, the lie detector test was over.

McIntyre led Russ into another small interview room at 3:55 p.m., where they were joined by Floyd and Rider. Russ sat in a corner with a wall to his left and a small table to his right. Floyd sat almost knee to knee with Russ, while McIntyre pulled up a chair at the side of the table and Rider sat at the far end.

McIntyre opened by saying, "All right. How do you think you did?"

"I *had* to have passed," Russ said emphatically.

"You had to have passed. OK. Well, remember when I was talking to you before the polygraph examination and I said in order for you to pass this test, you're going to have to be one hundred percent honest with me?"

"Yes."

"You were not one hundred percent honest with me. I do this for a living. You are not one hundred percent honest with me."

Russ was shocked. His voice turned plaintive, but exasperated. "I was. I was honest. I mean . . ."

As he would for the rest of the interrogation, Russ sat with his upturned hands extended in front of him and punctuated his comments with emphatic gestures.

"OK. Understand, like I said, I do this for a living," McIntyre said. "And this is how all the interviews start out. OK. 'You were not honest.' 'Yes, I was honest.' 'You were not honest.' 'Yes, I was honest.' And by the time it's all said and done, we both sit here, you know, for three hours and the truth comes out. You feel better. You get this huge weight lifted off your shoulders."

Russ didn't acknowledge this invitation to confess to something he *hadn't* done. "I did not—"

McIntyre interrupted. "I don't want to go that route. . . . I don't want to drag this thing out forever. OK? The fact of the matter is . . . is . . ." McIntyre spoke without any emotion. ". . . you stabbed Betsy."

Russ was beyond horrified. McIntyre had just accused him—bluntly, unemotionally, officially—of killing his wife. One of the police officers he assumed was there to help him in a time of trouble—as all kids are taught by their parents—had just announced he believed Russ was a cold-blooded killer. His mind began racing. What could he have said or done in the last eighteen hours that made the police believe he had been lying to them and, worse than that, was capable of murdering Betsy? He tried to keep his voice under control as he answered emphatically while shaking his head.

"No, I did not. I wasn't even there."

"You can be in denial with yourself," McIntyre continued, "but this is somebody looking from the outside, OK? And looking at the evidence and looking at the facts . . ."

Russ shot back with what was the most important fact of all. "I wasn't even there."

"Russ, you were there."

"No," Russ's voice was rising with a new air of urgency in the face of these more insistent accusations. "No! I found her like that when I came home!"

Russ realized McIntyre had concluded that Russ failed the polygraph test. How could that be? His answers were the absolute and simple truth. He wouldn't find out for some time that McIntyre had written in his report: *Upon careful examination of R. Faria's charted responses throughout the test series, it is this examiner's opinion; there were significant, consistent physiological responses indicative of deception when the above relevant questions were answered by R. Faria.*

McIntyre invoked a standard technique from the interrogator's handbook: We can help you—if you confess now.

"Let me explain something to you. OK? We're dealing with one of two people right here. We're dealing with somebody who lost it, made a mistake, and is remorseful—or we're dealing with some kind of fucking monster. You tell us who we're dealing with. You tell us who you would rather a jury see. OK? One of two people."

Russ was shaking his head. "It's . . ."

"Hey, hey, Russ, it's done. It's done. It's over."

Russ sighed and shook his head again and said as calmly as he could, "I did not do it."

"We're past that. There's too much here, Russ. . . . You're a churchgoing man, correct? Well, God is in this room with us right now."

Russ could only hope McIntyre was right. "And God knows that I did not do this. I could not do this. I found her like that when I got home."

McIntyre turned up the pressure in a soft voice that belied his new accusation. "Russ, you were fucking pissed."

Russ shook his head again. "No! I've not been 'fucking pissed' in a long time."

Floyd stepped in. "Something happened when you got home, Russ. . . . A lot of things have happened since we last talked to you. There's been a lot more physical evidence recovered from the scene, as well as from her body. And this is—"

Why weren't these guys listening? Russ interrupted, "Nothing happened when I got home."

Floyd wasn't buying it. Something happened that led him to kill Betsy in a rage.

Russ repeated again and again that nothing happened and he found Betsy dead when he got home.

"There's already been statements gathered that, you know, your relationship with your wife—not that anybody's perfect—but you guys were in a little bit of a rocky relationship," Floyd said. "This is coming from a friend that she's confided in. This is coming from some of her family members that she's confided in. And they're concerned about you, Russ."

What friend or family member would say something like that to the police? Russ sighed again. "I walked in the door and found her."

"There is no way that took place. There is absolutely no way that took place. A medical examiner has already ruled that out. You did not find her there. She was alive when you got home. She was dead by the time the police got there. What I need to know is what happened. . . . Russ, this is not suicide. This isn't a random killing. This is a crime of passion."

Russ's voice remained emphatic but desperate. "I did not do this. I'm telling you, I did not do this. . . . She was dead when I got home."

"Why did you assume suicide?"

"Because I saw slashes on her arms."

Floyd's voice was flat but disbelieving. "Slashes on her arms. And that was your only—that's why you assumed suicide? A knife protruding out of her neck didn't make you think that it may be something else? That story is not correct and you know it."

McIntyre asked, "Who did it, Russ?"

"I don't know!"

McIntyre spat out an exasperated "Bullshit!"

"I did not do this."

"Well, look, quit playing dumb. All right? This is what we do. The evidence is there. . . . Is it a crime of passion, or are you a monster? This happened. If you didn't do it, then tell me who did."

"I don't know who did this. I did not do this. I found this when I got home from my friend's house. . . . I have no reason to lie."

"You have a *lot* of reason to lie," McIntyre huffed indignantly. "That's probably one of the dumbest statements I've heard in a long time. 'I have no reason to lie.' You need to get this off your shoulders, Russ."

Floyd chimed in: "I wanted to believe you, but there's absolutely no way that I can believe you after talking to those detectives and those crime scene people that processed the scene that relayed the trace evidence. . . . She's already had an autopsy.

There's too much stuff pointing right at you. . . . It was a spur-of-the-moment thing, and I just need you to tell me . . . what sparked the incident happening?"

"I did not do this. I can't tell you what sparked it because I wasn't there when it happened." Russ's voice was louder and more emphatic and his hand gestures were more dramatic.

"You only have one person with a motive—money. It's the oldest motive in the world and I would hate . . ."

Money? That thought had not found its way through the fog in Russ's head until that moment. Betsy's insurance money? That was insane. "I don't have any need for money," he said slowly.

"Listen to me. I would hate to think that's your motive. I don't think it's your motive. I think there was a fight, an argument, or something like that."

Russ shook his head again in frustration. "There was no argument."

"Well, how many times did we practice putting a pillow over her face and suffocating her and telling her this is what it would feel like to die? How many times?"

Russ was flabbergasted and his brow furrowed. Putting a pillow over her face? Where did such an absurd allegation come from?

"I never did that!"

"Never? So her friends are just making this up? This is a story I'm just making up, I should say? You never put a pillow over her face and said . . ."

Russ could taste a new anger in his mouth. What "friends" could possibly be telling an outrageous and patently false story like that—and why?

"No!"

" '. . . you know, this is what it would feel like to die'?"

This was insane. "No!"

"Then why would they make that up? Why would her friends tell the police that you had done that and she was scared of you?"

Russ was set back again. "She had no reason to be scared of me. She's never been scared of me."

Floyd played the God card again. "And somebody well greater than both of us knows this."

"No! I had nothing . . ."

"You will . . ."

". . . to do with this."

". . . answer to that. You will answer to that as well. And that's why you need to get your conscience clean and come clean with what . . ."

"My conscience is clean. I had nothing to do with this—nothing at all!"

Rider said, "Russ, you've got two girls that just lost their mother. You've got a mom that just lost their daughter."

Russ's frustration was growing and his voice was rising. "And I'm being accused of something that I did not do."

McIntyre was more emphatic about Russ failing the polygraph. "One hundred percent deception. It wasn't eighty-five. One hundred percent deception."

Russ wondered if the police had talked to Mike Corbin and his game-night friends. They could prove he was twenty-five miles away when Betsy was killed. "There is no way I could have been there."

"How is there no way you could have been there? You left at nine o'clock. You got home at nine thirty, nine thirty-five. The call comes in around nine forty-five. That's why I need to know what happened in that ten-to-fifteen-minute time frame. . . . She was alive and healthy when you got home."

And there it was—the official conclusion by the police that Russ had managed to slaughter his wife and call 911 in ten or fifteen minutes after driving home from a relaxed evening watching movies with his friends twenty-five miles away. Russ couldn't even absorb the enormity of the errors in that accusation.

CHAPTER SIX

After accusing him of murdering his wife, Detective Ray Floyd didn't give Russ Faria time to catch his breath before the cop dropped the big lie—or in the best light, the big mistake—on him. Delivering what would become a foundation of the case against Russ, Floyd said, "She hadn't been dead hardly at all when the police got there—less than an hour."

Russ was shocked again. He was no forensic expert, but his brief moments with Betsy's body told him she had to have been dead longer than that.

"I was not there when that happened. I found her like that."

"You need to be honest for her family. You need to be honest for the daughters that you say are yours. . . . You need to be honest for the mother-in-law that you love. You need to be honest for your wife."

That stung and Russ suppressed a surge of anger. "I am being honest! . . . I am telling you what happened! I walked in the door. I put the dog food down. I took my jacket off and I saw my wife on the floor. That is exactly what happened."

"And I wanted to believe you all day . . . and I did believe you all day, until this other information came in and I realized you were lying to me."

Russ fought back. "I don't know what information you have that contradicts what I'm saying, but that is exactly what happened. That is exactly what happened when I walked in the door . . ." Russ was gesturing emphatically with his hands. "That . . . is . . . what . . . happened!"

Rider asked, "How many times have you played this story in your head to make sure you get it right? It's like a well-oiled machine. You're like a parrot regurgitating the same story the whole time."

"No! Because it's what happened!"

Floyd again: "I don't think you're a bad person, but I think something triggered and something happened and you lost control. . . . I was wondering if it was something to deal with the fact that she wanted everybody to move into this house . . ."

"She never mentioned that to me. . . . I never got a chance to hear it. The first time I heard about it was when you told me. . . . I don't know why you keep saying I'm not telling the truth."

"Because the crime scene has been cleaned," Floyd said as he shifted in his chair, leaned forward, raised his voice, and began speaking faster. "There's no reason for someone to break into your house and clean the crime scene. There's evidence the crime scene has been cleaned. There's blood . . . it's easily detected on some of your clothes at your house. That's why I'm telling you, you're lying. . . . The fact of the matter is, it's a sloppy crime scene. There's blood on your clothes, in your residence, in your bedroom."

"I didn't even go to my bedroom."

"How did the blood get on your clothes and also on your shoes in your bedroom, Russ? Somebody break into your house and put your shoes on . . . to kill your wife?"

How could there be blood on clothes and shoes he wasn't wearing in a room he never entered? "I have no idea. This is what I was wearing today . . .".

Russ continued to fence with the detectives, insisting repeatedly that he was wearing the same clothes he put on before he left the house at five o'clock, Tuesday. He had no idea how Betsy's blood got on clothing in the bedroom he never entered.

The cops were more insistent that Russ was constructing a ridiculous scenario that someone came into his house, put on his clothes, killed Betsy, changed out of his blood-spattered clothes, and left them on the floor in his bedroom. Their version was that Russ came home, changed clothes, killed Betsy, and then changed back into the clothes he was wearing now.

Floyd said, "You're in a bad spot, brother, and you need to be honest. . . . You come home. You got into a fight, an argument with your wife. You pulled a knife from your kitchen and stabbed her multiple times and killed her. . . . We know when it was done—who did it. . . . The only part of this whole puzzle that we haven't been able to put in place is the 'why' it happened. I don't want to believe you killed her for money. I don't want to believe that . . ."

"I did not kill my wife."

". . . because she was dying of cancer already. You could have waited, if you were in it for the money. . . . Time was on your side. All you had to do was wait."

Russ tried to ignore the disgusting implication that he was circling like a vulture waiting to collect her life insurance after her death from cancer or, even worse, that the money was a motive for killing her.

"I did not kill my wife! How many times do I have to say that?"

"Every speck of evidence secured at that residence points in one direction, and one direction only—you." With a pen in his right hand, Floyd jabbed his index finger toward Russ's chest. "That's it. It doesn't go anywhere else except straight ahead."

"I did not do it! I did not kill my wife. I don't care what the evidence says! I did not do this!"

Floyd began to stack lies upon lies—or bogus assumptions upon bogus assumptions.

"Who would have such a master plan that they would come into your house minutes before you got home . . ." A lie about the timing.

". . . put your clothes on so the blood evidence would be on your clothes . . ." A lie about blood on his clothes.

". . . and kill your wife, and then put your clothes back in your room . . ." The third lie in the same sentence.

". . . to be found by police? Who would have such a master, devious plan to be able to pull that off? . . . That's some serious planning. This is a big conspiracy. O.J.—'If the glove doesn't fit, you must acquit' . . . that's some major planning right there."

Russ was getting so numb to the accusations that even comparing him to O.J. Simpson failed to push him into an angry outburst.

"I did not do this. I don't understand what's going on here."

"What's going on is that your wife is dead."

Russ sucked in his breath and let some of the anger boiling inside escape through his voice. "I know that!"

"She's been murdered. She was stabbed multiple times with a knife from your residence, and there's only one person that was culpable, that had the means and the motive to do it. And like I said, the puzzle at this point is fairly easy. We're just trying to figure out the 'why' . . . and the 'why' could be the difference. . . . It could be a difference between murder first degree and a manslaughter—murder second degree. I mean, the 'why' is a big part of what is going on here."

The insanity just didn't end. "I did not do this. I had no motive to do this. I love my wife."

Rider asked if Russ would pray for forgiveness. Russ shot back that he did not need to seek forgiveness because God knew that he did not kill his wife.

Rider stayed with the religious theme. "God knows the truth. . . . He was looking down when all of this went down. . . . She died a horrendous death. . . . She's not coming back. . . . She's in Heaven now."

"I did not do this. I'm not capable of this." Russ pounded his left hand onto his knee with each word to emphasize his claim of innocence. "I don't know who did it."

McIntyre said, "Russ, there's too much evidence. It's going to bury you. How many times do we have to tell you? Man, help yourself out here. . . . It's overwhelming. . . . Russ, listen to me. Quit shaking your head no. This happened. It absolutely did happen."

Russ looked at the men across from him and told them another truth. "I know you *think* it did . . . and everybody here thinks it did."

"And all evidence says that it did."

McIntyre said, "This is not a tough case on our part. This isn't tough. It's done. It's a done deal. We're trying to give you the opportunity to tell us why. Something happened. . . . Were you high? Were you on drugs? . . . You smoked some weed last night. Right? . . . Did you go into a blackout and then, all of a sudden, there she was, dead? Is that . . ."

"No, no! I did not black out. I know I came in with the dog food and I took off my jacket and there she was. That is what happened . . . and I don't know what I can do to make you believe me."

"You're telling us a lie."

"I am not telling you a lie. I am not lying. I'm not a liar. I've never been a liar and I have no reason to lie."

McIntyre pounced, but his voice was soft and low. "Russ, you have a lot of reason to lie. We understand that. Something happened that wasn't supposed to happen."

Russ denied it again, but the detectives were on a roll, insisting repeatedly that something happened that drove him to kill Betsy. And then Rider dropped the bomb.

"Your wife was stabbed over twenty-five times."

Russ felt his heart shatter. "Oh, my God, no," he moaned as he dropped his forehead into his right hand. How could someone have stabbed his Betsy twenty-five times?

Rider repeated, "Over twenty-five times. Over twenty-five times. And they're not done yet. They're still counting."

Russ could only repeat, "Oh, my God."

Rider hammered away at a new and painful injury to his suspect. "Twenty-five times. Twenty-five times, Russ, and they're still counting. That's someone who was in a blind rage that lost control. That's not a stranger who did that. That's somebody who lost control of their emotions and couldn't stop until it was done."

Russ slumped farther down in his chair with his head bowed. "I did not do this," he mumbled again. "I did not do this. There's no way that I did this."

McIntyre snapped, "You cannot stick with that bullshit story. It is bullshit."

"It is not bullshit."

"It is so obviously bullshit. Nobody is going to buy . . . You have to come up with something better than that."

"That is all I have because that is the truth."

Russ and the cops seesawed repeatedly between "You stabbed

your wife" and "I did not do this." Floyd said the brutality made Russ look like a "cold-blooded killer who has no remorse for anything. . . . She sure didn't stab herself twenty-five times."

"No! I did not do this. I did not do it." And then, as if someone had flipped a switch in his brain, Russ realized there was only one way to stop this outrageous assault by the cops. He looked at the detectives and said, "If you're not going to believe me, then . . . then I need a lawyer."

McIntyre seemed incredulous and his voice shot up. "You're going to let the evidence speak for you? . . . Listen to me. Once we're done, we're done. When we walk out, we're done. This is your fucking chance, right now. This is it . . . and I'm telling you that this evidence is going to *bury* you. It is going to *bury* you. . . . Don't be stupid, Russ."

"I'm not being stupid."

Rider said, "You sound like you're trying to convince yourself, Russ."

"No, I'm not trying to convince myself. I'm trying to convince *you* that I'm telling the truth, because I am telling the truth."

The detectives made one last desperate attempt.

"We know you did it," McIntyre said.

"No, you *think* I did," Russ shot back.

"The evidence will prove that you did, Russ."

"Well, you guys sit here and accuse me of that."

"Russ, I have every right to accuse you because all of the evidence points to you."

Seventy-seven times in the last ninety minutes, Russ had said, "I did not do this" or "I didn't do it" or "I had nothing to do with it," or something close to those words. Dozens of more times, he had sworn he was not lying. It was now clear there was absolutely nothing he could do or say to convince them he did not kill Betsy. His grief was tearing at his insides while the cops were battering him with unrelenting accusations that he was a monstrous killer. He had spent almost eighteen hours under interrogation, with no contact with anyone from his or Betsy's families, and hadn't slept in more than thirty-three hours—and it was time for the madness to stop.

"Then I want a lawyer," he said with a new air of defiance and without a hint of emotion. "I want a lawyer right now. I want a lawyer."

McIntyre and Rider immediately walked out of the room as Floyd stood quickly and snapped, "We understand. Stand up and put your hands behind your back."

Russ stood slowly and turned his back to Floyd. At 4:36 p.m., Wednesday, December 28—some twenty-one hours after Betsy was murdered—Russ felt the cold steel of the handcuffs around his wrists and heard the click as they locked.

Russ heard Floyd say to one of the other detectives, "As soon as they want a lawyer, that means they're guilty."

CHAPTER SEVEN

Russ Faria stared blankly out of the window of the police car as the detectives drove him back to the Lincoln County Sheriff's Office in Troy. The unbelievable events of the last hour were beginning to force him out of the shock that had consumed his mind and body since he walked into his house the night before. He was still confused about what had happened and why, but he was beginning to understand that he was now in a new, tragic, and dangerous reality unlike anything he had ever experienced.

In just the last nearly twenty hours, he had discovered the brutalized body of his wife and, isolated from family or friends, had undergone the most prying examination of his personal life, his marriage, his religious faith, his integrity, and his honesty by a tag team of homicide detectives he had assumed was trying to help him. He willingly submitted to a polygraph test, only to be told he had failed and was a liar and a killer. He had endured the detectives' allegations that he was a raging monster who butchered his own wife. And now he was under arrest, his hands cuffed behind his back, riding in a police car with those same detectives on the way back to a cell at the Lincoln County Jail.

This insanity was real, he was beginning to understand as he watched the familiar countryside pass by the car window. He was vaguely aware the detectives were still talking to him, still trying to get him to confess, even though he had invoked his right to have an attorney present. He was done talking to them and was trying to tune them out. Once they arrived at the county jail, the detectives took him to a holding cell—a small room with several bunks like he had imagined a drunk tank would be. He asked again to make a phone call and was shown the telephone on the cell wall. Finally. He called his mother and told her he was OK, but had been arrested and jailed on suspicion of murder—of killing Betsy. He asked to speak to his cousin Mary Anderson, the person he trusted the most in the world. Only five months apart in age, they grew up more like sister and brother and remained close as adults. He called her his "sister cousin" and said the two were really the "wonder twins," who could almost read each other's mind. He asked Mary to call the only lawyer he knew, Andrew Beeny, who also attended the Morning Star Church. Mary had once worked for Beeny, so she knew him, too.

Mary was as stunned as her cousin that any of this could be happening. She knew to her very core Russ could not have killed Betsy. There had to be some horrible mistake, some crucial misunderstanding. She had just seen Betsy and Russ at a family Christmas party on Monday, December 26, and they were fine. She learned something had happened to Betsy when she got on Facebook early Wednesday morning and saw a posting from Betsy's daughter Mariah clearly implying Betsy was dead.

Mary called several family members and friends without getting any useful information before she reached Rachel Faria, Russ's sister, at the home of their mother, Luci Faria. Rachel shocked Mary by telling her the police were at Luci's house at that minute. Mary drove to Luci's and arrived while the detectives were interviewing Luci and Rachel. Mary asked the police repeatedly if Betsy was dead, citing Mariah's Facebook posting. The police would say only that Betsy had been accosted. When Mary asked where Russ was, a burly plainclothes officer, whom she would later identify as Sergeant Ryan McCarrick, told her Russ was out looking for the person who had attacked Betsy. She was furious when she learned later that afternoon that Russ had actually been undergoing police interrogation without an attorney—an interrogation she would soon learn had resulted in his arrest.

* * *

Despite being overwhelmed by exhaustion, Russ spent a restless Wednesday night in the cell, unable to find any comfort on the thin pad atop the metal bunk. He was barely aware of eating a little of the breakfast he was served Thursday morning. He was surprised when Detective Mike Merkel came to the cell at 10:30 a.m. to seize all of his clothes—the same clothes he had worn for the last forty-two hours on this long, strange trip to jail as a widower and accused murderer. Merkel presented Russ with a search warrant authorizing him to take the clothes: an XL-sized orange T-shirt proclaiming RHODE ISLAND, blue jeans, dark brown boots, white socks, a pair of black undershorts, a dark leather-strapped watch, and a dark leather belt. Merkel gave Russ a funky red-and-blue tie-dyed T-shirt and a pair of jeans, which he put on reluctantly, wondering about their previous inhabitants. The search warrant also authorized taking fingernail clippings from Russ's hands, which an evidence technician did with sterilized nail clippers.

Russ didn't know when Andrew Beeny arrived at the county jail at 4:30 p.m. to see if he could help Russ. Beeny couldn't imagine the friendly, mild-mannered man he knew from church being involved in anything as brutal as the murder of his wife. Beeny gave Detective Stephanie Kaiser and Sergeant Perry Smith of the Missouri Highway Patrol the names of two people Mary Anderson and other sources thought should be investigated—Pam Hupp and one of Leah Day's former boyfriends. And he added that there were thousands of people who would tell police there was no way Russ killed Betsy. After Beeny had talked to the detectives for thirty minutes or so, they surprised him by announcing they were about to release Russ from jail due to a lack of evidence.

Russ was as surprised as Beeny when detectives told him he would be released and Beeny was there to escort him out of jail. Russ felt a wave of relief wash over him, tempered by the awful reality that Betsy was dead and his life still was in ruin. He could only assume the police finally realized he could not have killed Betsy and were now developing other suspects. After a long wait for jailers to process his release, they took him to the lobby, where Beeny met him and told him he would drive him to his parents' house. Beeny was struck by how exhausted and shaken emotionally and physically Russ looked as he walked unsteadily into the lobby.

Russ and Beeny weren't prepared for the mob of reporters and photographers waiting outside as they walked into the parking lot. Beeny took Russ by the arm and told him to look straight ahead and not engage with the media in any way. Beeny had been interviewed on TV before, but he had never felt as physically assaulted as he did when the media pushed forward in such a rush that they actually separated him from Russ.

Russ shook off the shouted questions of "Did you kill your wife" with a terse "No comment," until one reporter pushed his microphone at Russ as he slid into the passenger side of Beeny's car. Without looking at the reporter, Russ snapped, "Get outta my face." At that moment, Russ couldn't begin to know how important that reporter, Chris Hayes from FOX 2 KTVI in St. Louis, would become in the long saga that was just beginning.

CHAPTER EIGHT

1997—O'Fallon, Missouri

Russ Faria had noticed the cute young woman behind the cash register the first time he went into the store at the service station where he had stopped for gas in O'Fallon in 1997. She had a huge smile that lit up her face and her blue eyes sparkled as the perfect reflection of the personality that everyone called bubbly. Her curly brown hair had blondish highlights, which Russ thought were a classy touch. He made a point of chatting her up every time he went to the station, including the extra stops he made just to see the girl he quickly came to know as Betsy Carter. She was genuinely nice and friendly—remarkably extroverted, really—and he hoped her response to his flirtatious banter was an indication she was interested in him. He was right. Although she was still going through a divorce, she asked Russ out on a date. It was the first step in a romance that soon led to their decision to live together in her mobile home in O'Fallon.

Russ was twenty-eight and Betsy was twenty-nine. She had two little girls—seven and three—from a relationship before the short marriage that was about to end in the pending divorce. Russ quickly grew to love the girls, just as he did their mother. After living together for two years, Russ and the now-divorced Betsy married in January 2000.

Russ Faria had grown up in nearby Florissant, Missouri, one of the popular middle-class communities on the northern edge of

St. Louis. He had spent a year in Florida with his parents when he was in the sixth and seventh grades while his father worked as a construction laborer and painter. After they returned to the St. Louis area, Russ went back to school in the Florissant area until he dropped out of Hazelwood Central High School in 1987. Two years later, he earned his high-school general equivalency degree from a nearby technical school. He had a series of jobs, including maintenance for a major grocery chain and ten years managing a liquor store during the time he met Betsy. He went on to work for an asphalt company and then a company that assembled bicycles for big-box and discount stores. But Betsy knew he was capable of a more substantial career and life. She encouraged him to go back to school and he attributed his associate's and bachelor's degrees in information technology to her positive influence. The degrees led to a good job in 2007 in IT technical support for Enterprise Holdings, the parent company of the massive Enterprise Leasing operation headquartered in St. Louis County.

Betsy Meyer Faria also had grown up in the St. Louis suburbs, the third of four daughters of a staunchly Roman Catholic family. She was a standout softball pitcher in grade school and high school and a member of state championship teams in 1984 and 1985. As a senior in high school, she had started her own DJ business, called PartyStarters. She attended classes in broadcasting that complemented her DJ business. It was the perfect outlet for her love of music and extroverted personality. She could get anyone out of their comfort zone and onto the dance floor. She operated the business part-time, and after Russ started seeing her, he often assisted at her DJ events by running the sound system. Betsy said she had performed at fifteen hundred weddings and other events. After broadcasting school, she landed a job as a DJ at a country-music station in the Florida Keys, where she began a long-term relationship with a man who moved back to St. Louis with her in 1989 and fathered her two daughters, in 1990 and 1994. They never married and he returned to Florida shortly after their second daughter was born. He had barely any contact with the girls as they were growing up. Betsy married Ron Carter in 1995, but it only lasted about a year before she divorced him.

Despite a happy start to the Farias' marriage, it soon proved far less than perfect. They argued often and Russ would admit that his sometimes-volatile temper could lead to angry words with Betsy and her daughters that he would later regret. They separated a few times, including once for about a year while he stayed with a friend across the Mississippi River in nearby southwestern Illinois. They both had relationships with people outside of their marriage. But each time they separated, they would forgive each other and decide to try again to make their marriage work.

In 2011, they were living in Troy and Betsy was fighting the cancer that threatened to take her life. In discussions with friends and family during the 2011 Christmas holidays, she developed a plan that would allow her to spend her last few years closer to her beloved family and friends in the area that really felt like home. She was going to propose that she and Russ buy her parents' old house in Lake St. Louis and move there, renting out the house in Troy. She didn't expect Russ to like the idea, but she was excited about presenting it to him when he got home from game night on December 27.

CHAPTER NINE

Thursday, December 29, 2011—*two days after Betsy Faria's murder*

Russ Faria's arrival at his mother's house for a reunion with his family after two long days of police interrogation and a jail cell—and the unbelievable accusations that he had murdered his wife—was bittersweet. He had ached to see his family while he was being questioned, but hugging them now made him that much more aware of Betsy's absence. With some of the fog from the last two days lifting, he was beginning to hope his family and Betsy's family could help him find his way toward an answer to the question haunting him since he found Betsy's body: What do I do now?

He was trying to put his experience with the police into some manageable perspective. Despite the aggressive accusations from detectives at the end, he was certain they released him because they realized he was not involved in Betsy's death. Surely, they would redirect their investigation now and find out who really killed her.

Mary Anderson knew her cousin was not capable of committing murder or harming Betsy in any way. Mary had seen them at a Christmas party just three days ago and they were happy and laughing. Betsy saved Russ a seat next to her on the sofa and happily invited him to join her there. But Mary's very nature required her to ask Russ one direct question when they had their first chance to sit down together.

"Is there anything you want to tell me?" she asked softly.

When he said no, he had not killed Betsy, she knew he was telling the truth. Beyond her confidence in the man she knew so well, his eyes and face told her unequivocally that he was innocent. She looked down and softly rubbed his wrists where she could still see the imprints from the handcuffs. She was glad Russ's ordeal with the police was over and he could begin to rebuild his life free from suspicion.

Russ also was pleased to find that Betsy's family seemed to harbor no suspicion that he was involved in her death and treated him with the compassion and affection he had always felt from them, especially from Betsy's mother, Janet Meyer. He always thought of her as a second mother and happily spent hours helping her with jobs around her house or apartment.

But Russ now had to turn his attention toward the painful task of arranging Betsy's funeral, which his family had agreed to pay for. Russ and Betsy always agreed they would be cremated, although Russ sensed disapproval from her Catholic family. He wanted the funeral to be at the Morning Star United Methodist Church, which had been so essential to the life the Farias were rebuilding together. But since Betsy had grown up Catholic—as had Russ—her family was adamant that there should be a Catholic service. Russ accommodated everyone by scheduling dual funeral services at St. Patrick Catholic Church in Wentzville at 10:30 a.m. the next Tuesday, January 3, 2012, and at seven o'clock that evening at Morning Star.

But it was the visitation and wake at a funeral home in Wentzville the night before the services that drew extraordinary and perhaps unforgivable conduct at a time reserved for compassion and consolation.

The first event roused Russ Faria from what others called grief so deep that he was in an almost zombielike stupor. Mary watched painfully as Russ stood over the open casket. A scarf hid the injuries to her neck and long sleeves covered the wounds to her arms. Russ began to speak directly to Betsy and then fell to his knees—a heartbreaking scene. But later one of Betsy's aunts angrily approached Russ, struck him in the chest, and spat out an accusatory "How could you!" in front of the other startled mourners. Some onlookers said they heard her call him a murderer. Despite his shock at this assault, he decided not to respond. The woman never liked him and made him the butt of nasty comments in the past. He avoided any contact with her for at least the last three years, placing her in that special category the Italians term "dead to me."

And despite this cruel and no-class attack now, Russ responded only with stoic silence. He would learn later that someone told his mother about the incident and she angrily confronted the woman. Russ knew that was sufficient. His mother was a tiny woman, but Luci was packed with Italian matriarchal power and was not someone to fool with. He nicknamed her "TNT" and called her "a firecracker in a small package."

The second event at the funeral home was just as shocking. Pam Hupp and her husband, Mark, walked in and inexplicably confronted a number of Russ's and Betsy's relatives with angry recriminations and allegations of somehow being responsible for Betsy's death. The confrontation soon became a shouting match, including Mark Hupp leaning into Rachel Faria's face and challenging her to hit him.

Mary quickly located the funeral director and asked him to throw out the Hupps. They saw the wisdom in a retreat after the funeral director threatened to call the police. Russ's and Betsy's relatives were outraged and offended, and they couldn't understand the Hupps' aggressive misconduct.

The day after the funeral services, Russ escorted Betsy's body to its final disposition—the funeral home's crematorium. He was supported by his best friend and an aunt, and they said a short prayer as they watched through a window as the box containing Betsy's body rolled into the flames and the door closed behind it. Russ compared the short process to the funeral pyres he had heard about in other cultures. He decided he would keep the urn with Betsy's ashes with him until the time came for his body to join hers.

CHAPTER TEN

Wednesday, January 4, 2012

The second time Russ Faria felt the click of handcuffs around his wrists seemed even more shocking—and terrifying—than the first.

The morning after Betsy's funeral services, Russ started trying to rebuild some of the wreckage that was now his life. Even the smallest things seemed so difficult. His sister took him to a mall so he could buy a new cell phone. The police still had his phone and he struggled to deal with the fact that it was part of the investigation into the murder of his wife. He was staying with his parents, and as gracious and welcoming as they were, he still felt Betsy's killer had not only taken his wife and destroyed his life, but had also destroyed his home—the house he could never enter again.

At 3:30 p.m. that day, Russ was on the computer in a back bedroom talking via Facebook with a cousin in Chicago about getting together for a visit, when he suddenly heard distressed voices in the front room. He walked in to face a shocking scene: Sergeant Ryan McCarrick and Detective Ray Floyd—their pistols in their hands—pushing past Russ's parents just inside the front door. Russ's sixty-five-year-old father, Richard, was adamantly telling the police they couldn't enter his home without a warrant. As they forced their way past him, they responded that they had a warrant, turned abruptly toward Russ, and leveled their pistols at him.

McCarrick barked, "You're under arrest for the murder of your wife. Get down on your knees."

Russ was flabbergasted. He was certain the police released him six days earlier because they had cleared him, the same assumption made by Mary Anderson and the entire Faria family. Russ's mind was racing, but he was thinking clearly as he dropped to his knees and followed the detectives' shouted orders to put his hands behind his back. As Floyd clicked the handcuffs around Russ's wrists once again, he forced himself to remain absolutely calm and quiet. He was being escorted to a police car when he heard one of the other officers crack sarcastically, "You forgot to check the drains. There was blood in the drains and on the mop." Even in the turmoil of that minute, Russ knew that blood or other evidence from the drains, the mop, or anything else could not be cause for charging him with Betsy's murder. He wasn't there and nothing the police found there could incriminate him.

As McCarrick ushered Russ into the front seat of the police car that Floyd was driving, Russ saw Mary's car pull up across the street. His cousin saw Russ in the police car and was headed toward it when an officer stopped her and told her to stay back. Russ heard a shouted warning from one of the officers: "Watch her!" Another absurd insult. What was Mary going to do? Break Russ out of the police car and escape with him to Mexico?

McCarrick slid into the backseat behind Russ as Floyd pulled away and drove down the street. And then Russ felt the cold steel of McCarrick's pistol against the back of his head.

McCarrick snarled, "If you say anything, if you even breathe the wrong way, I'm going to paint the windshield with your brains."

Russ was shocked again and had to wonder how seriously he should take this threat from the big cop. He had already decided to remain silent and McCarrick's threat confirmed the wisdom of that decision. Russ would do nothing to test McCarrick's intent.

When he arrived at the Lincoln County Jail, Russ was booked on two felony charges: one count of first-degree murder, which alleged he "knowingly caused the death of Elizabeth Faria by stabbing her in excess of twenty-five times," punishable by ten to thirty years in prison, life without parole, or the death penalty; and one count of armed criminal action, alleging that he committed murder while armed with a deadly weapon, punishable by a minimum of three years in prison and no stated maximum. He was informed a judge had set his bond at a crushing $1 million.

The indignities of the rest of the booking process followed quickly. Fingerprints. Mug shot. Pockets emptied. Stripped to his shorts and dressed in the uniform orange shirt and pants like every other prisoner wore. The guards gave Russ a thin mattress pad, as if he could possibly sleep now, and placed him in the familiar holding cell to await assignment to a regular cell. At least Russ could use the phone on the wall to call his parents and his cousin Mary to begin planning the next steps in this already-surreal fight for his life.

CHAPTER ELEVEN

Seven days a week, Joel Schwartz's morning ritual included a careful reading of the Law and Order section of the *St. Louis Post-Dispatch* to note the names of those newly arrested and the details of their alleged crimes. It wasn't a casual glance or idle curiosity. It was a smart habit by an experienced professional. As one of the top criminal defense attorneys in the St. Louis region, if not the Midwest, there was a distinct possibility he would be getting a call from one or more of the people whose names he had just read as being on the pointy end of criminal charges, from the most mundane to the most horrific. When those calls came, Schwartz wanted to be as informed and prepared as possible.

One of those calls did indeed come at the unusually late hour of 9:30 p.m. on January 4, 2012—and the woman on the phone dropped the name of Russell Faria. Schwartz knew exactly whom she was talking about—the husband charged in the stabbing of his wife in their home in Troy. From newspaper and TV reports, the only remarkable aspect of the case seemed to be the brutality of the attack. It wasn't cynical for a defense attorney to register no surprise that a husband was accused of killing his wife, or occasionally even the reverse of a wife charged with dispatching her husband. Except for drug deals gone bad and bar fights, there probably wasn't a more common crime scenario than a marriage ending with the violent death of one spouse.

But this late-evening call was different. It came from Mary Anderson, who was an assistant in the first law firm Schwartz worked in after he left the St. Louis public defender's office. He hadn't spoken to her for, what, twenty years. But she was now calling with the big ask: Would he represent her cousin, Russ Faria, on the murder charge in his wife's killing?

"Joel, I know he's innocent, with all my heart," she said.

Schwartz told her to meet him at his office first thing the next morning.

Mary had been in a near panic about finding a defense lawyer for Russ until one of her friends reminded her that she had worked for one of the best in the business. She called Schwartz immediately without any thought of the hour. At the meeting the next morning, she was pleased Schwartz already had accumulated a substantial amount of information and media reports. Even before the briefing by Mary, Schwartz had decided he probably would represent Russ Faria on what media reports were portraying as a fairly simple case of a husband murdering his wife.

Mary told Schwartz everything she could think of about Russ and Betsy, with special emphasis on Russ's remarkably detailed game-night alibi. Schwartz was impressed by the depth of her information and, even more so, by the look of certainty in her intense brown eyes and the set of her jaw when she swore there was absolutely no way in hell her cousin murdered his wife. Schwartz knew she believed it and he hoped her instincts were right.

And then she offered one more noteworthy observation. Based on some inexplicable, disgraceful, and—Mary thought—suspiciously aggressive conduct at the funeral home, Schwartz should look closely at the woman whom everyone was describing as one of Betsy's best friends and, more important, the last person to see her alive—Pam Hupp. Mary thought the attitude and actions toward Russ and his family by Pam, and even by her husband, were not only cruelly abnormal, but calculated to create hostility and suspicion toward Russ. Pam's unbalanced performance had far exceeded the righteous anger that could be excused from a grieving friend of the departed. Mary had never heard of Pam Hupp until her name was mentioned at the family Christmas party on Monday, December 26.

Schwartz told Mary he would meet with Russ that day, even before getting the small down payment on his fees that he requested. She was thrilled and, taking no chances with Russ's defense, hand-delivered the payment to Schwartz's office before the end of the day.

Joel Schwartz drove to the Lincoln County Jail in Troy shortly after noon to meet his new client. On the thirty-minute drive west on Interstate 70, Schwartz analyzed everything he knew about the case so far. One conclusion seemed obvious: unless the Russ Faria he was about to meet was a much different man than described by Mary Anderson, and unless his seemingly rock-solid alibi crumbled, the charges should be dismissed in fairly quick order. As Schwartz had said to Mary, this case surely was the result of some misunderstanding by the police and prosecutor that shouldn't be that difficult to clear up.

Schwartz thought the reports by the *St. Louis Post-Dispatch* and local TV news had been routine: brief stories with minimal police comment on December 28 and 29 about a woman stabbed to death in her home. There were mentions of her battle with cancer. The Major Case Squad of Greater St. Louis had been activated and one suspect—identified as her husband in some reports—had been questioned and released. An online story by a TV station on December 30 said investigators would work through the New Year's holiday to find grounds for a charge and arrest, and the county prosecutor was "fast-tracking DNA and fingerprint tests as well as cell phone records." One of the Farias' neighbors was concerned that the unnamed man had been released: "We are wondering why he got released and we are concerned that he is out—I will tell you that," the man said. Another report noted that a call to Betsy Faria's home phone number "gives listeners a chance to hear her bubbly message on the answering machine."

The media began hitting the story harder after Russ was arrested on January 4. More friends and relatives were quoted, including one the *Post-Dispatch* said "described a wake and funeral that were filled with tension because of suspicions about Russell Faria's involvement in his wife's death." The story also reported that Janet Meyer, Betsy Faria's mother, "declined to comment about the charges against her son-in-law, other than to say, 'I can't handle it; I've been close to him, as well.' "

While announcing Russ's arrest, Lincoln County Sheriff Mike Krigbaum told the cameras, "We want to make sure we arrest the right person and we have enough evidence to keep him in jail, and we do have it this time."

Schwartz thought that sounded wrong on both counts.

But the story by NBC affiliate KSDK also contained an even more interesting comment by Lincoln County Prosecuting Attorney (PA) Leah Askey: "We know from sources that she came home and laid down on the couch. We can assume she was likely resting or asleep at the time of the incident."

Schwartz wondered how Askey could know that now. Who could be her sources?

Fox 2 also quoted Sheriff Krigbaum's comment about getting the right man, but added that the arrest resulted from the discovery of unspecified key evidence in a second search of the Faria home the day Betsy was buried. And then FOX 2 quoted Askey with a surprising attack on Russ's alibi. She said the more police investigated, the more Russ Faria's timeline "unraveled," leading authorities to believe the murder was premeditated.

Schwartz was eager to see her evidence for that, given the alibi he had heard.

Schwartz was entering the lobby of the Lincoln County Jail when he was surprised to run into Sergeant Ryan McCarrick. Schwartz knew McCarrick was the lead detective on the Faria case and a tough, no-nonsense investigator. And McCarrick knew immediately why this top defense attorney was arriving at the jail. The cop didn't miss the opportunity to offer some candid, professional advice to the lawyer.

Talk some sense into Faria, McCarrick said, and get him to confess so everyone can wrap up this nasty case. Schwartz offered no reaction to the unsolicited advice and left McCarrick with a casual "See ya later."

Within minutes, Schwartz was seated in a small interview room across a table from Russell Scott Faria, a husky, formidable-looking man who seemed exhausted, but certainly not intimidated, panicked, or terrified. While he seemed physically capable of inflicting damage on another person, Schwartz saw something much less threatening in the man's face and especially his eyes.

After some general discussion, Schwartz delivered his stock opening gambit for a new client: "Tell me what they're saying you did."

Although that was designed to test a defendant's perspective on the crime rather than to elicit a claim of innocence or an admission of guilt, Russ Faria responded immediately with exactly what he had been telling the police and everyone else for the last week: "I did not kill my wife. I did not do this. I could not do this. I loved my wife."

Two decades as a criminal defense attorney had taught Schwartz not to jump to any conclusions on guilt or innocence. But the man in front of him now seemed genuine in his inability to comprehend how or why he had been charged with murdering his wife.

Russ maintained a calm and purposeful demeanor as he gave Schwartz the full account of Tuesday: the stops along the drive to game night, three uninterrupted hours with his friends there, the uneventful drive home while downing a couple of sandwiches, and then the soul-shattering discovery of Betsy's body. Schwartz found Russ's claims of innocence sincere and convincing, even if he was at a complete loss to suggest who could have done this to his wife. Everyone loved Betsy, Russ said. No one who knew her would ever be able to find enough anger or hatred to kill her, let alone inflict such ferocious wounds on this woman already fighting a likely losing battle with cancer. And he knew of no evidence that some intruder, a stranger who didn't know Betsy, had come into their house on a cold, snowy December night and inflicted such ruthless overkill in the glow of Christmas tree lights.

Russ ended his account with the troubling allegation of Sergeant McCarrick's armed threat to blow out Russ's brains on the ride to jail. That image of the cop with a gun to the back of Russ's head would haunt Schwartz. He had no reason to doubt Russ's honesty at that point. He just thought, Let's see where the evidence goes.

Schwartz had spent years honing an ability to assess people, their character, and their credibility fairly quickly and, more important, accurately. The police seemed certain this man had spent a pleasant holiday weeknight visiting friends before he rushed home, flew into a rage, and butchered his wife. That didn't fit the man sitting across the table—a man with such a solid alibi. And no man of even the most basic intelligence who had just sliced his wife to ribbons would tell police she committed suicide. Schwartz always retained a healthy skepticism about new clients and new cases. But he thought Russ Faria seemed to be an honest man caught up in a whirlwind of muddled facts and allegations. He didn't seem to be the kind of man who was capable of what the cops said he had done.

As Russ Faria's defense attorney, Schwartz offered some simple, essential advice to his new client: Do not talk to anyone about anything. Don't say a word to the police or a prosecutor without Schwartz's presence and permission. Expect the police to try to talk to you again; say nothing. Expect the police and prosecutor to put a snitch in your cell to get you to talk; say nothing.

Russ was impressed with this lawyer he had never met before—and who came with Mary Anderson's enthusiastic recommendation and full confidence. She assured Russ that Joel Schwartz was the best of the best. Russ appreciated the way Schwartz talked to him face-to-face in simple language. There was no big-shot lawyer attitude or arrogance. But there was a quiet confidence that spoke of experience and competence.

As Schwartz left, he said, "I'll get on this and I'll get you out of here."

Russ believed him. And he would always remember with a smile what the jail guard said when he came to get Russ for that first meeting with Schwartz: "There's a fancy lawyer in an Armani suit to see you."

The path that led Russ Faria to a jail cell was certainly bizarre. But in a different way, so was the one that led Joel Schwartz to this meeting as a renowned criminal defense lawyer.

For as long as Schwartz could remember, he wanted to be an actor—or perhaps, more specifically, a movie star. That desire to be a performer seemed to be in his genes. His mother, Susie, had been a dancer. His father, Arty, had dreamed of being a star on Broadway, and even though he now owned an auto-salvage yard in St. Louis, he still performed in local theater and sang show tunes around the house. His older brother, Brad, worked for a while as an actor after earning a master's degree in theater; he now operated the salvage yard with his father and performed in local theater, too.

But Joel Schwartz—blessed with classic good looks, a full head of curly brown hair, and an athletic build—had high hopes for a movie career after he graduated from Ladue High School in St. Louis. He spent his freshman year in 1980 at the University of California, Los Angeles, but decided to get the same quality education for less money at the University of Texas at Austin. Although he had no intention of practicing law, he went to law school to get a practical and marketable degree. While in Austin, he did a little acting and some modeling and appeared on the cover of *Texas Monthly* magazine after he published the first male pinup calendar in the state, drawing on experience with a calendar he saw produced at UCLA. His calendar sold well in all the major cities across Texas and even got noticed in *TIME* magazine. After he graduated with a law degree in 1987, he moved to Los Angeles to take acting classes, attend auditions, and look for that big break, while waiting tables and working for a theatrical agent.

When the writers' strike shut down the movie and TV industry in the summer of 1989, Schwartz went back to St. Louis for a visit. He ran into a friend who was an assistant public defender (APD) in the City of St. Louis and was trying a murder case. He invited Schwartz to sit in on the trial. "I think you'll like it," he said—and Schwartz did. His friend referred him to the public defender and he interviewed with a group of about twenty staffers, who mostly asked him two questions: Did he have any more of the pinup calendars? And could he start as an assistant public defender the next day?

Not long after starting his career as an assistant public defender, Schwartz won a nonspeaking role in a movie that was going to be set and partly filmed in St. Louis. But the schedule for his scenes was changed to days when he would be out of town for a friend's wedding. Schwartz decided that he had already committed to being a lawyer and the movie was unlikely to generate much buzz anyway. He went to his friend's wedding. Later, he heard that the actor who took his place got some attention and more work based on the role Schwartz skipped. It turned out that *White Palace*, starring Susan Sarandon and James Spader, had been pretty popular.

While regretting that missed opportunity, Schwartz was showing a natural ability as a trial attorney in criminal defense. He connected well with jurors—perhaps a function of his interest in performing before an audience. Just six or eight months after starting as a public defender, he tried his first murder case, and then a second and then a third and then a rape and then a robbery—all acquittals. In his second year, he tried sixteen cases. When he asked for a raise in his $29,000 salary in the spring of 1991, he was told he hadn't been there long enough. He and another assistant PD resigned a few days later and joined a private law firm.

After several months there, they opened their own firm. And a while after that, Schwartz started a partnership with two more of the region's most prominent defense attorneys, Scott Rosenblum and John Rogers. Rogers eventually was succeeded as named partner by Matt Fry to create the firm of Rosenblum, Schwartz & Fry.

But Schwartz would always remember his first day in the public defender's office in 1989. He immediately was introduced to the APD who would be his supervisor—Mary Ann Bogacki. It would be some time before they learned they had a connection from years before. While Schwartz was an undergrad at the University of Texas School of Law, he and a fellow student attended the annual spring break activities on Padre Island in 1982. When they learned that students from the University of Missouri School of Law were partying at the other end of the island, they decided to pay them a visit. Schwartz's friend talked him into participating in a push-up contest there, and while Joel was racking up an impressive number of push-ups, he could hear some of the audience yelling, "You're cheating. You're cheating." He found out they were actually delivering some good-natured harassment to the girl who would eventually win the women's contest, while he won the men's. And that girl was, of course, Mary Ann Bogacki.

Sometime after the push-up champions renewed their acquaintance in the PD's office, they were married. And by the time the Faria case came to Schwartz, they were the parents of two sons and a daughter.

And at fifty, Joel Schwartz was recognized as one of the top criminal defense lawyers in the region. He hadn't become a movie star, but he had found what he realized he was destined to do.

CHAPTER TWELVE

By the time the MCS's file in the murder of Elizabeth Kay Faria landed on Joel Schwartz's desk, Russ Faria's trial was set for June 26, 2012, before Lincoln County Circuit Judge Dan Dildine—an experienced and respected member of the bench—and Russ had already spent several long weeks in the county jail. He would describe that experience as living in a small bathroom with two strangers.

On his first day, the thirty to forty prisoners in the wing where he was housed knew who he was and what he was accused of. It seemed they all watched the TV news every day without fail. He was surprised none of the prisoners asked about the case and there were no threats or confrontations. The guards—called COs for "correctional officers" by the prisoners—also knew who Russ was and he thought they treated him fairly well. He worked to make friends with his two cellmates and as many other prisoners as possible. That included a big man named Mark, who was kept in a cell alone—a self-described "really bad dude." Russ played chess with Mark through the "chuck hole"—the opening in the steel door used to deliver meals. Mark warned Russ later that he was about to be put in a cell with a prisoner said to have been ordered by police to beat him. Mark had warned the prisoner not to touch Russ.

When Russ was moved to a cell with the supposed attacker, the man immediately said he had no interest in hurting Russ. To avoid more trouble and possible repercussions, the man suggested he and Russ pretend to have a fight. They tore their shirts and threw things around in the cell to make enough noise to convince the COs they had really gone after each other. Russ drew several days alone in a cell that had no lights; he couldn't even read to pass the time. He eventually went back to his regular cell—back to sleeping on a thin mat on a steel bunk and eating food that was adequate, but barely.

Trying to grieve for Betsy while coping with jail life was an incredibly contradictory reality. His heart was broken and his life would have been turned upside down, even if he wasn't behind bars with dozens of people who—although mostly still awaiting trials— probably had committed a wide variety of crimes. He often felt like weeping and crying out in pain, but he knew that was not the best image to project to fellow prisoners. He worked at keeping his spirits up, and regular visits from family members on Sundays and daily letters from them helped. He focused on the knowledge that Joel Schwartz was on the case, working to get him out of jail and, ultimately, to clear him of the charges.

That responsibility weighed heavily on Schwartz and he was eager to build a defense that would clear Russ. The initial pretrial court activity for a major felony case was dragging along at the usual frustratingly slow pace. Schwartz was pleased when Prosecuting Attorney Leah Askey delivered the Major Case Squad file as part of pretrial discovery—the required sharing of information by each side with the other.

He brought in a promising young associate, Nathan "Nate" Swanson, as his second chair. In nine months with the firm, Swanson, just twenty-nine, had shown a keen grasp of technical issues and a memory like a computer hard drive. He had a fascinating history. He was born in Chicago and lived in Omaha and Boulder before his parents divorced when he was young. After that, he divided his time between his mother, a Lutheran minister, in Los Angeles, and his father, a Lutheran minister, lawyer, and rancher, in Colorado. He was in San Francisco for the earthquake in 1989, in Los Angeles for the earthquake in 1994, and narrowly missed being on one of the subway trains that was bombed in the so-called 7/7 bombings in London in 2005.

Swanson had decided early on that he wanted to be a criminal defense lawyer and, at just twelve years old, had been fascinated by the O.J. Simpson trial. He graduated from the huge Santa Monica High School, got a master's degree from King's College in London, and graduated from a small law school in Colorado Springs. While he was there, he met his future wife, who was attending a nearby nursing school. He graduated in the down market for lawyers in 2009 and landed the job with Rosenblum, Schwartz & Fry in April 2011 after calling Matt Fry, an acquaintance who had also attended the same law school.

Swanson had seen the media stories on the Betsy Faria murder and wondered if the case would land at his firm. He wasn't surprised when Schwartz told him they would be defending Russ Faria.

When the MCS file arrived in discovery, Schwartz was out of town for a few days and he asked Swanson to begin going through the reports. When Schwartz returned, Swanson was waiting with a surprising conclusion. He handed Schwartz the police reports from interviews with one of Betsy Faria's friends and a thumb drive with audio recordings of those interviews, and said simply, "You've got to see this. These will tell you who killed Betsy Faria."

Schwartz began to read and listen to perhaps the most intriguing police reports he had ever encountered.Swanson wanted Schwartz to see and hear this story.

Pamela Marie Hupp answered the cops' knock on her door in O'Fallon at 6:40 a.m., Wednesday, December 28, with her dyed-blond hair still wet from a shower. And then the chunky, fifty-three-year-old, married mother of two young adults gifted detectives with a nearly three-hour recorded interview that provided intimate and revealing insights into what she described as the fatally-troubled marriage of Betsy and Russ Faria—with some ugly personal accusations about Russ thrown in, at no extra cost.

Detective Stephanie Kaiser and Sgt. Perry Smith tried to break the news of Betsy Faria's death gently, explaining that all they could say was that her friend was dead—not how she died or even whether it was an accident or natural causes. Pam sobbed and her voice choked as she told the detectives she had known Betsy for almost eleven years and saw her almost every day.

Were they best friends?

"Uhm, Betsy had a lot of best friends," Pam said, an apparently happy memory accompanied by a slight chuckle. "Zillions of best friends. But, yes, I saw her almost every day, every other day."

The detectives wanted to know everything about Betsy's last day. Crying again, Pam explained that Betsy had spent Monday night at the apartment of her mother, Janet Meyer. Pam planned to pick her up there and drive to her Tuesday chemotherapy session at the Site- man Cancer Center in nearby St. Peters, at 1:30 p.m. But Betsy texted Pam that morning to say she was getting a ride from a friend Pam knew only as Bobbi and wanted to spend one-on-one time with her while she was visiting from Texas.

Pam decided to join Betsy for the chemo session anyway and drove to Janet's apartment about the time she thought Betsy would need to leave. Betsy had already left with Bobbi, so Pam chatted with Janet for a while and then drove to the cancer center to join Betsy and Bobbi. After the chemo, Pam turned down an invitation to accompany the women to a Lion's Choice restaurant because she wanted to go home for dinner with her husband, Mark. After that, she drove back to Janet's apartment to wait until Betsy was ready for her to drive her home. Pam added that Betsy stayed at her mother's apartment most weekdays.

"Why was that?" Smith asked.

"Uhm, a lot of it, she didn't like the drive, and a lot of it, she didn't like going home."

"Why didn't she like going home?"

"Uhm, a lot of it was her husband."

Schwartz's eyes widened in surprise at Pam's unexpected allega- tion that Betsy had been avoiding Russ.

Pam began a depressing story about the Farias' marriage and Russ's behavior. "They had been separated—gosh—six, seven times all through the years that I've known her. . . . I don't know him that well. I've only met him maybe three times in ten years. He doesn't come to, like, functions and stuff. As far as her friends, it was just her. . . . He's not the most . . . he's kind of not nice verbally to her, you know, so he makes us uncomfortable sometimes."

"Have you heard him being not nice to her verbally?"

"Oh, yeah," Pam said almost casually. "He's kind of pompous. I mean, he seems nice enough. I just don't know him that well. The last time I saw him was at her fortieth birthday party that he had for her. . . . I think that was the last time I ever really talked to him. No, I take that back. I was at her house last week. She wanted to make me lunch. . . . He works in the house and I went down to say hi to him."

She said Russ had earlier given her directions to the house and asked why it had taken her so long to get there. She explained she was unfamiliar with the area, and Russ responded, "Oh, you women are such asses."

Pam clicked her tongue and said, "So we just went back upstairs. I just wanted to say hi."

Pam said Betsy talked often about leaving Russ. Betsy and a friend, possibly a cousin named Linda, whom Pam met once, spent the weekend before Christmas in the popular tourist center of Branson, Missouri, 250 miles southwest of Troy. Pam said both women were thinking about leaving their husbands and discussed moving into a place together in Branson and working at a college there.

Schwartz was surprised again. This was the first suggestion from anyone that Betsy was considering leaving Russ. Schwartz viewed that with great skepticism after hearing from others how well the Farias had been getting along.

Pam drove back to Janet's about 5:15 p.m. to pick up Betsy and take her home. She waited while Betsy finished playing a board game with her mother and Bobbi, and guessed it was after 6 p.m. when she and Betsy left. Pam called her husband after they pulled into Betsy's driveway to let him know she had arrived safely. "I don't really drive at night too much," she explained. Her husband had left his phone in his truck and didn't answer the call, so she left him a voice mail. Betsy took the phone to leave Pam's husband a cheery message of "Merry Christmas and Happy New Year."

"Did you go inside?" Smith asked.

"No. I helped her. . . . It was weird, because we drove up . . . and the reason she said she didn't have a car was because Russ had it. . . .

We drove up and the car was in the garage—or in the driveway—so we thought he was home. . . . I said, 'Well, there's no lights on. Maybe he took another car.' And she goes, 'No, he said he was taking my car.' " Pam said the car was a silver Nissan Maxima.

"And I said, 'Do you want me to walk you to the door?' And she said yes . . . so I walked her up to the door and in, until she could get a light on. And she got the front light on. And she walked in and turned on the living-room light and called for him, and he wasn't there. . . . Nobody answered."

"So, did you ever actually go inside the house?"

"I did. . . . I took her in."

Pam's answer startled Schwartz again. She had just contradicted her statement from seconds ago and admitted that, as the last known person to see Betsy alive, she had gone into the house where Betsy was killed at about the time she was killed.

"We just went in. She turned on the hall light. And Betsy doesn't like to be alone," Pam explained. "I went in and turned on her living-room light and then walked around and turned on her kitchen light so she would have the lights on. She was calling for him and he wasn't . . . Nobody was answering."

Schwartz recognized yet another contradiction within a few sentences. She just said she turned on the living-room light after saying before that Betsy turned it on. Either way, she had placed herself in the living room where Betsy was murdered, at just about the time Betsy was murdered.

Pam described how Betsy put the dog in the backyard because she was jumping up on the women—"driving us nuts"—as they stood talking. The two women discussed meeting for lunch the next day, and Pam said she had to take her mother to see her financial advisor in the morning.

Smith asked if she was there for ten to twenty minutes.

"It could be, yeah . . . I wasn't really paying attention. I was just trying to get out of there."

She said she called her husband again after she left, and the detectives wanted to know where she was when she made that call.

"Uh . . ." There was a long pause. "Actually, I don't think I called him. I called Betsy when I got home—or was on my way home—almost home. . . . I'm trying to think which one I called. I called Betsy to—that's right—I called Betsy to tell her I was home."

"Did she answer?"

"No, no. She did not answer and—which is not unusual for her if she's on the other line."

"And you left her a message?"

"I think I did, yeah . . . that I was home or almost home."

She called and texted Betsy again later that evening, but never talked to her again. Pam was worried because Betsy had been feeling sick and was sneezing, and she knew Betsy's white blood cell count was low from the chemo. She later called Betsy's mother to express her concern over not reaching Betsy.

Betsy had asked Pam to stay and watch movies with her until Russ got home. She knew Russ had a weekly card game or some activity with friends every Tuesday night. But she just wanted to go home and she told Betsy she should go to bed.

"So I just, you know, I left her. And she was sitting on the couch. She had a blanket on her and she was going to watch TV."

There it was, Schwartz thought. Pam was Prosecuting Attorney Askey's source for her comment to the media that Betsy was on the couch when she was killed.

Pam retrieved her cell phone for the police and pulled up the record of calls she made Tuesday night. The call to her husband registered at 7:04 p.m. The call to Betsy after she said she left was at 7:27 p.m. Detective Kaiser asked if she had arrived at home when she made that call to Betsy.

"Oh, yeah. When I was close to home."

Smith asked, "Do you remember about where you were when you made that call? Were you on the road still or at home?"

"Oh, I was on the road. . . . Actually, I called her because she's afraid. . . . I always get lost in Troy and it's really dark. . . . So, actually, I was still in Troy and said . . . I either said, 'I'm on my way' or 'I'm home already' . . . so she wouldn't worry."

After Pam got home and showered, she was concerned there was still no response from Betsy. Her phone showed she called Betsy's mother at 8:52 p.m. to ask her to check on Betsy.

Smith checked the phone's record of text messages between Pam and Betsy, finding several Tuesday morning as the women made plans for the day. He read one to Pam from Betsy at 10:35 a.m. saying that Bobbi was going to take her to chemotherapy: Have not spent any one-on-one time with her, Betsy had said.

Pam then told the detectives about an idea she and Betsy discussed at the chemo session—"a complicated controversy," she called it. The idea was for Betsy and Russ to buy the house where Betsy's mother and father lived before they divorced. One of Betsy's sisters was living there with her family, but they hadn't been making the payments and the house was about to be foreclosed or sold. Betsy and Russ would buy the house and live in the downstairs with Betsy's daughters, and Janet and Bobbi would live upstairs. The Farias would rent out their house in Troy to generate income toward Russ's recent goal of retiring to Florida. Betsy mentioned she was upset that the house in Troy was in Russ's name only and that he referred to it as "his house."

Betsy planned to talk to Russ about the idea when he got home Tuesday night, but said it would probably make him "very angry" and he would refuse to consider moving out of the house in Troy. Betsy didn't like living in Troy, so far away from her mother and sisters. She already spent most of her weeknights on the sofa at her mother's and did not look forward to weekends at home in Troy. Pam said Betsy didn't like to be "stuck" in Troy with Russ and stayed away from their house as much as possible.

"She had told me she doesn't like to go there on the weekends because, you know, sometimes he's in a good mood; they do lot of things together. But he's very degrading to her. He makes comments about how much money he'll have after she's gone because he's got—this is what she said; I don't know for sure. I haven't seen the financials. But he's got life insurance on her at work. She's got life insurance."

Pam added, "That's not uncommon for her to be away from him. . . . She goes to Branson as much as she can to get away with the girls. . . . I've been through several of her separations. . . . He is, according to her, verbally mean to her."

Smith asked the obvious question. "Is he ever physically mean . . . to her, that you know of?"

"I don't know. I never really got into that conversation because I don't know the guy. . . . I know him enough—a couple of times I've seen him, and he is pompous. Women are like . . . he just . . . He's a know-it-all. But I know a lot of guys like that. He smokes in the house, even though she's sick, and doesn't care."

"Sort of disrespectful?"

"Oh, he's very disrespectful, very disrespectful. He'll say disrespectful things. Uh-huh. She gets her feelings hurt a lot and she just doesn't care to be around him. . . . She's tired of the talk about what he's going to have when she's gone. And she got real tired of that. . . . She was afraid to be [there] on the weekends with him."

Schwartz was surprised again. Pam had just escalated Betsy's attitude from limiting her time with Russ to being afraid of him. She clearly was building a case against Russ as a menacing, potential killer.

Pam said Betsy had invited her to join her and Linda for their weekend in Branson to help make a plan for getting away from Russ. Pam didn't go because she didn't enjoy such trips, and her husband didn't like her to be away. Besides, she and her husband "flipped" houses—buying houses, renovating them, and then selling them for a profit—and they often did that work on the weekends.

She then delivered an accusation that Schwartz thought made her effort to incriminate Russ even more transparent. When she was with Betsy at her tennis club last week, Betsy said she had written a message to Pam "about something Russ was saying to her that was really disturbing to her." Betsy hadn't been able to send it to Pam because it was not in the body of an email, but on a "form" on her computer. She also said she was afraid to email it to Pam because Russ had been looking through her emails and she couldn't print it because the printer was in Russ's home office. Pam never saw the document, but Betsy had hinted at the content.

"She did say that the last weekend she was with him . . . that he'd start playing this game of putting a pillow over her face to see what it would feel like. . . . 'This is what it's going to feel like when you die,' or whatever, and then act like he was kidding. . . . She was very upset."

Smith was intrigued. "So she said he was actually putting a pillow over her face?"

"Yeah."

"Did she sound scared?"

"Oh, yeah. Very scared. But then she would laugh. And that's why she didn't—really, toward the end here, she did not want to go home. . . . She's been sleeping on couches for months."

"So she's talked about divorcing . . . her husband, Russell?"

"Oh, yeah. A lot . . . she always done that, though. . . . And she was desperately, like, talking yesterday that she wanted to get back in and live with her mom."

"But she was going to approach Russ yesterday evening with this deal with moving into her mother's house and renting out their house?"

"Uh-huh."

"He was going to get angry?"

"Absolutely. She said he would not leave his house. It's his house."

Schwartz couldn't stop shaking his head as he listened to Pam Hupp single-handedly build a case against Russ Faria as an abusive and scheming husband eager to cash in on the death of his wife—a man who could torture his wife by putting a pillow over her face in what easily could be seen as test runs for murder. She had even provided the cops with the trigger that could have set Russ off on a murderous rage—Betsy's proposal to abandon his house and move the family into a house twenty-five miles away. Schwartz now assumed Pam was the source for much of the information the police used to accuse Russ of Betsy's murder during that brutal last interrogation session. The cops seemed only too delighted to accept her allegations without the skepticism that was clearly warranted, and without acknowledging some glaring contradictions.

CHAPTER THIRTEEN

While Pam Hupp was explaining that she and Betsy Faria worked together in insurance offices for ten years, she almost offhandedly dropped a bomb that shocked Schwartz and clearly cast the entire story of Betsy's murder in a new light.

Pam said Betsy had recently talked more about Russ's fixation on the money he would have when she died, including his desire to buy a motorcycle from his uncle that Betsy said they couldn't afford. Betsy said Russ was her sole beneficiary on her life insurance policies. But before they got into that financial issue, Betsy mentioned another concern.

"She was talking—this was after she had mentioned that he was getting really creepy and kind of making her nervous with, like the pillow, you know, and I don't know what else he was doing. . . . She was just saying he was making her feel really creepy. Like, she would turn around and he just would be staring at her, and then again talk about, you know, wow, what he's going to have and he wanted to trade his motorcycle in . . . that kind of stuff."

Pam said she suggested Betsy change the beneficiary on her policies to her mother. But Betsy feared her mother would not handle the money properly, and she was sure her daughters would blow the money if they were the beneficiaries. Betsy said she might consider Pam's suggestion to make the beneficiary Betsy's sister Mary Rodgers.

And then Pam Hupp delivered an explosive bit of information that would become the focal point of the Betsy Faria murder case.

She said Betsy turned to her and said, " 'Would you be my beneficiary on my life policies and make sure my kids get it when they need it?' And I said, 'Well, I could. I don't feel real comfortable with that, but . . .' She goes, 'Well, I can't trust my mom because she'll give it to the kids.' I said, 'I don't—I guess, you know. To me, it's no big deal. Whatever.' "

Replacing Russ with Pam Hupp as the beneficiary on Betsy's life insurance had not been an idle thought. Betsy called the week before she went to Branson—Pam thought it was between Wednesday, December 14, and Friday, December 16—and asked her to meet at the nearby Winghaven Public Library, where Betsy surprised her by producing a change-of-beneficiary form on her policy with State Farm.

"She said, 'I'm going to make you the beneficiary. If you could, when my daughters are older, give them some money?' I said, 'OK. Well, how much is it for?' [Betsy said,] 'One hundred fifty thousand dollars' . . . and I said, 'Well, Russ is going to know. . . . I'm just assuming he would know if you changed.' And she said, 'No, the policy's in my name and I have the right to do that and I pick the beneficiaries. He's never going to know'. . . . [She] was real freaked out about him getting all this money."

She and Betsy sat at a table near the front windows of the library as Betsy filled out the form to change the beneficiary to Pam. They took the form to the front desk and asked Lauren Manganelli, the young woman librarian, to sign as a required witness to Betsy's signature. Both women produced their driver's licenses when Manganelli asked for identification. The librarian then signed the form. Pam remembered Betsy also checked out a book, but she had no idea if Betsy filed the form with the insurance company before she died.

Pam didn't think Betsy would have had time to follow through on the second step in her plan to keep the insurance money away from Russ by changing the beneficiary on another policy for $100,000 to her friend and relative named Linda.

Joel Schwartz rocked back in his chair and took a deep breath. Pam Hupp had just given herself motive and opportunity to murder Betsy Faria. This ominously odd woman had made herself a legitimate suspect amid a transparent attempt to frame Russ by creating a Frankenstein's monster version of him. But Pam now had the same motive to kill Betsy that she had been building for Russ: money. One hundred fifty K, free and clear.

It was a reasonable inference that Pam somehow convinced Betsy that making her the beneficiary was the best way to keep the money away from Russ while protecting it for her daughters. Pam then killed Betsy at the first opportunity—when she knew Russ would be away at game night—and happily spoon-fed the police a case against him. Pam Hupp had framed Russ Faria. She certainly could be the answer to the central question in this case: If Russ Faria didn't kill Betsy, who did?

But Pam wasn't finished talking. While Detective Smith took a bathroom break at 7:50 a.m., she and Detective Kaiser talked about whether Pam would have to miss an appointment at 8:30 a.m. with her brother to take their mother—who, Pam said, had dementia—to her financial advisor to talk about stocks she was holding from her late husband's employer. Pam called her brother to explain she couldn't make the appointment and said to him, "My friend—something happened to her last night and I have two police officers here asking me questions. . . . They just showed up at my door. I don't even know what happened."

She had a discussion with her brother about handling stock and annuity payments before and after their mother died. That conversation wasn't reported in the official transcript of the interview or the police report later, but it was captured on the audio recording. It didn't seem especially pertinent to Joel Schwartz when he heard it.

When the interview resumed, Pam continued to build a money motive for Russ. The Farias were struggling financially because Betsy's DJ business was down. Pam had recently taken Betsy to a Missouri state office to try to get food stamps for her daughters because they had such limited incomes. Betsy said she received a payment for her disability claim from Social Security and was expecting some money from her daughters' father—she mentioned $20,000—in back child support from his Social Security payments.

Before Betsy married Russ, Pam said Betsy had been married to a man Pam knew only as Ron. "Actually, I've probably met him more than I've met her husband now," she said.

Kaiser asked, "So, what was that relationship like between her and Ron?"

"Oh, they still saw each other up to this day."

"What's Ron's last name?"

"I don't know. Russ would know. He knows him. He doesn't know that they see each other, but—not often, but they do. . . . Betsy's funny. Betsy's—how can I say this? My husband says, 'Betsy's your little hoosier (a Midwest slang term similar to "hillbilly" or "red neck") friend.' Betsy would sleep with him to get things done in the house, and that's how she is."

"With Ron?"

"Yeah. They had that kind of relationship. He loved the kids . . . always has been there when she's fighting with Russ or if she says Russ doesn't give her sex, you know, Ron's there. . . . I've met him about three times. . . . It's just a weird arrangement. That's how Betsy is."

Detective Smith moved to the real question at hand and asked if she had an opinion "on who you think may have done this to Betsy."

Pam hesitated. "You didn't tell me what happened to her. You said there was an accident or whatever."

Kaiser offered an awkward explanation. "No, she's not accidentally dead. She's not naturally dead."

"What does that mean?"

"Well, let me ask you this, and I'm not trying to play word games with you, but we are trying to figure out what happened to your friend. OK? You understand that she's . . . she's dead? I told you that . . ."

"Yeah, you told me that."

"And I'm sorry. OK? I'm very sorry."

"OK."

"We're trying to figure out what happened. Do you think that she could kill herself?"

Pam's voice trembled slightly. "I don't know. . . . I don't think so, just because she's my friend, even though she's been very depressed. But no. I don't know. I don't think so. I wouldn't like to think that. She's Catholic, like me, and we're very serious about it. So I wouldn't think so."

"I'm just going to ask. Can you think of anyone that might want to hurt your friend?"

"No. Everybody loved . . . she had zillions of friends. . . . No, absolutely not. She was the nicest, sweetest—would give you anything you asked for if she had it."

"Anyone that scared her or that would want to hurt her?"

"Just recently, I mean, you know, she's been afraid of her husband. But that's been throughout their marriage . . . you know, and that's why they separate a lot, but . . ."

"And how would you describe that marriage?"

"Well, it's not a marriage. . . . They don't even really live, you know . . . she got back to him for financial reasons because she had the two girls."

She said Betsy had planned to divorce Russ so she could marry a man she was seeing the last time she and Russ were separated. She was devastated when the man decided to return to his wife; Betsy then returned to Russ only for financial reasons.

Pam began to cry as she talked about the recurrence of Betsy's cancer, her fear that she would not survive it, and her desire to stay away from Russ as much as possible. She cried even harder as she said Betsy had not wanted a prognosis from the doctor because she didn't want to know how much time she might have left. But Russ insisted and the doctor delivered an estimate that Betsy had just three to five years to live. Betsy was scheduled to get another scan that very day to determine if chemotherapy was shrinking the tumor. Betsy did not believe the chemo was working because she had started wetting the bed, which was angering Russ because he didn't want the mattress to smell.

Pam continued to cry as Kaiser tried to offer more of an explanation of Betsy's death. "She didn't die accidentally and she didn't die from an illness. So we're trying to figure out, then, if it's either by her own hand or somebody else's hand."

Pam asked, "Then how did she die? I don't think Betsy would ever kill herself. I mean, she's way too Catholic. She would not do that."

She was still crying as the detectives explained that they couldn't be specific about what happened to Betsy. Was there anything they hadn't discussed that could help them determine what happened? Pam said again that she knew that Betsy was really bothered by the fact that the house in Troy was only in Russ's name.

And then she said, "Maybe if you guys could find that letter that she was going to send me . . . if she really has it or if she deleted it or whatever . . . She said she was going to talk to me about changing her beneficiaries to me. And that he had done . . . started doing this weird thing with a pillow that had just started happening . . ."

Pam launched into a long diatribe about Betsy's fear of Russ, adding, "And though he's always been very nice to me, I do know over the years the hard-core stuff he has said to her. You know, he's just verbally . . . he's nasty . . . especially when he drinks."

She said Betsy talked about her decision to make Pam and her relative named Linda the beneficiaries on the insurance policies to protect the money, saying, "I want my kids to have it. I don't want Russ to have it because that's all he's talking about. . . . He said he would give the girls some money and give my mom twenty-five thousand dollars. And I said, 'OK . . . that's nice.' But then, the other day, he said, 'Don't you dare give Leah any more money. I'm sick of it. Don't give her a dime.' I want to give it to somebody that Russ can't get it from."

That prompted Detective Smith to ask about the Hupps' finances. Pam said they were set: $20,000-plus in a checking account and money in annuities and in traditional and Roth IRAs.

"Do you think Russ could have done this?" Smith asked.

"I don't know him well enough," Pam said as she began a convoluted debate with herself. "I know there was something going on there. I'm not sure what it was. I don't know if she was getting ready to permanently leave him. . . . But I can't imagine why he would. . . . When I talk about it and see how much she's been through in ten years in their relationship, I can see kind of her stage that she's going toward. But as far as him doing anything to her, I don't know why he would. . . . He thinks he's going to get a lot of money . . . unless she told him he wasn't going to get a lot of money. I mean, they can get in some nasty fights. I don't know what happened last night when she talked to him. . . . She was very excited to talk to him."

Joel Schwartz shook his head again. Her comment about not knowing what happened "last night" just confirmed that she knew when Betsy had died. And she had neatly supplied the police with the "trigger" they had been looking for—the "why" and the "something that happened"—that could explain Russ's rage and extreme violence against his wife. It seemed to Schwartz that Pam had just cleverly suggested that Russ snapped when his wife announced her plan to move him into a house he didn't want, with relatives he didn't want to be around, in a town where he didn't want to live, all while abandoning his first house that he had bought in the town where he wanted to live.

Pam had supported her suggestion that Russ would not want to live with Betsy's family by building stories of mistrust and dislike between him and Betsy's mother and daughters. She recounted several times when Russ had banned the daughters from his house and insisted Betsy not provide any financial support for them. And Pam knew Russ and Janet Meyer weren't getting along.

The detectives asked if Russ hurt Betsy physically. "I don't know physically. Never got into a lot of it . . . I can't say for sure. She would insinuate stuff that they would get in really big fights and stuff like that. I've never seen him hurt her. I've never seen bruises on her . . . and she really didn't complain too much about the verbal. I mean, people would be going, 'Your husband's an ass. That was just rude.' And she's like, 'Oh, he's always like that.' And I'm like, 'Damn.' He's just a smart-ass. Mean, though . . . he can say mean stuff."

When the detectives were about to conclude the interview, Pam asked about Betsy's death: "What time did this happen? This morning?" Smith said he couldn't get into that information.

But Schwartz immediately recognized another telltale contradiction by Pam. When she called her brother earlier to tell him she would be late for their appointment, she said something had happened to her friend "last night." But she had just asked the police if it had happened "this morning." That struck Schwartz as an obvious attempt to hide her knowledge that Betsy had been killed last night because the police had not disclosed that to her yet.

Kaiser and Smith turned off their recorder at 9:06 a.m., after two hours and twenty-four minutes of conversation with her. But then she remembered an incident the police might want to know about.

They turned the recorder on again at 9:17 a.m. as she described being at the gym with Betsy a week or two before the holidays. Betsy asked her to get a couple bottles of Gatorade from a bag in Betsy's car. Pam said Betsy took "a big gulp" from a bottle and started gagging. It tasted horrible and she asked Pam to taste it. Pam wouldn't taste it, but said it smelled OK. She held it up next to the other bottle and noticed Betsy's looked "cloudy." Betsy said Russ had bought the Gatorade for her because he wanted her to get electrolytes into her system to help combat the effects of chemotherapy. Betsy took her bottle to the restroom and poured out the contents.

As Kaiser began to close the interview for the second time, she asked if Betsy had ever hurt herself or talked about suicide. Pam recalled one time, when Betsy and Russ were separated and she was beginning to have problems with her teenage daughters. "She had said, 'You know, I just feel like killing myself. I can't do this anymore' . . . but I've had friends say that to me before. . . . Whether she's ever attempted, I don't think so. . . . She had talked about— she felt like killing herself. But Betsy is—can be down in the dumps and an hour later, be flying high."

The detectives ended the interview at 9:41 a.m. and left. But they returned at 12:15 p.m. with more requests for Pam. She signed a form agreeing to a search of her cell phone and one allowing the police to take a DNA sample from inside of her mouth—a buccal swab. Kaiser asked for the clothing she had worn the night before and accompanied her upstairs to retrieve a long-sleeved red T-shirt from a hamper in the bathroom and khaki slacks that were folded neatly on a shelf in the bedroom closet. She also gave Kaiser a pair of tennis shoes and a white coat that were in the dining room. She said she had not laundered any of the items. She consented to photographs of her face, neck, hands, arms, and feet. Kaiser noted in her report later that Pam Hupp bore no noticeable marks or injuries.

Kaiser also wanted a more detailed description of where she had been when she called Betsy at 7:27 p.m. on December 27. Pam said she had driven ten or fifteen minutes after leaving Betsy's and called her after reaching a familiar point in her drive home.

Less than twenty-four hours later, the detectives were back. On the morning of Thursday, December 29, Kaiser and Smith returned Pam's cell phone to her and then asked for more details about the visit to the Winghaven Public Library to complete the beneficiary form.

The police had essentially confirmed Pam's account when they interviewed Lauren Manganelli on Wednesday. The librarian remembered two women working at a table in the front window for less than an hour and then asking her to sign as a witness on some sort of insurance paper. She didn't remember the women's names, but described them as cheerful and friendly, dressed in workout clothes, both with short hair—one blonde and one with brown hair. Manganelli also confirmed that Betsy had checked out a book that same time—on Friday, December 23—confirming that as the date for signing the form.

The police paid their fourth visit to Pam Hupp's house Thursday evening so Detectives Mike Reiter and Donald Thurmond could interview her husband. The detectives sat in the living room with Mark Hupp—and then violated the first rule of Police Interviewing 101 by allowing Pam to join them. With his wife present, Mark said he knew Betsy, but did not know her husband. Mark confirmed his wife's statement that he had left his phone in his truck the night before and only learned later she had left him a voice mail at 7:04 p.m.

His wife's message said she had arrived at Betsy's house and would be leaving for home soon. Mark added that Betsy had taken the phone to leave him holiday greetings.

The detectives then made another amateurish error. Although Mark played the voice mail for them, they failed to seize his phone so they could preserve the recording. They would learn later that he erased it.

The detectives noted that Pam had commandeered the interview with her husband. In their report later, they wrote in grand understatement: *While interviewing Mark, Pam would begin to speak and engage us in conversation.* Actually, there was not another word from Mark in the report. The detectives quoted Pam as saying she had just visited Betsy's family that day and wanted to let the police know that Betsy's daughter Leah had forgotten to tell them how Russ would throw water on the girls to wake them up in the mornings and would drag them out of their beds.

Joel Schwartz was shocked again. The police had gathered absolutely no useful information from Mark in an incompetent interview they absurdly conducted in front of his wife. They didn't ask Mark what time his wife arrived home Tuesday night, what she was wearing, or what she said. The cops made no attempt to preserve the voice mail. And they allowed Pam to hijack the interview to heap on more unsupported hearsay about Russ Faria. Wasn't *any* cop paying attention to what this woman was doing—to how she was playing them?

Schwartz was struck by another bizarre element to Pam's contact with police. She agreed to Detective Kaiser's request to take a polygraph scheduled with Detective Gary McIntyre on Friday, December 30. But Sergeant Ryan McCarrick delayed the test because Pam said her attorney wanted to be there. Pam then told McIntyre she wasn't sure she could take a polygraph because she was on a variety of medications to address the effects of a head injury suffered in a fall some time ago that left her prone to seizures. McIntyre suggested she get a letter from her doctor saying she was medically fit to undergo the test. Three weeks later, on January 25, 2012, Pam provided a letter from Dr. Ronald L. Fischer that read:

To Whom It May Concern:

Pamela Hupp is unable to undergo a polygraph due to her medical condition. This was discussed with Pamela when she was last seen in the office on January 3, 2012.

Sincerely,
Doctor Ronald L. Fischer

It wasn't until later that the police learned that Pam had sent a handwritten note to Dr. Fischer the day before he wrote his letter. Her note said:

Dear Doctor Fischer,
*   Could you please write Det. Kaiser a letter stating that I was not able to do my polygraph due to medical reasons. Don't need any more detailed than that.*
*   Thank you.*

*   Pam Hupp*

*   Call if you need questions.*

Fischer would later tell Schwartz during a deposition that he was unaware of any medical reason Pam Hupp could not take a polygraph.

So Pam duped her doctor into giving her a medical excuse to avoid a polygraph. Why would she do that if she was telling the truth? And why didn't the police call her on such an obvious deception? Indeed, why didn't the police call her on the seemingly dozens of contradictions in her zealous effort to frame Russ Faria?

Schwartz met immediately with Swanson to discuss what they had learned about the case against Russ that they now realized should be the case against Pam Hupp. Russ's defense was built on the solid foundation of his unshakeable alibi and that fit, hand in glove, with what was called the SODDI defense—some other dude did it. The defense team now had the name of that other "dude": Pam Hupp.

CHAPTER FOURTEEN

Identifying Pam Hupp as the prime suspect in Betsy Faria's murder and the architect of the effort to frame Russ Faria didn't answer other glaring questions for Joel Schwartz and Nate Swanson. They still needed to know how some of the most experienced detectives in the St. Louis metropolitan region and Prosecuting Attorney Leah Askey had gotten this case so wrong. The defenders still had to dissect hundreds of pages from the Major Case Squad's investigation by twenty-three detectives and other forensic experts pursuing 104 leads over four days between Tuesday, December 27, and Saturday, December 31, 2011.

Schwartz continued his investigation with what surely would be the ugliest document in the police file—the autopsy report. The first thing Schwartz read made him shudder.

Betsy Faria was stabbed fifty-five times.

The cops had told Russ she was stabbed "twenty-five times and counting," and that had seemed an appalling level of brutality. But fifty-five times? Who does that to another person and why? Schwartz steeled himself against what he knew would be gruesome details as he read the fourteen-page report by Dr. Kamal D. Sabharwal, a forensic pathologist with the St. Louis County Medical Examiner's Office.

The autopsy had begun at 1 p.m., Wednesday, December 28— fifteen and a half hours after Russ found Betsy's body. First, the routine clinical observations: The deceased was a white female, forty-two years old, five-four, 160 pounds, with a mix of dark and light brown hair. Both blue eyes contained clear contact lenses. Both earlobes had two piercings and each ear contained a silver earring with a red stone. The body was dressed in a black T-shirt, blue athletic pants, black bra and panties, and white-and-green socks. Rigor mortis was severe in the jaw and the upper and lower extremities. The chest bore surgical scars from a mastectomy and breast reconstruction.

And then the pathologist documented with cold medical precision every one of the fifty-five stabs and cuts and slashes that rained down on Betsy as she surely fought for her life. The shape, length, width, and depth of each wound and the damage it inflicted created an almost unending list of horror and cruelty.

Ten wounds to the neck, including injuries to the thyroid gland, the trachea, and the right jugular vein. A knife protruding from a wound five and a half inches deep. A gaping wound almost three inches long by just over one inch wide on the left side of the neck below the knife.

Three wounds to the scalp, including one that caused a small fracture of the parietal bone above the left ear. One slitlike stab wound to the lower left eyelid. Two wounds to the left ear. Three wounds to the left shoulder. Five wounds to the left upper and back of the chest. Seven wounds to the abdomen, including two that were six inches deep and penetrated the liver. One wound through the left bicep that extended into the chest and penetrated the upper lobe of the left lung. Two wounds to the back, almost three inches deep, that penetrated the spleen and pancreas. One wound through the right bicep extending almost three inches. Ten wounds to the right arm, hand, and fingers, including a gash above the right wrist four inches long and an inch deep that cut through tendons, muscles, and blood vessels. Nine wounds to the upper left arm and seven to the left forearm and hand. One wound to the upper left thigh.

The pathologist entered a seemingly foregone conclusion: The cause of death was stab wounds to the neck, chest, and abdomen.

Blood tests identified only one substance: a low level of diphenhydramine, known as Benadryl, and commonly used to treat allergy symptoms or as a sleep aid.

There was another observation that may not have drawn much attention by the police. The pathologist noted the liver that suffered two stab wounds also showed several firm tan nodules, up to three and a half inches in size—the cancer that would have slowly taken Betsy's life, had not a sadistic killer inflicted a more sudden and violent end.

Schwartz next had to experience the sounds of Russ Faria's overwrought 911 call. His first reaction was that Russ's hyperventilating hysteria did not seem excessive for an average guy who had just come home to find his wife's bloody body on the living-room floor. And Russ's assumption that Betsy had committed suicide didn't seem outrageous or even incriminating, given the wound to her right forearm, her background of depressed suicide threats in the past, and a recent diagnosis of terminal stage-four cancer. The cops' allegation that Russ had tried to misdirect them with a bogus claim that Betsy committed suicide now seemed even more absurd. How could a killer who had just inflicted fifty-five stab wounds on the victim expect a mere suggestion of suicide to cause the police to overlook the overwhelming evidence of murder? It was a ridiculous proposition that the police had set as the cornerstone of the case against Russ—and, Schwartz thought, perhaps the element of the State's case that would be simplest to overcome.

Schwartz thought the average person would find the sounds of Russ's agony, grief, and shock genuine and believable. Surely, people would understand that every person would react differently and unpredictably to the scene Russ Faria had just encountered. Surely, people would find nothing in the sounds of Russ's pain to suggest he was anything but an anguished husband.

CHAPTER FIFTEEN

The official investigation into the murder of Betsy Faria began when Lincoln County Sheriff's Deputy Chris Hollingsworth arrived at 130 Sumac Drive just minutes after Russ's 911 call. The first to respond to the dispatcher's call of a possible suicide, Hollingsworth knew as soon as he saw Betsy's body that he was looking at a murder. He took Russ to a chair on the front porch to protect the crime scene inside. Although Hollingsworth pointedly noted that he saw no tears being shed, Russ's erratic breathing and speaking and apparent state of panic and shock made the deputy fear Russ could collapse or pass out.

Joel Schwartz realized it had taken bare minutes for the first cop on the scene to cast suspicion on Russ with an observation—a rather early judgment—about the way this husband was reacting to his wife's death. No tears, Hollingsworth reported before noting the husband seemed to be about to pass out.

Sitting in Hollingsworth's patrol car to get warm, Russ chain-smoked cigarettes as he described Betsy's cancer, the couple's schedule of activities that day, and his discovery of Betsy's body just minutes before. Hollingsworth wrote in his report: *It should be noted during this conversation Russell appeared to be calm, laughing at times.* But Hollingsworth also wrote, when he got out of the car to get another cigarette for Russ: *I observed a few tears in Russell's eyes as he stated that he needed to contact his mother and is unsure how he is going to tell his daughters.*

Captain Robert Shramek of the Lincoln County Fire Protection District (FPD) arrived moments after Hollingsworth had led Russ out of the house. The first official to examine Betsy's body, Shramek felt unsuccessfully for a pulse on her upper arm and noted how cold and stiff the body was. When he tried to lift her hand, the hand and fingers didn't move, but her entire arm lifted up. To Shramek, that meant the victim had been dead long enough for the onset of rigor mortis, which usually begins two to four hours after death. The blood under Betsy's head and the other streaks of blood on the carpet around the body appeared to be cold and coagulating, more evidence that death had occurred at what he estimated to be two to three hours earlier.

Supervisor Mike Quattrocchi and two paramedics from the Lincoln County Ambulance District arrived at 9:51 p.m., right behind Shramek. One of the paramedics wrapped a light-colored blanket around the shivering Russ Faria as he sat on the porch. Quattrocchi didn't know who the man under the blanket was, but he would remember him sitting with his face in his hands, noticeably distraught and probably in shock.

Shramek met Quattrocchi at the doorway and told him the victim was dead and in rigor mortis. "Stiff as a board," Quattrocchi would remember Shramek saying.

Quattrocchi leaned down and touched the victim's arm—cold and stiff, just as Shramek had said. He saw the knife protruding from the neck and noticed the wide, deep gash across the right forearm. The drying blood on the carpet confirmed what the condition of the body indicated—the woman had been dead for some time. There was no need for the emergency medical services of Quattrocchi and his team; they left immediately.

Recognizing the complexity of this investigation, the Lincoln County Sheriff's Office filed an official request at 1:30 a.m., Wednesday, for assistance from the Major Case Squad of Greater St. Louis. The MCS is a multijurisdictional organization of local police departments that calls out detectives and other resources from across the region to provide massive and unmatched manpower and expertise to investigate a case—usually a homicide. MCS has a stellar reputation and a record to match. MCS directors quickly activated the squad and early-morning calls went out across the region for member detectives to report to Lincoln County. Detective Sergeant Ryan McCarrick of the sheriff's office took the role of MCS deputy report officer with the responsibility to keep track of all of the activities by detectives and the results of the overall investigation.

Teams of MCS detectives immediately fanned out across the area searching for witnesses and information that might shed light on the life and death of Elizabeth Kay Faria, the woman known to everyone as Betsy. The deceased was universally described to police as bubbly, upbeat, effervescent, extroverted to the extreme, friendly with everyone, and loving to her family and friends. She had a zest for life that even the shadow of terminal cancer couldn't diminish. No one in her circle could begin to think of anyone who would wish her harm, let alone kill her so brutally.

Neighbors on the few streets in the Waterbrooke Estates Subdivision said they hadn't heard or seen anything suspicious or unusual that night. They had few concerns about neighborhood safety because there had been no break-ins or other troubling events there for years.

Crime scene investigators had begun combing through the Faria house even before Betsy's body was taken to the St. Louis County Medical Examiner's Office. They took hundreds of photographs documenting every corner of every room, as well as the outside of the house, the two cars in the driveway, and the third in the garage.

The bloody carpet under the body was cut from the floor and sections of the sofa upholstery bearing bloodstains were removed. A second knife that looked like the one still in Betsy's neck was found under a pillow on the sofa, but did not bear any blood or other obvious evidence.

What the police thought looked like a print from a dog's paw on the left rear hip of Betsy's pants was marked for testing. If the dog had touched Betsy after she had been killed, that could contradict Russ's statement that the dog was outside when he got home and was never back in the house. A photo captured a sad scene as a detective actually took inked paw prints from a patient Sicily to compare to the mark on the pants.

The police made some of the most dramatic and potentially valuable discoveries early in the search, and Schwartz finally learned more about what the police had been talking about in their assault on Russ during the interrogation. Tossed casually in the rear of Russ's bedroom closet, but certainly within easy view, investigators found a pair of tan size-11 men's house slippers bearing smudges of what appeared to be dried blood. To the police, they were the first direct link between the husband and the wife's bloody body and a potential contradiction to his claims of finding her already dead and never changing his clothes.

There also appeared to be smudges of dried blood on the white plastic switch plate for the ceiling light just inside the master bedroom doorway and near the closet where the slippers were found. Had the killer used a bloody hand to flip on the light?

Found on the kitchen floor, the yellow ball cap Russ had worn that night showed a stain that appeared to be blood inside the crown. A search of the bathroom led to the seizure of two washcloths, four bath towels, and a brown bath rug. Swabs were taken from the vanity sink, the shower, and both drains. Investigators lifted what appeared to be two good palm prints from the glass sliding doors that opened from the dining room onto the rear deck, where the dog still was chained in the cold.

They picked up Russ's black leather Harley-Davidson jacket from the chair in the foyer and a pair of black leather gloves folded on the back of the love seat near Betsy's body. From various locations throughout the house, including Russ's basement office, the police seized two cell phones, four laptops and computers, three hard drives, a mini thumb drive, an Apple iPod, two MP3 players, more than two hundred writable compact discs (CDs), and a Fuji-film camera.

Great care was taken to process Russ's blue Ford Explorer in the driveway, including the installation of a hidden GPS transmitter that could be used by police to track the vehicle, if that became useful later. Swabs for blood or DNA were taken from interior and exterior door handles, window frames, interior door panels, armrests, the gearshift, and the steering wheel. Luminol, a liquid that glows in the dark when exposed to a substance that might be blood, was sprayed on the driver's seat and door panel.

But it was other evidence the police found inside the Explorer that made Schwartz smile. On the front passenger seat, there was an Arby's paper bag from Lake St. Louis that contained a receipt for $3.01 for two junior cheddar-melt roast beef sandwiches—time stamped at 9:09 p.m., Tuesday, December 27. Two bottles of Brisk iced tea—one nearly empty and one unopened—and a carton of cigarettes, with one pack missing, were next to the Arby's bag. Those simple items should irrefutably prove Russ Faria's account of his stops on his routes to and from game night.

CHAPTER SIXTEEN

Russ Faria's alibi should have seemed even more air-tight, rock-solid, unshakeable—name the cliché—after the detectives investigated all of the elements. Everything they learned added proof upon proof that Russ was driving to game night between 5 and 6 p.m., watching movies with four fellow gamers twenty-five miles from his house between 6 and 9 p.m., and driving home between 9 and 9:35 p.m. He called 911 at 9:40 p.m. Betsy surely had been dead long enough for her body to become cold and stiff—maybe as long as two hours—when police arrived about 9:50 p.m. Joel Schwartz wondered how anyone could still think Russ Faria murdered his wife in their living room that evening after compiling that evidence.

Schwartz began his review of the alibi investigation with the interviews of the game-night participants by Detectives Mike McCann and Dean Frye. They opened their report on arriving at Mike Corbin's mobile home on Fox Trotter Drive in O'Fallon in the predawn darkness of Wednesday, December 28, by noting they had barely started up the short sidewalk when they smelled what they recognized as "burnt marijuana." The smell was even stronger inside the house. But a little weed passed among friends in a private home was not why the detectives were there and it drew only that cursory mention in their report.

Mike and his partner of twenty years, Angelia Hulion, confirmed every detail of Russ's account of a night watching movies. Russ arrived about six o'clock and left at straight-up nine o'clock. He seemed fine—completely normal. In fact, he was so relaxed that he got a bit drowsy and dozed off. They all had smoked a little marijuana, but nobody had a drop of alcohol.

McCann and Frye then checked out the game-night scenario by stopping by the O'Fallon home of the missing player, Richard May. He confirmed he had been unable to attend game night because he was making deliveries for a Chinese restaurant. His boss would later confirm that Richard had indeed been on the job.

After that, the two detectives began looking for proof that Russ had made that series of stops on his way to and from game night— and proof was exactly what they found. Video from the Conoco station in Troy showed Russ pumping gas into his Explorer at 5:16 p.m. He was on video at the counter at the U-Gas station in Wentzville buying a carton of cigarettes at 5:31/32 p.m. Greene's Country Store in Lake St. Louis had no video, but there was a receipt for a charge on Russ's VISA credit card for $41.87 at 5:52 p.m. for the purchase of a thirty-five-pound bag of dog food. He appeared on video again as he entered the QT station in Lake St. Louis at 5:56 p.m., bought two bottles of iced tea, and left the store at 5:58 p.m. For the trip home, police learned the video camera on the drive-through lane at Arby's in O'Fallon wasn't working. But Schwartz thought the Arby's bag and receipt in Russ's car were just as good.

Detectives carefully followed Russ's routes to and from game night, but failed to find any video or surveillance cameras facing the roads that could have recorded Russ's car as it passed, or, on the other hand, could have proven that it never passed.

Reports timing both legs of Russ's route were perfectly consistent with his account. Detectives Floyd and Rider timed the drives from Russ's home to the Conoco station, then to the U-Gas station, then to Greene's Country Store, and then to the QT at a total drive time of forty-one minutes and thirty seconds—a route the MapQuest website measured at 24.86 miles. Adding time for stops and purchases at two service stations and two stores, Russ's claim of a sixty-minute trip to Corbin's seemed right on the mark.

Checking Russ's drive home, Floyd covered the distance from Arby's in Lake St. Louis to Russ's house in Troy in twenty-six minutes and thirty seconds. Detective Roger Mauzy covered it slightly faster, at twenty-four minutes and fifteen seconds. The police concluded that Russ's departure from Mike Corbin's at 9 p.m., and a stop at Arby's, should have put him at home no later than 9:31 p.m.—some fourteen minutes earlier than Russ's estimate of 9:45, and nine minutes before he placed the 911 call at 9:40.

Despite confirming Russ's alibi details and timing, Schwartz learned the police and prosecutor concocted a theory that Russ had time to kill Betsy between his arrival at home and his call to 911—a superhuman feat in less than ten minutes. Schwartz wondered how anyone could believe a man arrived at home, changed clothes, stabbed his wife fifty-five times, cleaned up the scene, changed clothes again, called 911, and presented himself believably as a shocked and grieving husband, all in a mere nine or ten minutes. Then he was able to withstand more than forty hours of intense police grilling without exposing a single contradiction or weakness in his story.

Detectives had called the four game-night players to the Chesterfield Police Department for another round of interviews on New Year's Eve, just three days after the police had first talked to them. Schwartz assumed the hours of interrogation of Russ on December 27 and 28, and the results of the checks on drive times, had motivated the new round of questioning of the gamers to try to punch holes in their accounts of that night. As he watched videos of these second interviews, it was clear to Schwartz that the police pulled nothing new or even slightly incriminating about Russ or his behavior from his friends.

Mike Corbin told detectives he had known Russ for fifteen years and had never seen him lose his temper or be violent. Russ and Betsy had separated for a while, a long time ago, but Mike didn't know the details or much else about Russ's private life. He described the game they played every Tuesday, explaining that he was the referee and Russ's character was a monk named Gi, who never used weapons. Mike repeated the group's insistence that no one, including Russ, left his house during the three-hour double feature.

"We were all within eight feet of each other all night," Mike said. He assured Floyd that he was being truthful, adding he would never lie about Russ or assist him in the commission of a crime.

Floyd and Rider got very much the same story during the second interviews with Angelia Hulion, Marshall Bach, and Brandon Sweeney—all of them sincerely seeming to cooperate with police. They were regulars at game night and saw each other at an occasional Saturday viewing of mixed martial arts fights on TV, but they didn't socialize much beyond that. They didn't know details of Russ Faria's marriage or his relationship with his wife. But they certainly had never seen Russ angry or violent enough to hurt or kill anyone, especially his wife.

CHAPTER SEVENTEEN

Informing family members that a loved one has been killed is one of the most gut-wrenching jobs a police officer ever faces. Joel Schwartz had to sympathize with Detectives Paul Barish and Jana Walters as he read their report about arriving at 7:20 a.m., Wednesday, December 28, to deliver that news to Betsy Faria's older daughter, Leah Day, and Betsy's sister, Julie Swaney, at Julie's house in St. Louis. There was nothing the officers could do to soften the blow as Leah and Julie burst into tears.

When the women composed themselves enough to talk, they said they knew nothing about what had happened to Betsy or who could have wanted to harm her. But they were able to provide information that Schwartz thought established an approximate time of Betsy's death. Leah said she and her aunt went to a U.S. Cellular store about 7 p.m., Tuesday, to upgrade Leah's cell phone. Since her phone was a line on Betsy's plan, Leah knew she would need Betsy's approval. Leah called Betsy at seven o'clock to ask her to answer her phone later when Leah called from the phone store. Betsy said Pam Hupp was driving her home then and she promised to answer Leah's call later. But when Leah called Betsy from the store three times, there was no answer. Leah said she hadn't been concerned; it wasn't unusual for Betsy not to answer her phone. When the police checked Leah's phone, they found the unanswered calls to Betsy at 7:21, 7:26, and 7:30 p.m.

Those calls were more evidence that Betsy was killed long before

Russ arrived home after 9:30 p.m. Schwartz thought Betsy was either dead or was being attacked when Leah called.

Confirming what Russ had told the detectives, Leah said she had been staying with her Aunt Julie, who was forty-four and the middle of Betsy's three look-alike sisters.

Leah offered some criticism of Russ and his behavior. He would sometimes get angry, mostly over financial issues, and would yell at Betsy. Betsy was afraid to stand up to him and began staying often at her mother's apartment. Leah said things were not good between Betsy and Russ, but Betsy would act like everything was OK to keep peace in the family.

Detective Roger Mauzy and Officer Steve Queen were spared the emotional task of breaking news of Betsy's death to her seventy-four-year old mother, Janet Meyer, and Betsy's younger daughter, Mariah Day. By the time the cops arrived at Janet's apartment in Lake St. Louis, Julie had already called with the grim news. Mariah and Janet could not offer any insight into Betsy's death, but they could describe her final hours at her mother's apartment. They had been with Betsy all day Tuesday and were joined by Bobbi Wann, an old friend visiting from Texas. Bobbi had driven Betsy to her chemo session at the Siteman Cancer Center, where they were joined by Pam Hupp. They had returned to Janet's after chemo and spent the rest of the afternoon playing Upwords, one of Betsy's favorite board games. Janet said Betsy had begun to feel "blah" and left with Pam for the drive home at about 6:30 p.m.

Janet said Pam called at 8:52 p.m. and said she tried to call Betsy after she had dropped her off at home, but got no answer. Pam was worried that Betsy was mad at her because she didn't stay until Russ got home. The police quoted Janet as saying Pam said she hadn't gone into the house with Betsy because it was dark and the front door was unlocked.

Schwartz was shocked by yet another obvious Pam Hupp lie, this time telling Janet that she had not gone into Betsy's house. Pam told the police she was in the house for as long as twenty minutes, but she lied to Betsy's mother about it. Why all of the lies?

Janet told the detectives she called Russ's cell phone about 8:30 p.m.

to ask him about Betsy, but got no answer. She left a voice mail, also with no response. She said that wasn't unusual because Russ often would not answer his phone on game night.

Mariah told detectives about the depression that had gripped her mother in recent years. Mariah found a suicide note written by Betsy and folded on her bed pillow after her first cancer diagnosis. Mariah gave the note to Russ and didn't remember what it said. She thought Betsy might have gone to a mental-health facility after that. Her mother appeared to be handling the new cancer diagnosis well and seemed happy over Christmas. She was planning to take Mariah on a cruise over spring break, next March, so she was making plans for the future.

Janet confirmed Betsy had received psychiatric treatment at a local hospital several years ago. But she believed the Farias now had a great relationship, their marriage was going great, and they were in great financial shape.

While at Janet's apartment, the detectives also interviewed her friend and houseguest, Bobbi Wann. She said Betsy had been in good spirits and mood all day Tuesday, including at the chemo session where Pam Hupp joined them.

Bobbi was able to answer one of the remaining questions. The idea Betsy planned to discuss with Russ when he got home was for the Farias to buy Janet Meyer's former home in Lake St. Louis, where they would live with Betsy's daughters, Janet, and Bobbi. The Farias would rent out their home in Troy to build up their finances so they could retire to Florida when both houses were paid off in twenty years. Betsy never liked living in Troy and said she just couldn't do it any longer. She didn't think Russ would like the new idea, but she was excited about it and was going to talk to him Tuesday night. Bobbi added that Betsy said Russ was "very abusive verbally" to her.

Detectives had to make several calls on Thursday to locate the biological father of Leah and Mariah Day at his home in Cape Coral, Florida. Tremus Day, forty-three, partially paralyzed and suffering from lupus, quickly convinced police that he had been at home with his wife and two children when Betsy was killed. His mother had notified him of Betsy's murder after she saw something about it on Facebook. He last talked to Betsy two months ago when he called in an unsuccessful attempt to get her to drop her claim for child support.

Betsy's sister, Mary Rodgers, provided a little more fodder for suspicions about Russ when she arrived at the Lincoln County Sheriff's Office at 10:15 a.m., Wednesday, to be interviewed by detectives. Forty-six, and the oldest of Betsy's sisters, Mary said Russ had ordered her to leave the Farias' home six or seven years ago when she attempted to intervene in a "verbal altercation" between him and Betsy, which was alarming enough for her to call the police.

Mary said she heard Russ say about her, "I'm going to cut her up and put her in a bag." Detectives would later check a report from January 2005 to learn Russ and Betsy told police they argued because she had come home to find that Russ had not cleaned the house, as promised.

Mary described the early years of the Farias' relationship as "rocky." She knew Betsy had cheated on Russ several times—and Russ knew it, too. But she said Betsy and Russ had worked through those problems and they now loved each other very much. Russ had come a long way, earned a college degree, and changed his behavior. Russ now "loves and takes care of Elizabeth," Mary told the detectives.

She recalled twice in the past when Betsy had been suicidal. She was admitted to a hospital for "psychiatric issues" in 2008 and again in 2010 after she made statements a police officer interpreted as suicidal. Betsy had been understandably sad after the doctor delivered the terminal cancer diagnosis two months ago, but she seemed to get past that quickly and returned to her happy self. She continued to play tennis, which she loved so much that she joked she would probably die on the tennis court.

Betsy's eldest sister confirmed that Betsy was married to Ron Carter before Russ. Betsy and Ron maintained a good relationship, and he had been very supportive during her illness.

When police interviewed Ron Carter later at his home in St. Peters, he described a rather more intimate relationship with Betsy that continued even after their one-year marriage ended in 1996. They still had sex about every two weeks, including two weeks before she was killed. She would come to his home when she was upset with Russ and that often led to sex. Betsy would visit him when she "needed a release." He talked to Betsy on the phone on Christmas Eve and she seemed upbeat, not at all depressed. Ron said Russ frequently disrespected Betsy and they argued often, but he didn't think Russ had ever struck Betsy.

Betsy's youngest sister, thirty-nine-year-old Pamela Welker, said Betsy's history of suicide threats and depression made her think Betsy must have killed herself. Pamela also knew about Betsy's hospitalization after making disturbing statements to a police officer. When she was with Betsy at the family Christmas party on Monday, Betsy had seemed normal, but was "feeling down from the cancer treatments."

Detectives Mike Reiter and Donald Thurmond began interviews with Russ's family when they arrived at his mother's home at 9:30 a.m., Wednesday. Luci Faria, sixty-five, and her daughter and Russ's sister, Rachel Faria, thirty, could offer no leads on Betsy's killer. Luci had last seen Russ and Betsy at the family Christmas party on December 26, when they were in good moods and ate well. In fact, Russ's family had been amazed at Betsy's positive attitude in light of the new cancer diagnosis. Russ and Betsy even talked about taking Mariah to Florida for a vacation in March 2012. Luci noted that Betsy was still playing tennis and loved her job as a DJ. Asked who in Russ's family would be closest to Betsy, Luci named Linda Hartmann. Luci also confirmed Russ's statement that he had called her about 5 p.m., Tuesday, to say errands would keep him from attending the family dinner at her house.

Rachel Faria showed the detectives a posting on Facebook by Betsy's daughter Mariah shortly after she learned of Betsy's death. It read: *RIP, mom. I'm sorry I was never the best daughter, You were such a strong person, didn't let nothing get you down, not even chemo. I love you and miss you already. : (Love, Mo.*

Later Wednesday, Mary Anderson and Rachel Faria tried to see Russ while he was still being interrogated at the Lincoln County Sheriff's Office. They arrived at 12:40 p.m., saying they knew Russ was there, his family was concerned about him, and they wanted to see him. The police wouldn't talk to Mary because she wasn't Russ's immediate family. But they told Rachel that Russ was unavailable because he was being interviewed. Rachel told police the only information she could provide was a vague description of an earlier incident when "Betsy was off her meds and depressed" and threatened to kill herself with a knife, which Russ took away from her. Asked about Russ's relationship with Betsy's daughters, Rachel offered only that Russ considered them his own children.

Joel Schwartz was eager to see if Linda Hartmann—Russ's fifty-four-year-old aunt by marriage—would confirm Pam Hupp's story that Linda and Betsy were discussing leaving their husbands. To Schwartz's surprise, the police report on Linda's interview never mentioned that at all. It quoted Linda as saying she had been friends with Betsy for two years and they had gone to Branson for a girls' weekend from December 19 to 22. She had seen Betsy over the holidays and remarked that she remained very upbeat despite her cancer battle.

It was Linda's daughter, Ashley Frost, twenty-three, who addressed the report about dumping husbands and fleeing to Branson. Ashley had accompanied the women on their weekend in Branson and said any such discussion was "a joke . . . not serious talk."

Schwartz read every word of the police reports on their interviews with dozens of more friends and acquaintances of the Farias over the first few days after Betsy's death. The results offered nothing that advanced the cops' case against Russ beyond varying personal opinions and anecdotes about Russ and Betsy and the state of their marriage. No one could think of anyone who would want to harm Betsy.

With so many references to the Farias' involvement with the Morning Star Church, detectives interviewed all three pastors. Mike Schreiner confirmed that Russ and Betsy were involved in church activities ranging from leading a youth group to operating audio equipment for services. He had last seen them at the Christmas Eve service and they both appeared to be in high spirits. Schreiner said the only issue facing the couple that he was aware of, besides Betsy's cancer, was personal conflicts with her daughter Leah; he didn't know much about the details. The other two pastors echoed Schreiner's comments.

Kathleen and Edward Meyer (not related to Janet Meyer) said they had known Betsy for seventeen years, even before her marriage to Ron Carter. Kathleen considered Betsy her best friend and said the loving, caring, friendly, happy, outgoing Betsy had no enemies. The Meyers also called Russ a devoted husband—Edward Meyer described him as "one of the most devoted husbands ever"—and said Russ often referred to Betsy as his angel.

Detective Mike Merkel got an interesting view of Russ from high-school classmate Jimmy Crenshaw. He had not seen Russ much during the last fifteen years, but said Russ had a temper in his younger years. Jimmy had seen him get into a fistfight over a girl. He said he couldn't see Russ killing Betsy, adding, "Unless he was really, really pissed."

Jimmy recalled Russ being in a "zombie state" at Betsy's wake at the funeral home. He was sitting with Russ next to Betsy's casket when he heard Russ say softly, "I don't understand why you think you would have to leave me."

The police report then quoted Jimmy as saying, not only had one of Betsy's aunts struck Russ, but Pam Hupp also slapped him. He quoted Pam as saying that she knew there was going to be a problem when she dropped off Betsy at home and Russ was already there. The police were able to confirm that Russ took the blow from one of Betsy's aunts. But the report about Pam hitting him proved to be false, and Jimmy's quote from Pam couldn't be accurate because the police knew Russ wasn't at home then. They had proven Russ was at Mike Corbin's house when Pam delivered Betsy at home about 7 p.m.

Betsy's longtime friend Rita Wolf told police the day after the murder that she had spoken with Betsy by phone at 5:08 p.m. the day before while Betsy was playing a board game at her mother's. Betsy complained about how painful the chemotherapy was and said that, if she had to continue to endure that kind of pain, she would stop the chemo and "just live out the rest of her life."

Rita said she had known Betsy for thirty years and considered Betsy one of her best friends. Rita couldn't think of anyone who would want to harm Betsy. And Rita thought Betsy's dog would protect her if she was attacked by a stranger in the house.

Janet Meyer had told Rita in a call that day that Pam Hupp called her the night before and said Betsy wasn't answering her phone after Pam dropped her off at home. Janet assumed Betsy had gone to bed and didn't try to contact her. Rita told the police she thought it was odd that Pam would repeatedly call Betsy so soon after leaving her house.

One of the last interview reports in the MCS case file surprised Schwartz, but he thought it was unlikely to be evidence in a trial. An anonymous caller suggested that police talk to Darlene Fuller, who had left comments about Betsy's murder on a TV news website. When police interviewed her on Saturday, December 31, the thirty-nine-year-old woman said she had an affair with Russ for about four months in mid-2010. She said Russ ended all contact with her when she sent him an angry message after seeing photos on Betsy's Face-book page of a vacation trip Russ took with Betsy and her daughters. Months later, Darlene sent texts to Russ, but he did not respond. Nor had he responded to a call she made after hearing about Betsy's death. She said she did not believe Russ was capable of killing Betsy.

Schwartz knew an affair by a husband whose wife reportedly had a number of affairs certainly was not evidence that the husband killed the wife. There seemed to be nothing about an affair with Darlene that was connected to the case.

He took a similar view of the witnesses suggesting Russ had been verbally abusive to Betsy. Some were nothing more than hearsay—somebody said they heard somebody say Russ was verbally abusive or rude or mean. For every witness who said they had heard less-than-kind comments to Betsy by Russ, there was another witness who said Russ was a loving husband and his marriage to Betsy was solid and improving. And, Schwartz knew, what a friend or relative might view as a harsh comment could easily be the standard level of discourse between spouses. In the end, occasional angry or sharp comments by a spouse certainly did not portend murder.

CHAPTER EIGHTEEN

Earlier on the same day that police arrested Russ Faria—January 4, 2012—Detective Sergeant Ryan McCarrick filed a probable-cause statement with Lincoln County Prosecuting Attorney Leah Askey—the statement of facts that, the police investigators contend, establishes a reasonable belief that someone committed a crime. McCarrick's three-page, single-spaced, and unusually detailed document—written as an affidavit signed under oath and penalties of perjury—started with his direct statement: *I have probable cause to believe that Russell Scott Faria . . . committed the criminal offense of Murder in Lincoln County, Missouri.* He added that he was not including all of the facts he was aware of, only those sufficient to establish probable cause to arrest Russell Faria. Askey used McCarrick's statement as grounds to file charges of first-degree murder and armed criminal action against Russ and to authorize his arrest.

To Joel Schwartz, the statement completely failed to establish probable cause to charge Russ while relying on numerous mistakes, unsupported assumptions, and guesses.

McCarrick began with the basic facts of Russ's call to 911, his description of finding Betsy's body, his belief that she committed suicide, and the details of his game-night alibi. But he quickly challenged part of Russ's account by stating he should have been able to see Betsy's body as soon as he entered the house, not after he set down the bag of dog food and took off his jacket. The detective said evidence included human blood inside Russ's ball cap, on his slippers in the master bedroom closet, and on the switch plate for the bedroom light.

Recounting statements by the last person to see Betsy alive—Pam Hupp—took up a long paragraph and presented her statements as unchallenged gospel. There was no acknowledgment that nearly all of her statements were unsupported and came from someone with her own motive to kill Betsy. McCarrick wrote: *Hupp said Russell was not very nice to Elizabeth, and Elizabeth said she was thinking of leaving Russell. Hupp said Elizabeth was growing increasingly uncomfortable with Russell. Hupp said Elizabeth told her of an incident that occurred the week before Elizabeth's death, where Russell put a pillow over her face and told Elizabeth that was what it would feel like to die . . . Hupp said Elizabeth was planning to change the beneficiary information for her insurance policies, which, at the time of her death, listed Russell as the primary beneficiary. However, Hupp said there were delays in the changes because Elizabeth started to be very cautious of the business she conducted on the computer. Hupp said this was because she believed Russell was monitoring her emails.*

Schwartz hadn't found much damning evidence in McCarrick's statement until the end of the third page, when he recounted the search of the Faria house on January 3, 2012, the day before he filed the statement, secured the charges, and arrested Russ. Police looked for blood evidence, using what McCarrick called "illuminating materials," a reference to luminol that illuminates a substance that might—emphasizing *might*—be blood.

Although luminol was a "presumptive" test, meaning that it only indicated the possibility of blood, and was known for resulting in false-positive reactions, McCarrick used the tests to offer what Schwartz thought were some surprising and unfounded conclusions. McCarrick said the tests "illuminated blood evidence." He detailed: *[It] had been cleaned from the crime scene, on the vinyl floor between the area where Elizabeth was found, and the patio door used by Elizabeth and Russell Faria to let the dog inside.* Blood evidence cleaned from the crime scene also was illuminated on the floor in the kitchen, on the kitchen sink, and the handle of the drawer holding towels, which suggested "prior knowledge of the towels' location." He wrote: *These items, along with a sink trap and a mop head found in the laundry room, were seized.*

McCarrick took a final shot over the polygraph test: *Russell showed extreme deception to all the answers he provided . . . When questioned about his deception during the exam, Russell requested counsel.*

Just above his signature, McCarrick wrote, *I hereby state that the facts set forth in this Probable Cause statement are true and correct, and are made by me with the knowledge that false statements made herein are punishable by law.*

Schwartz was glad he already had the results of the lab tests on evidence McCarrick cited. The lab found no blood on any of the items listed by McCarrick, nor in sink or shower drains or the water collected in them or the attached drainpipes. There were no stains— blood or otherwise—on the two washcloths and one of the bath towels seized by police. Stains on two bath towels could not be excluded as coming from Russ, but were not from Betsy. Red or brown stains on a brown bath towel showed a weak presence of DNA consistent with a mix from Betsy and Russ.

The palm prints on the sliding door in the kitchen came from Russ, but that certainly wasn't incriminating for the man who lived there.

The best of the lab results in Schwartz's mind showed there was absolutely no blood on the clothes Russ wore from five o'clock, Tuesday, during his discovery of Betsy's body, until police seized them at 10:30 a.m., Thursday. They would have been spattered with Betsy's blood if Russ had inflicted that savage knife attack. The spot of blood inside Russ's yellow ball cap was his. There was no blood on Russ's hands and arms. Clippings from Russ's fingernails contained only his DNA. Fingernail clippings from Betsy contained her DNA and a tiny sample not from Betsy or Russ that was insufficient to compare to anyone else. The handle and blade of the knife removed from Betsy's neck were heavily coated in blood that came only from her.

One other result caught Schwartz's attention. The switch plate from the light in the master bedroom was stained with DNA from at least two people—mostly by Betsy's blood, but also by material from a man who could not have been Russ. Did that indicate another man with Betsy's blood on him touched the switch plate and left her blood and his DNA?

Russ's slippers stained with Betsy's blood would be the only evidence Schwartz knew he would have to address later. Schwartz was confident that, given the lack of any other bloodstains on Russ's clothing or body, he could make a convincing argument that someone else had applied Betsy's blood to Russ's slippers and then left them in an obvious location in the closet to be found by police. There were no bloody footprints leading from the living room to the bedroom or to the closet, even though there was some blood on the soles of the slippers. Someone carried them to the closet.

DNA samples from inside the slippers proved nothing. The manufacturer's tag inside the left slipper, however, showed a mix of DNA from Russ and another contributor that could not have been Betsy. Once more, had someone else handled Russ's slippers, perhaps to stain them with Betsy's blood, and then planted them in the closet?

The last two items confirmed Russ's statement that he and Betsy had sex Sunday night—Christmas night—less than forty-eight hours before she was killed. A vaginal swab showed a mixture of eight sperm cells, seminal fluid, and other cells that DNA identified as equal parts from Russ and Betsy. A swab from the exterior of the rectum also produced a mix of material from at least two people. The major contributor was Betsy, but the material from the second source was too small for comparison and identification. Since there was no evidence of anal penetration, the pathologist concluded that the material was the result of seminal drainage from the vagina after intercourse—not an uncommon finding in postmortem examinations.

As Joel Schwartz studied the police investigative file, he kept looking for something that would hurt the defense's case. He never found it. Instead, he was left with questions about how experienced detectives could have been manipulated so easily by Pam Hupp and misread all of the evidence and witness statements. And he wondered how a prosecuting attorney could believe that this investigation had established a case for a murder charge that could be proved to a jury beyond a reasonable doubt.

Schwartz knew Askey had only been prosecuting attorney for eighteen months, a hometown girl elected as a Democrat in a small, largely Republican county. She had graduated from St. Louis University School of Law and opened her own practice in the county in 2006 before running for prosecutor in 2010. Schwartz thought that level of inexperience still was no excuse for filing a murder charge against Russ Faria based on the evidence in that file. Schwartz just hoped Askey would be open to taking an unbiased look at the facts he could present to her.

"I know who did it."

Joel Schwartz turned to look at his fourteen-year-old son, Jonah, who had just made that surprisingly confident announcement. After thirty minutes of reading through the police reports with his father, Jonah—already an aspiring attorney—sat across the desk with a calm air of certainty.

Schwartz chuckled slightly and asked, "Who?"

"Pam Hupp," Jonah said without a hint of doubt.

The elder Schwartz nodded slightly at his son, smiled, and said, "You are absolutely correct."

The police investigation of the murder of Betsy Faria had indeed uncovered the real killer and revealed her to Jonah Schwartz. It should have been that obvious to the police and prosecutor. The murderer's identity nearly exploded off the pages of the Major Case Squad's reports. And Joel Schwartz was as flabbergasted as he was perplexed that the cops and prosecuting attorney had completely and ineptly misread the evidence and charged the person who had irrefutable proof that he could not have committed this crime—all while ignoring the evidence against the one person who was at the epicenter of the murder with unmistakably incriminating motive and opportunity.

If a high-school freshman—regardless of the advanced levels of intelligence and insight his father might impute to him—could so readily see the real killer emerge from those pages, how could some of the region's top detectives so blatantly miss the obvious solution as it sprang up right before their eyes? How could they misinterpret proof of Pam Hupp's guilt that came mostly from her own mouth and was so clear in a careful reading of the statements of other witnesses and in the reality of the hard evidence? Could the case against Pam Hupp be any more obvious? Could the case for Russ Faria's innocence be any more obvious?

CHAPTER NINETEEN

June 25, 2012—six months after
the murder of Betsy Faria

The big, bald cop had no reaction when his prime witness casually tossed off the most unexpected, shocking comment Joel Schwartz had ever heard in a police interview. He watched the video of this new interview intently as Pam Hupp explained to Sergeant Ryan McCarrick that the many personal issues she was juggling—selling a house, buying a new house, her own medical issues—also included handling the financial affairs for her mother, who was suffering from dementia and Alzheimer's, while living in a residential care center.

In the middle of that lengthy diatribe, Pam casually told the cop, "And if I really—hate to say—wanted money, my mom's worth a half a million that I get when she dies. My mom has dementia and doesn't half the time know who we are. . . . I know this sounds morbid and stuff like that, but I am a life insurance person. But if I really wanted money, there was an easier way than trying to combat somebody that's physically stronger than me. I'm just saying."

What was she just saying? Schwartz backed up the recording and played it again. Yes, he had heard it right the first time. Pam Hupp had just raised the question of whether she killed Betsy Faria and suggested it would have been easier for her to kill her own aged, ill mother if she wanted money. And she had added—apparently as a factor she thought counted in her defense—that Betsy was stronger than she was and would have been more difficult to kill.

Schwartz stared at the image of this bizarre woman in the video for a long time. Had she just actually weighed the options of killing her mother or Betsy? Had she actually pondered her level of risk in each option? Had Betsy Faria died because she came up on the fatal end of a monstrous calculation by this disturbed woman?

Schwartz was learning that Pam Hupp was an unfiltered font of inappropriate, off-the-wall, inexplicable comments—shockingly ill-conceived utterances that often were self-incriminating. Why in the world would she raise with the top cop on the case the question of whether it would be easier to kill her mother for $500,000 or her friend for $150,000?

Schwartz watched the exchange on the video again and again. On June 25, 2012, just two days short of six months after Betsy's murder, Sergeant McCarrick—the case officer for the Major Case Squad investigation into the Betsy Faria murder, and the detective who probably knew more about it than any other cop—had not even blinked as Pam discussed her options for killing for profit.

He just leaned forward with his arms folded on the table in front of him in a small interview room in the Lincoln County Sheriff's Office and continued to look at Pam with no change in expression. He didn't even make a note on the legal pad in front of him. And she simply moved on to a discussion of how Betsy's family had harassed her over the insurance money.

"As soon as the phone calls started with her family—it was her father, her mother, her sisters, calling. 'Pay for the funeral. Pay for this. Pay for that.' I was like, 'I'm not paying for a funeral that her husband killed her. I'm not having Betsy pay for that.' I'm sorry. That's my view."

"OK," McCarrick said flatly.

Pam Hupp's voluntary discussion of the advantages of killing her mother versus killing Betsy had come shortly after McCarrick mentioned her receipt of Betsy's insurance money as an issue the defense was sure to raise when she testified against Russ Faria at his trial set for a month later in July. McCarrick scheduled the interview—meeting Pam for the first time—to "hammer out" some of the discrepancies in her comments to various detectives. But it was clear to Schwartz that McCarrick and, by extension, the rest of the detectives and the prosecutor were not addressing suspicions that Pam Hupp could be a suspect in Betsy's murder. The meeting clearly was to prepare Pam to be a valuable witness against Russ Faria and to stand up to questioning by the defense.

McCarrick had opened by explaining that Russ's family had spent a lot of money to hire a "pretty good law firm" to defend him.

Pam—dressed casually in a yellow T-shirt, gray capri pants, and flip-flop sandals and sipping on a bottle of soda—listened intently as McCarrick said, "Their whole job is to make sure that Russ is not prosecuted for murder and to try to find anyone else on the planet to blame, but him, so their client gets off. You've seen TV. You know how these things go, what they try to do." And then he casually dropped the kind of cheap shot Schwartz was used to from cops like McCarrick. "This guy . . . this guy will put his mother up for the murder if he can get his client off. OK?"

Schwartz chuckled and shook his head.

Thirty minutes into the interview, the burly detective had rolled his chair back from the table and was leaning back casually when he unexpectedly broached the subject that had to be worrying the cops and prosecutors.

"The insurance policy," he said without a hint of drama.

Pam's head bobbed down and then back up as she said softly, "Uh-huh."

"Huge in this case, obviously," McCarrick explained. "The biggest doubt that they are going to try to create is that you . . . prior to her murder . . . wound up being the benefactor of $150,000 in cash."

"Uh-huh."

"What you're originally telling investigators is that she wanted you to do this to try to take care of . . . make sure the kids are taken care of because . . . she's afraid Russ and the kids will blow through it. However, now you have this money and have not turned any of this money over to the family or the kids."

"That's correct." Pam nodded without a hint of concern.

"That's a huge problem. . . . I'm not telling you you've got to do that. I'm just telling you that it's going to be a huge issue of doubt in court because, by your own volition, Betsy has told you that she wants you to hold on to this money to make sure the family . . .the girls are taken care of. Yet they haven't seen a dime of that money. You still have it and—"

"I think if you really look at my wording, it wasn't exactly she wanted me to make sure the girls are taken care of," Pam interrupted as she began a shameless rewrite of history to justify refusing to give any of the insurance money to Betsy's daughters. Rattling off a list of the daughters' alleged issues and problems, she declared she had intentionally avoided any involvement with them. "Honestly, they're not that nice to her (Betsy) . . . have never been nice to her. . . . I know all of the problems with them . . . all that crap. . . . Again, not my world."

In fact, Pam now maintained, Betsy did not want the girls or her family to get the money. "She did not want them to have their hands on the money. . . . Not that she didn't want me to help or do whatever I wanted with it. 'Do not let them get their hands on it, or the family, because the family will give it to them.' That was her major concern. . . . They'd 'piss it away.' "

Pam added with that same smugness that $150,000 was not a lot of money to her and she had not spent a dime of it. And, almost as an afterthought, she said she had been planning to set up a revocable trust for Betsy's daughters, but had not done anything about that yet.

McCarrick said he had already received calls from people wanting to make sure he knew Pam had put her house up for sale and had bought a new house. Pam insisted she hadn't used any of the insurance money for the new house and had, in fact, paid $65,000 less for it than she made from the sale of her previous house. Downsizing to a smaller ranch house was part of the Hupps' ten-year financial plan for retirement after her two adult children left home, as well as an accommodation for her physical limitations resulting from a fall in 2009.

And then she casually tossed out her stunning consideration of whether it would be easier to kill her mother or Betsy.

Without any real reaction or discussion about that, McCarrick returned to the issue of a trust for the Day sisters with another reminder that Pam would help the prosecution's case against Russ if she set it up before the trial. She nodded and then reminded McCarrick, "I had told you on the phone originally, it will be set up before the trial. My husband believes in that. We're all on board. That's not a problem."

She said her issue with providing money to the girls was whether they were responsible enough now to handle it. Betsy had entrusted the money to Pam so she could help the girls if they built more solid financial foundations. She would establish criteria for them to receive the money. "Like Mariah—you will go to school and you will graduate before you touch anything. . . . Leah, the same thing. And I'm doing that in honor of Betsy, because that's the right thing to do."

Schwartz wondered why Pam Hupp's head didn't explode in flames. How could the person who was responsible for Betsy's death get away with saying anything she had done was in honor of Betsy, especially when it also involved screwing the rightful beneficiaries out of Betsy's money?

A few more minutes into the interview, Schwartz was surprised again when McCarrick bluntly asked Pam *the* question that hung over this case like a summer storm cloud. As Pam was saying she had probably only spoken to Russ Faria once on the phone, the cop asked abruptly, "Did you have anything to do with Betsy's murder?"

Pam was unfazed as she calmly responded, "No, absolutely not."

McCarrick quickly retreated from what could have seemed an accusation by adding, "That's exactly what's going to be asked of you. You know what I mean?"

"That's what the detectives asked me, too," she said. "I expect that."

"And it's going to come sooner or later, you know? I mean, that's . . . that's unfortunately the way of the beast."

"That's fine . . . I don't mind that. I know myself . . ."

"Uh-huh."

". . . I'm not physically able to do . . . maybe if I had a gun. . . . I'm not physically able to do that."

"I'm not suggesting that you murdered Betsy for real. . . . I'm saying that they're going to suggest that you may have had something to do with the planning or the conspiracy to commit that murder because of your financial windfall . . ."

"OK."

". . . which either way, like I said, it helps, obviously, if that trust is going to be set up for the girls before the trial."

"It will. And I told you that in the first phone call."

He repeated his prediction that the defense attorney would challenge her as a suspect in the murder. Was there anything the defense could find to attack her? Financial problems?

"No . . . nope. Never had financial problems, other than the normal when I was eighteen and on my own . . . whatever. Lack of money—not problems."

She said speeding tickets were the only other thing the defense might find. McCarrick tossed off a casual "Well, I ain't worried about that."

Pam launched into a confusing ramble about the timing of the change in beneficiaries and Betsy's murder that again seemed self-incriminating. "She has to be killed. . . . How does that work? She has to be killed or they have to receive it (the beneficiary form) before she's killed. Otherwise, he's still the beneficiary. . . . So, why wouldn't I wait a few more days? I mean, I just . . . That's practical to me. . . . Why didn't I just wait until Friday to be sure they got it?"

Schwartz shook his head again in frustration. Pam couldn't wait until Friday because Russ was at game night on Tuesday, giving her the opportunity to take Betsy home and be alone with her—or perhaps to bring in someone to assist in the murder. Pam's timing was so obvious that Schwartz couldn't believe McCarrick was looking right past it—and past her.

Pam's warped logic and circuitous, rambling style of responding to questions had been remarkable to Schwartz throughout the interview. And she constantly employed one of her annoying verbal habits—substituting a bored "blah, blah, blah" for details she apparently found too tiresome to repeat.

McCarrick began addressing the primary reason for the interview—the contradictions in her various statements. He asked her to commit to one of her two versions of where Betsy was when she left—on the couch under a blanket or waving good-bye from the front door. What he got was a loopy monologue, which either demonstrated a memory so muddled, as to destroy her credibility, or, as Schwartz believed, a deviously evasive response that made it impossible to pin her down to one factual account.

"I know she was on the couch," Pam began, "because she was put . . . she was going to put in a movie. She was going to watch a movie. I want to say she walked me to the door—now—but she may have been still on the couch because she had her blanket."

"OK."

"And she had her blanket on her. And at one time, she was sitting there showing me something she got for Christmas. But I know she always puts a blanket on her and she had it on her. Right now . . . and it may just make sense to me—she walked me to the door. She may not have. She may have still been on the couch. But today, it makes sense that she walked me to the door . . . but she could've been still laying on the couch. . . . All that happened really fast and I'm used to her walking me to the door. . . . Maybe not, but I want to say—today—she did. . . . Maybe she was still on the couch. . . . She was off and on the couch that, you know . . ."

Schwartz was amazed that any rational human being—especially an experienced detective—could think that string of illogical reversals and half-completed thoughts could even approximate an answer to the question. But McCarrick seemed to accept her tortured dithering with a series of understanding interjections: "Right. Sure. OK. Uh-huh."

Had he found some logic in Pam's rhetorical meandering, or was he simply willing to accept her verbal gymnastics so he could continue to rely on her long list of accusations about Russ? After all, he had applied many of them in his probable-cause statement that Leah Askey used as grounds to charge Russ with murder. Schwartz thought anyone who found Pam's answer to this basic question to be reasonable, let alone mentally competent, was either amateurishly naïve or unabashedly biased toward her as a witness.

As McCarrick continued his questioning, Pam made her disapproval of Russ a centerpiece of her relationship with Betsy, even adding an arrogant claim of being socially superior to him and Betsy. Despite a close friendship between the women, the Hupps and the Farias did not socialize. "This is going to sound bad," she warned. "Me and Betsy are very different people. We come from very different worlds, though we liked each other genuinely. I didn't really care for Russ that much, or his type."

"When you say 'his type,' what . . ."

"His type to me—he is a hoosier," she said, trotting out the Midwestern slang for a redneck or hillbilly or even the uglier white trash. "I'm just going to be honest with you . . . he's a hoosier. He does things that are inappropriate in my social circle, and I'm very uncomfortable in that. . . . He's a heavy smoker. He's a drinker. He doesn't really care for women that much. He's a hoosier to me."

"OK."

"And I just . . . you know, I've known her a long time and she's been married to Russ the whole time. I don't like him. My husband has never socialized with him—nor would he."

McCarrick said he was good with her explanation that she called Betsy from the road soon after leaving her house because she was worried that Betsy was angry with her for not staying longer. But McCarrick said the defense would attack her justifications for calling her husband, Betsy, and Janet Meyer and then texting Betsy, all so shortly after she left her at home.

Pam said multiple phone calls and texts were a normal practice for her and Betsy. She had made some of those calls because her husband and Betsy worried about her driving at night. "My sense of direction is horrid and always has been. It's gotten worse since my accident," she explained.

If driving at night in an unfamiliar area was so risky, why did she volunteer to drive Betsy home?

"Because she wanted to go home," she said with a shrug that suggested it was no big deal and certainly not suspicious. She often helped friends or family like that and didn't worry about getting lost, because she eventually found her way home. "My friend who I was at chemo with wants to go home. That's not abnormal for me. It just happened to be at night."

McCarrick reassured his witness by interjecting, "You realize I'm not being accusatory. I'm trying to get some of these things hammered out. . . . I'm not pointing a finger at you. I'm telling you that the defense attorney is most certainly going to do that."

"Right . . . and I get that."

Two weeks after his interview with Pam Hupp, McCarrick filed a three-and-a-half-page, single-spaced report detailing her recollections, comments, and explanations in response to his questions. Near the end of the report, he offered this conclusion: *I asked Pam about the subtle difference in her statements to me from the statements she originally gave. Pam said she had documented memory loss due to her accident, which involved a head injury. Pam said she has to write things down on a regular basis to remember them. Pam said I could ask her questions again in two days and her statements probably would be somewhat different.*

The cop and the defense attorney couldn't know it then, but there would be so many more interviews with Pam Hupp—and describing some of her statements as "different" would be a world-class understatement.

CHAPTER TWENTY

September 11, 2012—*nearly nine months after Betsy Faria's murder*

Movement in the case against Russ Faria was routinely slow through the summer of 2012, and it was finally scheduled for trial in November before Circuit Judge Dan Dildine. At Leah Askey's request, the Missouri Attorney General's Office had assigned one of its trial lawyers, Richard Hicks, to assist her.

The standard pretrial motions and activities continued to inhibit Joel Schwartz's goal of a full-out assault on the charges that he hoped would lead to their dismissal by the judge. He was haunted by the image of the innocent Russ Faria sitting in a cell in the county jail in Troy, counting on Schwartz to rescue him. Russ was patient and understanding of the court's glacial momentum, but he still wanted to get out of that cell as quickly as possible. And he remained confident Schwartz would get the charges thrown out. Russ's unfaltering confidence weighed heavily on Schwartz as he thought about Russ spending every agonizing second behind bars.

Schwartz was relieved when a hearing on his motion to reduce the unattainable $1 million cash bond was set for September 11. In a forceful and almost angry tone, he argued that there was virtually no evidence against Russ Faria, and certainly not enough to justify the high bond that was keeping him in jail. Russ had strong ties to family and the community that made him an unlikely flight risk if he was free on bond.

Prosecuting Attorney Askey argued the polar opposite: The case against Russ was strong and backed by significant evidence, the brutality of Betsy's murder marked a free Russ as a threat to society, and none of the defendants in the dozen charges of murder or manslaughter she had filed during her eighteen months in office had been released on bond before trial or disposition of their cases.

Judge Dildine agreed with Schwartz that the bond was too high and reduced it to $25,000 cash It was a Pyrrhic victory; Russ still lacked the financial resources to meet the bond. He would stay in jail.

But at the end of the hearing, Schwartz got an unexpected hint of the tone he might expect from the prosecutor from then on. He overheard Askey say to a colleague that Schwartz was the "biggest asshole defense lawyer" she had ever encountered. Schwartz made a quick decision not to escalate the situation with a really biting response, but he couldn't let it pass.

He breezed past Askey as he said in a fairly sarcastic tone, "Your depth perception is miserable when you whisper—and you're wrong. I'm not even in the top three assholes in my office." He left his affectionate reference to his good friends and partners, Scott Rosenblum and John Rogers, unfinished.

He didn't look back as he left the courtroom. But he feared PA Askey's remark signaled a sharp new edge in her demeanor that did not bode well. Personal animosity between the prosecutor and the defense attorney added an ugly and complicating dimension to the natural conflict between them. He hoped he and Askey could get past this initial skirmish and focus on the mutual goal of both of their jobs—to find justice for the victim and the defendant. But he not only could not foresee how wide the chasm would become between the State and the defense, he also could not imagine the depths to which the prosecution would sink.

Schwartz was aware of what appeared to be Askey's reluctance to try the case before Judge Dildine. She had even tossed off a remark privately that she might have to reconsider the entire case if Dildine continued as judge. Schwartz had begun to hear rumors that Dildine was planning to retire soon and a surprising tactical move by Askey to delay Russ Faria's trial date of November 27 seemed to confirm that. Askey filed a *nolle pros* motion on November 16 that dismissed the charges against Russ on the grounds that the prosecution had decided not to prosecute them. That canceled the scheduled trial before Dildine. Askey then had a grand jury return a new but identical indictment against Russ on the same charges on the same day, essentially restarting the pretrial process from the beginning.

Judge Dildine soon announced his retirement, and on December 5, a quite-literally new judge was assigned. Circuit Judge Christina Kunza Mennemeyer was not just new to the case—she had just been elected judge a month earlier as a Republican in an upset victory by less than 1 percent of the vote over a more experienced Democratic associate judge. She had never participated in a jury trial during the months she had served as an assistant prosecuting attorney handling traffic and juvenile cases under Askey's predecessor, or while she was in private practice after getting her law degree from the University of Missouri-Columbia in 1997. She had tried a civil case shortly after she was elected judge, but Russ Faria's case would be her first venture into felony criminal law.

Mennemeyer was an unknown quantity to Schwartz and he could only hope she wouldn't become another disadvantage to the innocent man she was about to try.

CHAPTER TWENTY-ONE

March 18, 2013—nearly fifteen
months after Betsy Faria's murder

Pam Hupp was a money-hungry bitch, but she didn't kill Betsy
Faria.

Janet Meyer's head was tilted up slightly and her jaw was set—
the pose of someone who knows what she knows, and nothing, not
even an avalanche of facts or logic, would change her mind. Her
daughter had been murdered and her granddaughters cheated out of
the life insurance money they should have received. And Janet knew
what she knew. Pam Hupp was the cheater, but not the killer.

Joel Schwartz had deposed other witnesses with conclusions set
in concrete like Janet Meyer's and it could be maddening. But he
had to know what she would say when she testified in Russ's trial,
and this was his chance.

He had just asked Janet for her thoughts about the change in the
beneficiary on Betsy's life insurance policy to Pam Hupp.

"That she's a money-hungry, grabbing *B.I.T.C.H.* OK?"

"We're talking about Ms. Hupp?"

"We are. Sorry, but that's the way I feel. She didn't commit the
murder, but that's the way I feel."

"When you say she didn't commit the murder, how do you know
that?"

"Because I know who did it. That's why," she said with just as
much certainty.

"Who did it?"

"Russ! No ifs, ands, or buts."

"How do you know that?"

"You know he did it, too," Betsy's mother quipped. "It's just you have to defend him. That's a murder of passion, of betrayal. He loved her. There's no doubt in my mind . . . and that's where it comes into murder because it was . . . she took his name off the policy. And nobody stabs anybody fifty-five times unless they loved that person and they were betrayed. Nobody's going to do it any other way. Pam Hupp did not kill her."

Schwartz needed to know how this grieving mother would explain and defend her unshakeable conclusions when she testified at Russ Faria's upcoming trial. He had to challenge those opinions now.

"Now, initially, when you found out about Betsy, you couldn't believe that Russ would do something like this, did you?"

Her eyes narrowed. "You want to know something?"

"What?"

"Yes, I did. And don't ask me why. I just . . . It all came together to me, in my mind."

Schwartz asked who gave her the "crime of passion" phrase. She said they were her words.

"Did a detective meet with you or a sergeant meet with you and tell you those words?"

"I don't recall that. I just feel it's a crime of passion."

Schwartz repeated the phrase with an emphasis on the important word. "You *feel* that way?"

"I just feel . . . yeah."

"Because she was stabbed so many times?"

"Right."

Someone clearly had provided Janet Meyer with the "crime of passion" talking point, and Schwartz was fairly certain he knew who. He challenged her again.

"So, it was either a crime of passion or somebody wanted it to look like a crime of passion?"

"It was a crime of passion. No doubt in my mind."

Janet believed Russ killed Betsy and cleaned up the blood. When Schwartz pressed, she couldn't remember who had told her that, but it was probably a police officer. She believed Russ killed Betsy after he got home from game night. He had been very angry about her decision to remove him as beneficiary and lost his temper. Janet believed Russ found out about that when he got home or possibly even earlier.

"Has anyone indicated to you when he got home?"

"Yeah, we've talked about it."

"Who's 'we'? Ms. Askey and Mr. Hicks?"

"McCarrick."

There was the name Schwartz had expected. It seemed that Sergeant Ryan McCarrick was making sure witnesses who would testify against Russ Faria were equipped with the pertinent details to support the State's theory—à la "a crime of passion."

"Officer McCarrick," Schwartz repeated slowly. "And what were you told?"

"That he came home after he played the games—and took care of business."

Yeah, Schwartz thought, that sounded like McCarrick. And the sergeant's turn on the hot seat was coming up the next day.

CHAPTER TWENTY-TWO

March 19, 2013—nearly fifteen
months after Betsy Faria's murder

The big, bald cop was one of the most defensive, if not outright hostile, witnesses Joel Schwartz had ever deposed. Questioning Sergeant Ryan McCarrick in a conference room in the Lincoln County Prosecuting Attorney's Office in Troy, with Nate Swanson, Leah Askey, and Richard Hicks, Schwartz hoped even reluctant and petulant comments by McCarrick would expose facts demonstrating how the police incompetently, or perhaps corruptly, focused solely on Russ Faria, ignoring all of the evidence that should have made Pam Hupp a suspect.

Schwartz started his interrogation of McCarrick at ground zero. Hadn't the police been advised by first responders that Betsy's body was cold and stiff when they arrived?

McCarrick offered a different view: "What we got was an opinion from a medic that said that she felt like she could've been stiff."

"Well, there was a medic and a fireman. Correct?"

"The only one I remember was the medic. If there was a fireman, I apologize."

Schwartz named EMT Supervisor Mike Quattrocchi and fire Captain Robert Shramek as the first responders quoted in police reports.

"I'm aware that there's reports that are written discussing those individuals being on the scene. What I'm telling you is what I remember here today is that Mike Quattrocchi is the one that said he felt she . . . thought that she was stiff."

McCarrick wouldn't even acknowledge that Quattrocchi and Shramek said Betsy's body *was* cold and stiff, only that they *thought* it *might* have been. Schwartz ignored the equivocation and asked, "Now, assuming she was cold to the touch and stiff, what does that indicate to you?"

"We're making a lot of assumptions," the cop responded.

Schwartz replied that Quattrocchi and Shramek—with fifty years of experience between them—said in police reports that Betsy's body was cold and stiff. McCarrick discounted their experience— "Those are all fifty years of being human"—and referred to their reports as opinion he couldn't confirm because he wasn't there. After more back-and-forth about assumptions and opinions, McCarrick finally said if a body was cold and stiff, "it usually means that somebody's been dead for a couple hours, at least."

Schwartz asked if McCarrick had any information to suggest the first responders were wrong.

"I don't know any of them. . . . Therefore, I can't tell you whether or not their opinions could be validated or not. They may be complete idiots. I don't know."

Schwartz realized that bit of evasion—beyond making McCarrick look unprofessional for throwing the first responders under the bus—could force the cop into a revealing admission.

"So, for you to validate an opinion, you need to know them personally?"

"Yeah, if I'm going to validate somebody's opinion."

Schwartz pounced with an unexpected question he hoped would draw an unscripted response. "Is Pam Hupp telling you the truth about where she was that night?"

That sudden challenge seemed to rock McCarrick. "Do what?" he replied awkwardly.

"Is Pam Hupp telling you the truth about where she was that night?"

"Don't know."

"You have no idea, do you?"

"No." McCarrick tried to regain his footing. "I have no idea whether or not she's telling me the truth, other than what I can tell you from my training and experience and talking to her. I did speak to her personally. I didn't speak to those other three individuals. I spoke to Pam."

Schwartz upped the pressure with one word. "And?"

"And based on my opinion of speaking with her, I did not visibly observe any deception when I was speaking to her."

Schwartz tested the basis for McCarrick's confidence in Pam's statements.

Did McCarrick know what she was wearing that night?

No.

Did he believe her statement that she left Betsy's twenty or thirty minutes after she had called her husband at 7:04 p.m.?

"My opinion doesn't matter, sir."

"Well, you're the one who filed the probable-cause statement that caused his arrest."

"I did file a probable-cause statement based on what I gathered during that. OK? But my opinion here, or in court, doesn't matter."

Schwartz asked if much of the information in the probable-cause statement was now known to be incorrect. McCarrick said he believed the information to be accurate when he wrote it—as he had stated in the first paragraph.

Schwartz was surprised when McCarrick said he had no reason to believe the game-night players were lying and no reason to doubt Russ Faria was at Mike Corbin's, as they said, or that he left at nine o'clock. That was a significant admission. Schwartz thought the whole case should turn on whether Russ could have been home to kill Betsy sometime around 7:30 p.m.—at least two hours before her body was found, in order to be cold and stiff.

McCarrick confirmed it took twenty-three minutes to drive from Arby's in O'Fallon to the Faria home in Troy. Schwartz asked if McCarrick believed Russ Faria made that drive and then killed his wife when he got home.

"That he went home and murdered his wife? Yes. I believe he got home sometime around nine thirty–ish or so."

"And murdered his wife?"

"Yes, I do."

"And then what did he do?"

"Called 911."

Schwartz thought about how much he was going to enjoy cross-examining McCarrick in front of a judge and jury. Judges usually won't let a witness get away with equivocal or vague answers. And jurors generally know when a witness is shading his testimony, being unnecessarily combative, or stubbornly denying an obvious fact—and they discount that witness's credibility.

McCarrick agreed Betsy had not answered three calls from her daughter between 7:21 and 7:30 p.m., but wouldn't agree that indicated she was in a struggle or already dead. "Maybe she's in the bathroom. Maybe she took a nap. They said she was tired. Maybe she was getting something to drink. Maybe she simply didn't answer her phone because she didn't want to talk to anybody. . . . You're asking me to make assumptions about a woman I never met."

Schwartz asked what McCarrick's assumption that Russ killed Betsy was based on.

"It's based on one hundred five—"

"What is it based on specifically?"

"If you want me to answer the question, then stop talking. . . . One hundred five leads."

"All right," Schwartz sighed.

"I don't know why you're getting so frustrated with me, sir," McCarrick said. "But I am trying to answer your questions. . . . It's based on one hundred five leads of investigative information during a Major Case Squad callout. It's based on the previous information gained prior to that Major Case callout. And it's based on the information gathered following the deactivation of the Major Case Squad. It's based on about six months' worth of work."

"All right. Now I'd ask you to answer this question. Give me one fact it's based on—one fact."

"It's not based on 'one fact,' sir."

"It's not based on any facts, is it?"

"It's based on one hundred five different leads and information prior to and after. It's not based on 'one fact.' "

McCarrick had to agree that some of the "facts" he was citing had come only from Pam Hupp, such as Russ putting a pillow over

Betsy's face, and Betsy writing a letter to Pam, which couldn't be found. And Pam was the only person to get $150,000 from the change in beneficiaries four days before the murder and the only person known to be alone with Betsy two hours before she was confirmed dead. Of the 104 leads McCarrick cited, he had to agree not one confirmed where Pam Hupp went after she left the Faria house.

Was Pam's husband asked to confirm when she arrived at their home?

McCarrick didn't know.

Was that ever confirmed?

"We asked her where she was. She explained to us where she was. That's the only thing I can do. . . . How do you want me to confirm it? Do you want me to pull a magic trick? That's the best I can do for you."

"Ask her husband?" Schwartz suggested.

"OK. Well, that's the best I can do for you. . . . Her husband was interviewed. And I can't tell you exactly what the interview said right now."

McCarrick had to admit he would not have handled an interview with Mark Hupp the way the police did.

Should Pam Hupp's account of that evening have been checked out more extensively?

"Again, that's why I reinterviewed her. And when I reinterviewed her, I didn't see any signs of deception . . . indicating anything that was untrue, to me."

Would McCarrick agree that the actions of Russ and everyone else involved in the investigation *except Pam Hupp* were accounted for until nine o'clock?

Yes.

Did Pam Hupp tell McCarrick that she had been fired from two insurance jobs for forging signatures?

"No . . . this is the first I'm hearing of it that I can recall. Obviously, if . . . if I would've been told that somewhere along the line, I probably would've asked her about that."

McCarrick said he assumed Betsy turned to Pam to control the insurance money because she didn't trust Russ, her mother, or anyone in her family to get it to her daughters correctly. He added, "So, outside of that, again, I can't tell you what was going through Betsy Faria's mind before she was murdered by your client."

"Well, you're assuming that, right? . . . That she was murdered by my client?"

"No, I'm not assuming that."

Schwartz couldn't let that go unchallenged. "You were there?" he asked with justified sarcasm.

"I'm saying that based on one hundred five leads or one hundred four leads, as we're sitting here, not 'one fact,' like I said before, but several facts."

Schwartz asked again for one fact indicating Russ's guilt.

McCarrick said Russ's story about his activities that night changed more than anyone else's in the case. He once reversed the order of two of the places he stopped on the way to Mike Corbin's. Russ claimed he got home at 9:45 p.m., which was several minutes after he placed the 911 call. Russ said he had lain on the floor in front of Betsy's body, but he had no blood on his clothes.

"I'd like to know how that's possible when we've got wet blood on the floor. Your client changes his story as much as everybody else. Your client failed his polygraph. How many facts do you want?"

McCarrick's mention of the polygraph reminded Schwartz that he suspected the police had not really given Russ a polygraph, but had faked it so they could tell Russ he failed to get more leverage as they badgered him to confess. Leah Askey had told Schwartz the police could not find a copy of the test, and the camera and audio recorder that Detective McIntyre told Russ were recording the test apparently did not work. Lying to a suspect about polygraph results is a court-approved tactic in Missouri, but the test results must be turned over to defense attorneys. In Russ's case, Schwartz thought the results didn't exist because there had not really been a test—and failure by the State to disclose a faux test was unconstitutional.

Schwartz asked if Pam Hupp claimed the effects of her brain injury meant she might give different answers to the same question if asked on different days. McCarrick said that was part of her explanation for her memory problems, but he had not reviewed her medical records.

Didn't he think it was necessary to confirm her medical condition?

"She is telling me that she's got a head injury—and there you have it, and there you are."

Schwartz moved into what he thought was significant misconduct by McCarrick—his suggestion to Pam Hupp that funding a trust for Betsy's daughters before Russ's trial would be helpful to the prosecution. McCarrick agreed he asked her three or four times to open a trust when he interviewed her on June 25, 2012, just before the trial date in July that was postponed.

Why did it need to be before the trial?

"It's what the family wanted. . . . They wanted it done before the trial. . . . The family wanted to make sure that they've got some kind of peace of mind."

"So you don't want it together before the trial because you think it would look better—it would make your case better if it . . ."

McCarrick had to agree: "Oh, I'm sure it will look better for us. Yeah. Absolutely."

Schwartz switched back to the contradictions in Pam Hupp's stories that McCarrick had called "subtle differences." She said the last time she saw Betsy, she was wrapped in a blanket on the sofa, watching TV. But then she said Betsy waved good-bye from the front door as Pam was leaving. Schwartz asked, "Those are subtle differences, or those are major differences?"

"Yeah, I . . . and that's why I asked her to follow up with it."

When Schwartz asked about the several contradictions in why she made a phone call after she left Betsy's and whom she called, McCarrick said he only remembered Pam saying she called Betsy because she was afraid Betsy was angry with her. When Betsy didn't answer, she became worried and called Janet Meyer.

Schwartz asked if McCarrick remembered that Janet said Pam told her during that call that she did not go into Betsy's house. McCarrick didn't remember ever hearing that. Schwartz showed McCarrick the detectives' report on the first interview with Pam Hupp when they quoted her as saying that.

Schwartz asked, "Is that a big difference to you—'No, I didn't go in the house'?"

The cop was ready with an excuse. "No. If she's just been told that her friend's dead, and she corrects herself immediately on a statement—no, I can deal with it."

"You can deal with that. So when Russ was told his wife—or knows his wife is dead, and he's making a statement that night and he got the order of two stores wrong, at least initially, that's a big deal to you?"

"When you're being asked what your chain of events was and you're under the gun for murder—yeah, I consider that to be a decent deal."

McCarrick agreed Russ's correction about the order of his visits to stores had been confirmed by police. But Schwartz's next question pushed the difficult deposition into open hostility.

"Pam Hupp's never been confirmed as to where she was, what she did. And she's not under the gun—"

"What's your question?" McCarrick interrupted abruptly.

"Pam Hupp's stories have never been confirmed, have they?"

"What's your question?" McCarrick's tone took on a more hostile edge, and Schwartz was getting frustrated and a little angry.

"Listen, please," the defense attorney said with a sigh.

"I'm trying, but you're not asking a question."

Schwartz tried again. "Pam Hupp's stories, as to what she did and where she went, have never been confirmed?"

McCarrick snapped, "We answered that thirty minutes ago. . . . It's still no."

It was time to call McCarrick on his obstinacy. "Why are you so angry?"

"Me?"

"Yes."

"I've stayed in my seat the entire time, Joel. You're getting up, walking around, swinging your chair around, getting mad, calling me 'Sergeant McCarrick,' and huffing. . . . I'm trying to agree with you, Joel, but at the same time, we're still having this problem with you asking me the same questions over and over again."

Schwartz wasn't going to let McCarrick dictate questions or control the deposition. "Because I'm getting different answers the entire time."

"You're not getting different answers. You're getting the same answer, Joel."

Schwartz's tone intensified as he began, "Do you believe . . ."

Hicks tried to defuse the conflict by jumping in. "Hey! Hey!"

"What?" Schwartz snapped.

"Objection. This is argumentative."

McCarrick kept talking. "I find it funny—" he began in a condescending tone.

"On whose part?" Schwartz interrupted.

". . . that you think I'm aggravated with you. I find that humorous."

The cop and defender also disagreed about the way McCarrick's probable-cause statement characterized the tests on kitchen floor tiles and front of the towel drawer. McCarrick wrote that the tests indicated "blood evidence, which had been cleaned from the crime scene." Didn't later tests show no blood was found?

McCarrick insisted that, because of dilution of the evidence, the lab was unsure if there was blood, but the reports suggested there was "blood evidence."

Schwartz asked if the lab reports had concluded there was no blood on the mark on Betsy's pants, the floor tiles, or the drawer front, or the mop head and sink traps. McCarrick repeated that he had based the evidence he cited in the probable-cause statement on what he had been told by investigators at that time.

Schwartz ended the difficult deposition with a couple of simple questions:

When McCarrick saw Pam Hupp earlier that day, did he ask her about the trust for Betsy's daughters?

No.

When they analyzed her computer, did police find the letter she said Betsy was writing to her about things Russ was doing?

No.

Did the insurance company tell McCarrick how or when they received the change-of-beneficiary form?

No, they just said it was "imaged" into their system on December 28 or 29—one or two days after Betsy was murdered.

When Schwartz turned over the deposition to prosecutors for

questions, Hicks held up his hands and cracked, "No more questions. I ain't asking any."

Sergeant Ryan McCarrick had been an obstinate and surly witness, but he had basically confirmed Schwartz's suspicions that Mc-Carrick and, by implication, Leah Askey had based their conclusion that Russ Faria murdered his wife on suppositions and conclusions unsupported by even one solid fact that pointed beyond a reasonable doubt to Russ as the killer. And while they were trying to twist evidence to conform to their conclusions, they were not only ignoring the obvious prime suspect, but they were also accepting her contrived and contradictory statements as damning evidence against Russ.

Schwartz couldn't wait to depose Pam Hupp the next day.

CHAPTER TWENTY-THREE

March 20, 2013—*nearly fifteen
months after Betsy Faria's murder*

"I did not kill Betsy."

The unsolicited declaration from the woman sitting across the table from Joel Schwartz caught him by surprise. He would never have expected Pam Hupp to initiate a conversation about suspicions that she killed Betsy Faria. But that was exactly what she had just done as Schwartz was taking her deposition, with the same participants, in the same conference room, where he had deposed Sergeant McCarrick the day before. She had been explaining that, although she and her husband were financially secure, she could not afford health insurance after an injury kept her from working. Her husband, who worked for a building rehab company, had also been without health insurance for a while, but had it now. Schwartz started to ask why someone who had sold life insurance hadn't maintained health insurance, but she interrupted.

"I sold life insurance for over twelve years," she said, "and I don't have that, either."

"Why not?" Schwartz asked in surprise.

"I don't believe in it for myself," she said.

"But you obviously believe in it for other people if you were selling it."

"That was my job."

"So I'm not clear what you're saying. You sold . . ."

"My job was to sell life insurance. If I had to sell grapefruits, I would. But that doesn't mean I'd eat them."

"Fair enough. . . . Does your husband have life insurance?"

"Yes, he has life insurance."

"And . . ."

"I sold him that, too, and, amazingly, he's still alive."

What did she just say? Schwartz caught his breath. "I'm sorry?"

Pam responded with smug aggression. "I said, 'Amazingly, he's still alive,' because it's a lot, and I sold it to him, so . . ."

Schwartz was stunned. "What do you mean by that?"

"I mean, I guess if I wanted a lot of money, I could kill him instead of her."

For a second time, Pam Hupp had analyzed the dollar value in killing someone besides Betsy Faria. First, Pam's mother, and now, her husband.

"Who said you killed Betsy?"

Pam was calm, but defiant. "You did—or at least your private detective told my friends that."

"And you didn't kill Betsy?"

"I did not kill Betsy."

Schwartz asked if she was willing to take a polygraph. No, she didn't want to now. She denied sending her doctor a note asking him to say she could not take a polygraph for medical reasons. Schwartz was surprised by her willingness to lie about things that could be so easily proven. He had a copy of the note she sent to her doctor asking him: *Could you please write Det. Kaiser a letter stating that I was not able to do my polygraph due to medical reasons?* Did she not realize her note would be found by the police or the defense attorney? Did she just not care?

Pam was delivering exactly what Schwartz hoped to draw from her in this deposition. The more he could get her to open up and talk, the more likely she was to lie and contradict herself and make up more absurd stories. The more she talked, the more ammunition she provided Schwartz when he tried to impeach her testimony and credibility as a witness against Russ at trial. She would prove herself to be a pathological liar, a person who couldn't be trusted to tell the truth about anything, especially what happened at the Faria house between seven and eight o'clock on Tuesday, December 27, 2011. With so many lies and contradictions, how could a jury believe anything she said—especially about Russ Faria and the supposed danger he presented to Betsy?

Pam said a neighbor named Susan, with a Hispanic last name, told her Schwartz's investigator said she killed Betsy.

"And you didn't kill Betsy?"

"I did not kill Betsy."

Schwartz broached the possibility that someone had helped her kill Betsy—perhaps an accomplice more physically suited to the demands of a violent murder.

"Did you have someone kill Betsy?"

"No, I did not have someone kill Betsy."

"You would agree—if Betsy died, you had a considerable amount of money to gain?"

"In your opinion."

"In my opinion what?"

"That's a 'considerable amount of money.' "

"You had money to gain?"

"Absolutely" was her more brazen response.

Pam Hupp had just supplied her motive to kill Betsy, so Schwartz moved to opportunity. Why did she drive Betsy home from her mother's that night?

"Because she asked me to."

"Actually, *you* asked her if you could take her home."

"No, she asked me when we were at chemo if I could take her home."

"So, if the text messages say you offered a ride to her, that would be incorrect?"

"That would be incorrect."

She agreed Betsy sent her a text that afternoon saying Russ would drive her home that night. But she said she had not seen the text because she was driving and she does not "text and drive." So she didn't know Betsy had arranged for Russ to drive her home, until Betsy mentioned it when she and Pam were on the way home.

Pam said her husband was lying on the sofa when she got home that night and she sat there to watch TV with him for a while before taking a shower and going to bed. She confirmed that she also took a shower when she got up the next morning, as she always did.

"That's my normal routine because, honestly, I don't like messing around with somebody who's been sweaty from all day. So, yes, that's my routine."

Another curiously odd and inappropriate remark in a deposition in a murder case.

Schwartz turned back to the money—the motive. Pam said she had not set up a trust for Betsy's daughters, but had been thinking about it. McCarrick asked her in June 2012 to set up a trust fund and she told him she would.

"Why did Betsy leave you the money? Why did she tell you she was leaving you the money?"

"She trusted me. She liked me. Her family dynamics at that time, as all the time, had a bunch of stuff going on with it that she couldn't trust with the money."

"She just gave [the money] to you free of any stipulations?"

"That's right. She just wanted me to take care of it and make sure that her daughters and her mom didn't 'piss it away'—were her words."

"Do you intend to give it to the daughters?"

"I don't know. It's on my mind to set up a trust."

Schwartz asked repeatedly why she never told the police she had gone to the post office with Betsy.

"They didn't ask me that," she said. "They asked me if Betsy ever mailed that. And today, I don't know for sure. They never asked me if I went to the post office."

Pam denied telling Janet Meyer that she did not go into Betsy's house when she took her home. Betsy's mother must have been confused if she told police that. "Janet's quite often confused."

He quickly caught her in another significant contradiction when he asked why she had gone to the chemo session after Betsy texted her that she wanted to spend some "one-on-one time" with Bobbi Wann. She said she probably hadn't read that text yet and didn't remember it at all. He read her the transcript of their texts that day, including the one Betsy sent at 10:35 a.m.: "'Bobbi is going and I want to spend some one-on-one time with her.'"

Schwartz added, "One minute later, you responded, 'Bummer.' Would that indicate to you that you read the text?"

"Yes."

"Do you remember reading the text?"

"No. I don't remember the reply, either."

Pam said she would have gone to the chemo session even if she had seen Betsy's text. "Because Betsy is—was—a good friend of mine and she was dying and I wanted to spend as much time with her as I could. It didn't matter what she said."

The next contradiction was even more glaring and equally inexplicable. Schwartz asked if she and Betsy had gone door-to-door collecting money for cancer research. She said they had not gone door-to-door, but were trying to raise money for a woman who was dying of cancer. When Schwartz asked how they were raising funds, Pam said, "Just door-to-door collecting."

"Didn't you just say you didn't go door-to-door?"

"Did I? I don't know. Did I say that?"

"You said it."

"I don't know."

She said she gave the money they collected to Betsy, but didn't have any paperwork related to the effort.

Schwartz asked what condition qualified her for monthly disability payments through Social Security.

"I'm not sure what they classify it as. . . . I know I have drop foot and balance problems. I don't know what the classification is."

She said her injuries occurred in 2009 when she worked for UnitedHealthcare. She tripped in the office and hit her head on a file cabinet. She filed a worker's compensation claim, which remained unresolved.

Pam said she worked in insurance for more than twelve years and had met Betsy Faria the day in October 2001 that she applied for a job with Bob Davenport's State Farm agency, where Betsy worked. She said Davenport had been "let go" by State Farm, but she didn't know why.

"You were never told that Mr. Davenport was accused . . . that people in his office or somebody in his office was forging documents?" Schwartz asked.

"We weren't told anything by corporate. There was a lot of gossip."

"What was the gossip?"

"Some that he was forging documents; other that he was selling insurance across state lines. A bunch of stuff like that."

"That he was forging documents or someone in his office was forging documents?"

"I think it was somebody forging—Irma Donley."

"Irma Donley was forging documents? What kind of documents were being forged?"

"I have no idea. I wasn't with her when she was doing that."

"Were there any repercussions as a result of some of the rumors and innuendoes—to you? Specifically, was your car keyed?"

"Yes. Yes."

Pam said she later went to work for another State Farm office run by agent Al Wansing, but he eventually let her go without explanation and rehired a former employee.

"Did he ever accuse you, to your face, of forging notary seals on documents?"

"No . . . no, he never said any of that."

Pam agreed that she and Betsy would have known how to write a life insurance policy with contingent beneficiaries. She showed no recognition that Schwartz was implying they easily could have added Betsy's daughters as contingent beneficiaries on Betsy's policy without taking the radical step of making Pam the sole beneficiary with only a verbal, unwritten agreement to use the money for the girls.

Schwartz wanted more information about Pam's medical condition, but she said she couldn't name the injury to her head. "I have balance problems. Why? I don't know what that's called."

She said she had had a CAT scan, but the doctors' conclusion was "'We don't know what's wrong' . . . I think."

She said she wouldn't release her medical records to Schwartz or Askey "because that's my business and I don't want my business out, medically."

She said she had stopped seeing her doctor because she couldn't afford the visits; her health insurance had lapsed and she was not old enough to qualify for Medicare. She said her last visit might have been January 3, 2012—just seven days after Betsy's murder.

"What kind of symptoms do you have as a result of your head injury?"

"I have balance problems—fall down. I can get migraines from fans."

"Do you have memory issues?"

"Yes."

"Tell me about those. How do you know you have memory issues?"

"Well, because you're asking me questions and I don't remember."

Schwartz closed his questioning by addressing one more contradiction. Had she told police initially that she had been driving her Nissan Sentra when she took Betsy home that night, when she was actually driving a Honda Accord?

"Well, I might have, but I don't know why I would say that. I haven't had one for a long time. Don't even know anybody who has one."

The prosecutors didn't have a single question for their primary witness and Schwartz's first confounding exposure to Pam Hupp was mercifully over. He had gained an important insight about this strange woman: she knew there were suspicions that she was Betsy's killer and she was driven to proclaim her innocence.

And he had reached one defining conclusion about the prosecution's star witness. She was as slippery and slimy as a fish coated in oil.

CHAPTER TWENTY-FOUR

May 28, 2013—seventeen months
after Betsy Faria's murder

The one-page order from Circuit Judge Christina Kunza Menne-meyer was the most catastrophic four paragraphs Joel Schwartz had ever read in one of his cases. The judge had just prohibited the defense from arguing, presenting testimony or evidence, or in any way implying that Pam Hupp could have been Betsy Faria's killer. In fact, Schwartz would not even be able to cross-examine her in a way that suggested she had motive and opportunity to kill Betsy or that her long list of contradictory and inconsistent statements about almost every aspect of the case suggested any guilt on her part.

He couldn't question her about becoming the beneficiary to Betsy's life insurance, just four days before her murder. He wouldn't be able to point out that she had said repeatedly that Betsy made her the beneficiary so she could give the money to Betsy's daughters later, but was now denying that and saying the money was all hers. He would not be able to argue that the real killer could have been Pam Hupp, even though the essence of an alibi defense is "some other dude did it" because the defendant was elsewhere at the time of the murder.

The judge had agreed with Leah Askey's position that none of the issues involving Pam Hupp qualified as the "direct connection" to the murder, as Missouri case law required. Russ's bloody slippers and his claim that Betsy had committed suicide established a direct connection to Betsy's murder, but there was no such connection for Pam. Askey insisted case law decided motive and opportunity were not enough unless the person also had a direct connection to the crime.

The judge's decision was wrong on the law and wrong on the facts, and Schwartz was almost as furious as he was astounded. In a hearing before Judge Mennemeyer a week earlier, Schwartz had explained meticulously how scores of cases in Missouri—if not more than a hundred—supported the defense's right to treat Pam Hupp as a suspect. Case law established that a person with motive and opportunity to commit a crime, who makes inconsistent and contradictory statements, or who was with a victim at or near the time of death had a direct connection that justifies the defense treating them as a suspect. Case law gave the defense the unrestricted right to cross-examine a witness who had any kind of interest in the outcome of the trial—such as maintaining a claim to $150,000 in life insurance or helping convict someone else of a crime the witness may have committed. Schwartz argued the facts involving Hupp created more of a direct connection for Pam Hupp to Betsy's murder than any of the State's evidence against Russ Faria.

Over the next few months, Schwartz would make repeated efforts to convince Judge Mennemeyer to reverse her decision—all without success. He would become so frustrated during one hearing—when he had carted in a huge stack of cases to support his position—that he would risk a contempt-of-court citation by proclaiming, "Judge, I don't know what to do to get you to listen. Would it work if I strip down and bang my head against the bench?"

Russ Faria likened the judge's decisions to sending Schwartz into a boxing match with one hand tied behind his back—or perhaps both hands. But he agreed with Schwartz that they could still convince a jury of Russ's innocence even without mounting a full-frontal assault on Pam Hupp. Russ had an invulnerable alibi for his time between 5 and 9:30 p.m. The forensic evidence proved Betsy had been dead for some time, perhaps as long as two hours, before Russ called 911 at 9:40 p.m. Even with this wrongheaded decision by Mennemeyer, the jury would hear that Pam Hupp was the last person to see Betsy alive in the place where, and about the time, she was killed. There wasn't a speck of blood on Russ or his clothes from a savage knife attack on Betsy. And Russ's bloody slippers appeared to have been dipped in her blood—an act anyone could have committed as a fairly obvious attempt to frame Russ.

Surely, a jury would see the obvious truth.

About a week before Russ's trial was scheduled to begin on November 18, Leah Askey called Joel Schwartz and asked what it would take to make a deal for a guilty plea. Schwartz almost laughed before he said, "Dismiss the charges against Russ and hire me as a special prosecutor. I guarantee I'll get a conviction against Pam Hupp."

Askey wasn't interested.

CHAPTER TWENTY-FIVE

*Monday, November 18, 2013—first day
of testimony in Russ Faria's trial*

Prosecuting Attorney Leah Askey was barely five minutes into her opening statement to the jury of seven men and five women—the first five minutes of the murder trial of Russ Faria—when she handed Joel Schwartz the grounds for his first motion for a mistrial. He had expected the trial to be contentious, but he was surprised how quickly Askey had stepped over the line on a key issue. She had begun her opening statement by attacking Russ's shocked and confused initial assumption that Betsy had killed herself, and she used his own words against him.

"'I just got home from a friend's house and my wife killed herself.' That is what the defendant said when he called 911 after he saw his dead wife lying on the living-room floor with some fifty-six stab wounds [the correct number was fifty-five, but it was often misstated] in her, after he saw her arm nearly severed off, after he saw a knife still protruding from her neck. 'My wife killed herself.' That's what the defendant said. You'll hear him wailing in despair on the phone with the 911 operator as he's moving about, trying to convince her and himself, likely, that that is, in fact, what had happened."

That last sentence, just her fifth of the trial, drew Schwartz's first objection as improperly argumentative in an opening statement.

Askey withdrew the comment before Judge Mennemeyer could respond. Just several sentences later, Schwartz made another "argumentative" objection when Askey told the jurors, "Folks, this is a murder about greed." Again, Askey withdrew the remark.

But the first real explosion occurred just sentences later as Askey said, "You'll hear evidence the defendant was well aware that Betsy had three insurance policies totaling—"

Schwartz quickly interrupted with an objection and asked for a sidebar conference with the judge at the bench. He argued that the judge's rulings on motions, including one that very morning, prohibited either side from discussing the insurance policies. He motioned toward Askey and said, "She just said, 'You'll hear evidence that Betsy Faria had three insurance policies.'"

Askey parsed her sentence more precisely. "That's not what I said. What I said was the defendant knew she had three policies. That's what he tells the detectives."

Schwartz was furious about the entire insurance issue and the State's position now. "I will ask for a mistrial based upon that statement to the jury at this time."

Richard Hicks seemed flabbergasted as he spat out, "What?" Which rulings by the judge, he asked, could be interpreted as prohibiting the prosecution from saying there were life insurance policies listing Russ as beneficiary? "That's establishing black-and-white, motive evidence that there were three insurance policies in his name," he said.

Schwartz noted the judge had granted the prosecution's motion barring him from mentioning the change in beneficiary to Pam Hupp and had just denied his motion that morning for her to reconsider. "The State cannot get into the fact that there was an insurance policy that exists and then keep us from arguing that the policy had been changed," he said. Surely, the judge hadn't ruled that the defense was barred from alleging that being a beneficiary gave Pam Hupp a motive to kill Betsy, but the prosecution was allowed to argue that being a beneficiary gave Russ a motive to kill Betsy.

Judge Mennemeyer rifled through her file and said all she could find was rulings barring the defense from mentioning the change in beneficiary and from arguing that someone else committed the murder.

"At this point," Mennemeyer added, "the court is not granting a mistrial. We're just going to direct the parties to stop talking about insurance at this time."

Schwartz then asked the judge to instruct the jury to disregard Askey's last statement about the insurance policies. And then he added, ". . . and I would then request a mistrial."

Hicks asked the judge to reconsider banning the mention of insurance. "Judge, this is a vital issue. . . . This evidence that he knew about the existence of three insurance policies goes right to motive." He argued again that a lack of direct evidence linking Pam Hupp to the murder made the change in beneficiaries irrelevant, while direct evidence against Russ, such as his bloody slippers, made the policies with him as beneficiary relevant as a motive.

Mennemeyer continued to search her rulings until she found two that she said supported the prosecutors' position. She told Askey to proceed with her opening statement.

Schwartz asked again, "Your Honor, so I can make a record . . . the last order from the court correctly stated that the issue of any insurance policies is inadmissible and will only serve to confuse the jury."

Mennemeyer shook her head. "That's a mischaracterization. . . . I'm saying the fact that they mentioned it at this point doesn't mean anything."

"So my motion for the jury to disregard is overruled?"

"Right. That's correct."

"And my motion for a mistrial . . ."

"Is overruled. . . . The State may proceed."

As Askey stepped back in front of the jurors to resume her opening, Schwartz returned to the defense table with the confirmation that unjust rulings by this judge would continue. He glanced at Russ and was pleased that his client remained unruffled, even stoic. Russ certainly was not surprised to see more of the adverse rulings the defense had suffered for almost two years. But he remained optimistic that, with Joel Schwartz and Nate Swanson conducting his defense, the jurors would see the truth.

Askey picked up where she had stopped when she was so rudely interrupted by Schwartz's attempt to ensure a fair trial. She explained that Russ knew his wife was insured for between $300,000 and $400,000. And then she began to create a version of Russ Faria the jurors might be able to see cutting his wife to shreds.

"You are going to hear that the defendant had a short temper, a short fuse. He oftentimes would instigate arguments that would result in name-calling and disrespectful statements to his wife and her daughters. You're going to hear that his language that he chose to use is some that I don't even feel comfortable saying to you, frankly. You're going to learn that sometimes his anger got so far out of control he was even abusive to the family dog."

Askey began to attack Russ's alibi by offering a warped view of game night. "Now, this wasn't a game like you guys are probably thinking about. I'm not talking about poker. Not pitch. Not blackjack. No three-card stud. No, this is a role-playing game where this band of merry men dressed like hobbits, act like monks, sorcerers, all sorts of things that I don't really understand, and they do this every Tuesday night while they smoke pot and drink beer."

Schwartz bristled again, but still decided not to object. Askey had just lied to the jury. No one had ever said the players dressed like hobbits or acted like their characters. That was an intentional lie designed to cast the players as vaguely threatening weirdos involved in sinister activity fueled by drugs and booze. Yeah, there was a little pot, but there was seldom even a beer. And this harmless game was not that much different from any board game, even the dangerous, mind-bending adventures in capitalism called Monopoly.

Askey was on a roll. She cast the texts between the Farias that day like this: "You'll see text messages from Betsy to Russ where she says, 'Do you have a game tonight?' Do you think he says no? No. Instead, he starts orchestrating a plan with the same people. 'I know we can't play the game tonight, but how about, instead, let's get together and watch *Conan the Barbarian* or something.' He waits until he gets some commitment from them that they are all going to get together anyway, and then he tells her, 'Yeah, I'm playing.'"

Orchestrating a plan with the same people? Schwartz and Russ looked at each other, marveling at how Askey could make friends getting together to play a game or watch a movie sound like Osama bin Laden and his cadre of terrorists designing the 9/11 flight plan.

Askey's next target was Russ's call to his mother while he drove to game night to explain that errands would keep him from attending dinner at her house. "The errands are my favorite part," Askey quipped. And then she reached for the absurd again by saying, after Russ talked to Betsy and his mother, "The wheel gains momentum."

She trotted out a neat little semantic trick when she began to attack Russ's stops on the way to game night. Each time she mentioned his stops for gas, cigarettes, and iced tea, she emphasized, "Got a receipt. Got on video." Three times. "Got a receipt. Got on video." She had to break her pattern to mention his stop to buy dog food because he only "Got a receipt." She mentioned his stop at Arby's on his way home: "Guess what? Keeps the receipt. That's his alibi."

She told the jurors that first responders at the scene would testify, "This guy's emotions were all over the place. He was really up, wailing, crying. . . . You'll hear the 911 tape, and the only time he's not wailing and crying—with no tears, by the way—is when he's answering their questions or asserting his alibi. He can just shut it off, answer a question, and then commence the wailing."

She started her listing of evidence against Russ with the alleged paw print in Betsy's blood on the hip of her pants left by the dog who, Russ said, was outside. There would be "evidence and testimony that there were cleaning agents used on the floor between where her body was found and the back door where the dog chain was." Betsy's blood was found on the switch plate for the light in the master bedroom, where Russ told police he had not gone, and on the slippers Russ always wore that had been "tossed in the back corner of a closet—a very disheveled closet."

To close her attack, Askey moved to Russ's account of arriving home to find Betsy's body. After saying he should have been able to see Betsy's body as soon as he walked in the front door, she said, "He tells the detectives how he was so distraught he laid down next to her. He shows them he laid this close to her, just trying to get it together and figure out what to do, realizing she was gone. But you're going to find out, not only did he not have one speck of blood—not on his hands, not on his clothes—but he lay next to her.

"A woman who has been stabbed fifty-six times, who has a knife protruding from her neck, whose wrists are lying upright and are almost—her hands are almost cut off—and he lays this close to her. And yet, when he calls 911—'I just got home from a friend's house and my wife, she killed herself.'"

Askey let her last line reverberate for a second before she ended with, "Ladies and gentlemen, after you hear the evidence, the State trusts that you will return a verdict of guilty."

Across the courtroom, Joel Schwartz wasn't impressed by Askey's presentation or her evidence. He knew how he would address each part of the specious story she had just tried to sell to the jury. And he would begin by acquainting jurors with a family not much different from theirs—a husband and wife just struggling to build a good life with each other.

"The evidence is going to show that this is absolutely a tragedy," he began as he stepped before the jury. "It's a tragedy for the Meyer/ Faria family. It's also a tragedy for Russ Faria. His wife of eleven years was brutally murdered on December 27, 2011—and he's the one who found her."

Calling the Farias "a typical family today," with a stepfather, a mother, and two stepdaughters, Schwartz explained how they had moved to Troy in 2010 when they found a house at a good price. He recounted the fatal diagnosis of Betsy's cancer and her decision to keep her plans for a cruise with family and friends in November. He took jurors through family parties over the Christmas holidays and Betsy's stay at her mother's in Lake St. Louis on Monday night to be closer to her chemotherapy session the next day in St. Peters. Russ spent that Tuesday working a normal day in his home office and exchanging texts with Betsy about getting dog food on his way to his regular game night from six to nine o'clock, which Schwartz emphasized as "a cheap, fun, easy way for them to enjoy their evenings." But the absence of one of the usual players meant they couldn't play Rolemaster and, after some exchanges of texts among Russ and the players, game night became movie night.

Schwartz explained the pivotal change in plans that originally called for Russ to pick up Betsy on his way home. Betsy texted Russ that afternoon—while mentioning the essential detail that she had picked up toilet paper—that her friend Pam Hupp would be driving her home early so she could rest. Russ asked if Pam was taking Betsy home to Troy, and Betsy responded, Yes, she offered and I accepted.

At five o'clock, Russ started his drive to Mike Corbin's house and stopped at Conoco to get gas. Schwartz pointedly rebuffed Askey's misleading attempts to deride Russ's alibi. "He doesn't 'get' on video, but it later turns out he is 'on' video getting his gas and it shows the time he's there . . . approximately five sixteen to five twenty."

Schwartz hoped the jury would catch the difference in how Russ's appearances on surveillance videos at three of his stops that evening were portrayed. Askey's snarky "gets on video," implying a devious scheme, versus Schwartz's explanation that Russ simply appeared on the video in the normal course of conducting his business. And, Schwartz noted, the videos showed Russ was wearing the same clothes he was when the police seized them for testing that showed "not one speck of blood on that clothing. Not one speck of blood on his hands. No blood—anywhere."

All four of the players at game night would testify that they were with Russ every second between six and nine o'clock as they watched movies. And, Schwartz said, records from cell phone towers would show that Russ's phone was in exactly the locations he said at the times he said.

Schwartz drew the first objection from Askey when he recounted the texts between Betsy and Pam over attending the chemotherapy session. Before Schwartz could tell the jurors that Betsy had texted Pam that she preferred to have some one-on-one time with Bobbi alone, Askey objected to citing Betsy's text as hearsay. The attorneys gathered before the judge for Schwartz to argue that it was not hearsay because police documented it when they examined Pam's phone. But Judge Mennemeyer agreed with Askey that there was no hearsay exception for texts by Betsy to Pam and sustained her objection. Schwartz was limited to telling jurors that Betsy and Bobbi went to the chemo session together and Pam showed up later.

Schwartz emphasized Pam's insistent insertion of herself into Betsy's plans that day, explaining to the jury that Pam went to Janet Meyer's apartment later and took Betsy home about 6:30 p.m., in time to arrive at Betsy's and call Pam's husband at 7:04 p.m. He also explained Betsy had agreed to answer a call from her daughter sometime after seven o'clock, but her calls went unanswered at 7:21, 7:26, and 7:30 p.m. He hoped the jurors would see that as establishing the first half of the seven o'clock hour as the time of Betsy's death.

Firing an opening shot in his attempt to impeach Pam Hupp's expected testimony, Schwartz explained that cell phone analysis showed that Pam's call to Betsy at 7:27 p.m., when she had, at first, told police she had arrived at her home in O'Fallon twenty-seven miles away, was actually placed from the same sector of the cell phone tower as the call to her husband from Betsy's house at 7:04 p.m. Schwartz followed that quickly by telling the jurors that Pam, at first, told police she did not go into Betsy's house, but then changed her story and admitted she did.

Askey asked for a sidebar with the judge to say Schwartz's mention of the cell phone location and Pam Hupp's contradictory statements about going into the house signaled he was going to suggest Pam "committed this crime." Under the judge's earlier rulings, Schwartz could not argue that, and, therefore, his last two statements to the jury had to be stricken.

Schwartz offered a simple defense: "It's the facts and it's the evidence." Swanson added that legal statutes said prior inconsistent statements by a witness were admissible to impeach the witness. Hicks said the cell phone tower locations, and whether Pam entered Betsy's house, could only be relevant if Schwartz could argue that Pam killed Betsy—and the judge had already prohibited that. Judge Mennemeyer agreed with Hicks and prohibited Schwartz from getting into those matters.

With an edge of incredulity in his voice, Schwartz asked Mennemeyer, "So I can't open regarding the statements that she made to the police that are inconsistent. Is that what you're saying?"

She responded, "I don't think they're relevant at this point. That was a prior ruling. I don't know how that would change."

When Schwartz said, "That has nothing to do with the court's ruling that I can't get into her motive or opportunity to commit the crime," Mennemeyer snapped, "Just no. It's sustained. Let's move on."

Schwartz returned to the jurors to explain that the timing of pings from Russ's phone off the cell phone towers showed that the earliest he could have arrived at home was 9:38 p.m. He did indeed tell the police he thought his wife had killed herself, but the jurors would hear testimony that Betsy had threatened suicide in the past. As he started to recount what Betsy's sisters would say, Hicks objected that testimony from them was hearsay. Schwartz and Swanson disagreed with the State again, saying the testimony would not be hearsay because it would include only the women's knowledge that Betsy had threatened suicide in the past. Hicks said if that testimony was admitted, he should be able to introduce evidence that Betsy was happy and excited about talking to Russ when he got home that night about her idea to move into her mother's former house. The judge said that testimony might be admitted at the proper time; she told Schwartz to proceed with his statement to jurors.

Schwartz decided to be less specific. Referring to Russ telling the police she had committed suicide, Schwartz said, "You'll hear an explanation and you'll understand as to why that was stated."

He hoped to establish the time of Betsy's death as some two hours before Russ got home by quoting the paramedic and fire chief who were first to inspect her body. "They will each tell you that the body was stiff, they will tell you the body felt cold, and they will tell you that the blood was matted, coagulated, and drying."

Schwartz took on the prosecutors' number one piece of evidence—the bloody slippers—describing them as "soaked in blood, including the bottoms of those shoes." And then he added, "But what you won't see is any bloody footprints anywhere in that blood. What you won't see, after fifty-five stab wounds and incisions, is a speck of blood anywhere on Russell Faria."

And finally, what about Russ's alibi? Schwartz said the police interviewed the four alibi witnesses from game night and found the receipts and videos, all confirming Russ's account of his whereabouts during the crucial time when his wife was murdered.

"After you hear the evidence," Schwartz said, "I will stand before you and I will ask you to return a verdict of not guilty."

CHAPTER TWENTY-SIX

"A lot of bickering and fighting," Mariah Day told the jurors. "A lot of cussing at each other."

Leah Day echoed her younger sister when she testified next: "It was just a lot of bickering and fighting."

Betsy Faria's daughters were Leah Askey's first two witnesses and she quickly led them into accounts of squabbling between their mother and stepfather. Askey asked nineteen-year-old Mariah if the cussing by Russ was aimed at her mother.

"Usually toward my mom. Sometimes toward me and my sister," Mariah said.

As Askey began to ask if Mariah's occasional fear of Russ played any role in her decision to live with her grandmother, Mariah began crying and trembling so badly that Askey handed her a cup of water and suggested taking a minute for her to calm down.

Her sister, Leah, now twenty-three, had the same emotional response while testifying next. Askey started by asking for more information about the words her stepfather had used.

"The *C* word."

"The *C* word," Askey repeated for effect. "And would that word be used, directed, at you?"

"Yes." Now Leah was crying.

"Would it be directed at your mother as well?"

Leah was struggling. "I don't know. I don't know."

Askey handed Leah a cup of water and promised the questioning wouldn't last too long.

"Tell the jury about the situation with regard to your dog."

"Like, I don't want to do this," a sobbing Leah said. "I really don't. I don't want to do this."

Schwartz interrupted with a request to approach the bench to argue the judge had already ruled that prosecutors could not bring up any prior "bad acts" by Russ, and Askey's questions suggested she and Leah had a discussion about some incident involving the dog that was never disclosed to the defense—a discovery violation. Askey and Hicks said discovery rules only require information to be disclosed to the defense if it was memorialized in a report based on a witness's statement. Judge Mennemeyer decided to prohibit discussion of any incident involving the dog until she had a chance to research the situation in the *Missouri Rules of Evidence*.

Russ Faria felt an intense ache in his heart as he listened to the two young women he had loved as his own daughters tell twisted, exaggerated stories of their lives with their mother and him. He soon found the word to describe the ache: betrayed.

On cross-examination, Schwartz asked Mariah if Russ and Betsy's relationship hadn't gotten better after Betsy was diagnosed with cancer in 2009. Mariah offered no support: "I couldn't tell you about that."

The judge sent the jury out of the courtroom so Schwartz could make an offer of proof—an on-the-record presentation without the jury of what the evidence would be if the defense was allowed to present it to the jury and a tactic that also preserved the evidence or legal point for consideration by the appellate court. With the jury out, Mariah testified that, about an hour after Russ was arrested, she went to their bank, withdrew approximately $9,000 from an account in Russ's and Betsy's names, and deposited it in her savings account. She said she didn't get Russ's permission to do that, but her account was linked to her parents' and it was legal for her to transfer the money.

She also said she and Leah had never received any of the money from her mother's life insurance that she assumed Pam Hupp had.

Schwartz tried to get Mariah to repeat the comment she made to police that her first thought was that Betsy had committed suicide. Mariah resisted, saying instead that she had been confused and hadn't known what to think.

"But you had told the police that you had found a note several years before of your mother contemplating suicide?"

"Right."

Judge Mennemeyer said she would decide later whether Schwartz could question Mariah about the bank withdrawal in front of the jury. She would eventually decide against it.

Leah Day had been on the witness stand for only a few minutes when Schwartz filed his second motion for a mistrial. Askey had Leah identify photos of the jewelry box Russ gave Betsy for Christmas as it leaned against the wall in the master bedroom with a broken leg and some chips to the finish.

When Schwartz objected on relevance, Askey responded, "It shows a struggle ensued. You typically don't struggle when you are committing suicide."

Schwartz's temper flared again. With the jurors listening, he said Askey was intentionally distorting Russ's suicide remarks, again, to imply he had been lying and trying to mislead the police.

"Your Honor, I would ask that be stricken from the record and I would ask for a mistrial."

The judge ignored the mistrial request, but said, "The last statement will be stricken from the record. At this time, the exhibit (the photo) will not be admitted into evidence."

Schwartz was again realizing that he would not only have to be extraordinarily vigilant to put all of the evidence into the proper perspective for the jurors, but he also would have to combat Askey's improper implications and snide insinuations. She was quickly proving to be a master of ringing the bell—as in the old courtroom adage that you can't *un*ring a bell once a jury has heard it.

On cross-examination, Schwartz focused on Betsy's promise to answer the call from Leah sometime after seven o'clock the night of the murder. Although she said she was getting confused when

Schwartz quoted the exact times of her three unanswered calls, she readily agreed that Betsy had not answered the calls she made at 7:21, 7:26, and 7:30 p.m.

Askey called another pair of sisters to the witness stand after that—Betsy's sisters Pamela Welker and Mary Rodgers. Much like Betsy's daughters, Pamela and Mary focused on allegations of Russ's poor treatment of their sister. Pamela described Russ as condescending to Betsy. She said Betsy was "really not herself" at the family Christmas parties. "She just seemed tired and just not her cheery self."

Schwartz had Pamela confirm that she, Russ, and some of their friends from church had gone on the cruise the month before Betsy was killed and that she was undergoing chemotherapy during the holidays, when she seemed tired and not herself.

And then Schwartz told the judge in a sidebar that he wanted to ask Pamela if her first reaction to news of Betsy's death was that she had committed suicide. Mennemeyer seemed ready to prohibit Schwartz from asking about this, but Hicks said the prosecutors would stipulate that Pamela had told the police that—a rare agreement between the sides that would avoid the need for Pamela to testify about that. The judge would explain the stipulation to the jury later.

Mary Rodgers's criticism of Russ was a stronger than her sister's. She called Russ's behavior toward Betsy demeaning and recounted getting a frantic call while she was at work six or seven years earlier from Mariah and Leah because of an argument between Betsy and Russ. Mary said she went to the Farias' mobile home and heard Russ calling Leah and Mariah—the younger daughter was only around twelve years old—the C word. Russ pushed Betsy and that was when Mary called the police and took the girls out of the house.

"When I was walking out of the house, I heard him say something like, 'I'm going to cut her up into several pieces and bury her,' or some kind of . . . grotesque . . . that I can't even imagine," she said.

On cross-examination, Mary agreed with Schwartz that the incident had been six or seven years before Betsy's death. When

Schwartz asked if Russ and Betsy got along better after her cancer diagnosis, Mary said, "For a spell."

The prosecution called Russ's mother, Luci Faria, in a veiled attempt to cast suspicion on his game-night alibi. Adopting a friendly and solicitous approach to Russ's mother, Richard Hicks asked if Russ had called to alert her that he could not make her usual Tuesday night dinner the night Betsy was killed. Yes, she said, he called and said he wouldn't be there because he had some errands to run.

Schwartz was ready with a very short, but pointed, cross-examination. How often did Russ call and say he could not attend?

"Oh, I'd say at least, might be, twice a month," she said.

"So, fair enough to say half the time?"

"Yes, half the time. Correct."

CHAPTER TWENTY-SEVEN

Pam Hupp took the witness stand, embodying Joel Schwartz's greatest challenge in the trial. He had to overcome her ability to make lies sound reasonable, while also working around the judge's ruling barring any implication that she could be Betsy's killer. He was still optimistic that, first, he could reveal to the jurors the real Pam Hupp—a lying, conniving narcissist and likely murderer whose testimony had to be viewed with the greatest skepticism—and second, that he could plant enough clues about her motives for the jurors to suspect that she had framed Russ Faria because she was the killer.

But before he could try to accomplish any of that, Schwartz had to listen to another muddled recitation of her version of the life and death of Betsy Faria as Richard Hicks questioned her. Pam started by explaining that she was wearing a TENS unit on her waistband. (TENS is an acronym for transcutaneous electrical nerve stimulation.) It stimulated the nerves to reduce pain in her right leg resulting from an injury in an accident that left her unable to work and on disability payments.

"I lost some discs. I have a plate in my neck," she said. Before the accident, she was working in an insurance office, when she met Betsy Faria and they became close friends. Betsy began to confide in her about the problems with her health, her daughters, and—especially—her marriage to Russ. "I ended up being a sounding board for her and a lot of things going on in her life," Pam said.

What were her observations about interactions between Betsy and Russ?

"To me, he was very degrading to her. Talked down to her. Made her feel like she was simple, not that smart. . . . My husband and myself never socialized with him, nor did our group of friends, and their husbands did not want to socialize with him . . . because he made people feel uncomfortable, the way he talked to her."

Pam said she often accompanied Betsy to her chemotherapy sessions and joined Betsy and Bobbi Wann there on December 27, even though Betsy asked her not to come.

"Selfishly, I went there to spend time with her." Pam said Betsy asked her to drive her home from her mother's later that evening. They arrived at Betsy's home between 7 and 7:05 p.m. Pam called her husband to tell him she was in Troy, but got his voice mail. She left a message and Betsy took the phone to wish him happy holidays. Still sitting in the car, they "gabbed for a few minutes because she was trying to talk me into staying all night with her . . . and then we went into the house." After turning on some lights, Betsy took her dog, Sicily, outside.

"We're goofing, talking about Christmas, what we got, what the kids got. Blah, blah. Girl stuff . . . then she wanted to show me her Christmas present in the bedroom."

"So you went into the bedroom?"

"Yes."

Pam said she was in the house "twenty, thirty minutes or so." Betsy tried repeatedly to get her to spend the night or at least stay and watch some movies; she was angry when Pam refused.

"She said [Russ] was on his way home, or should be home shortly, and I just really did not want to be there. I had never been around him that much or socially. So that made me uncomfortable."

Pam said she left and called Betsy from the car to make sure she felt OK and wasn't still angry at her, but got no answer. She called Betsy's mother later that evening to alert her that Betsy had not answered her phone. She didn't know Betsy was dead, until six o'clock, the next morning, when the police knocked on her door.

*   *   *

Schwartz wasted no time attacking Pam Hupp's thick catalogue of contradictions that he hoped the jury would see as manipulative lies. After quoting her testimony that Russ degraded Betsy, made her feel simple, and made people uncomfortable, Schwartz got her to agree that she had told police in her first interview: "I don't know him that well. I've only met him maybe three times in ten years."

Schwartz wanted to add some perspective to Pam's decisions to go to the chemo session on December 27 and then go back to Betsy's mother's to give Betsy a ride home. "Were you trying to track her down?"

Pam's voice reflected her objection to Schwartz's implication. "'Trying to track her down'? I knew she was going to chemo, so I didn't have to 'track her down.'"

Schwartz zeroed in on the witness's lie about who suggested giving Betsy a ride home later. She said again that Betsy asked her for a ride and denied knowing until later that Russ was planning to pick up Betsy and take her home. She said she hadn't seen Betsy's text about that, until she had arrived at Janet Meyer's apartment on the way to the chemo session.

Schwartz pointed out that Pam lived about ten minutes from Betsy's mother's apartment, suggesting she could have easily gone back home from there rather than driving to the cancer center, driving home, returning to Betsy's mother's, making the thirty-minute drive to Troy to take Betsy home, and another thirty-minute drive back to her own house. That was a lot of extra effort to furnish a ride Betsy didn't need.

"Yes, because she asked if I could just take her, then she would tell Russ."

Schwartz put Pam Hupp in the house with Betsy about the time of the murder. She agreed she had gone into the house after calling her husband, Mark, from the driveway at 7:04 p.m. and stayed twenty minutes or even longer. She agreed that 7:27 p.m. would be about the time she left, if that was what the police said her cell phone showed.

"Did you tell the police that you called Betsy to tell her you were home?"

"Yes."

Schwartz decided to mix things up. "Let's step back for a moment. Initially you told the police, when they interviewed you, that you never went in the house?"

"Correct."

"And then you changed it and told them, 'Yes, I did go in the house,' and [you] went in this room and went in that room?"

"Right."

"'I went in the bedroom.' Correct?"

"Correct."

But Pam said she didn't remember telling Janet Meyer in a phone call later that she did not go into the house.

Schwartz let another lie by Pam hang in the air and then moved back to her call to Betsy at 7:27 p.m. Did she tell the police she called Betsy "'when I got home to tell her I was home'"?

"That's not what I said."

"Are you certain?"

"No."

Richard Hicks asked for a conference at the bench to object to questions that could lead to a suggestion that Pam Hupp was the killer. Schwartz defended cross-examining her on this point: "It's prior and inconsistent statement." He said Pam had not really answered the question of whether she told police she called to tell Betsy she was home; Hicks said she had. Schwartz offered to narrow the question.

Schwartz read Pam Hupp's statement from the transcript of the interview: "'I called Betsy. That's right. I called Betsy to tell her I was home.'" Pam agreed that was accurate. She also agreed it was impossible for her to be home by 7:27 p.m. So, why had she said that to police?

"Because that's not exactly what I meant. As we continued our conversation, what I said to them was that, when I got out of her neighborhood, because I don't know Troy that well, and I get to the interstate, I give her a call and always say, 'I'm home,' which means I'm on my way home. I made it out of your neighborhood. I made it home free. That's what it means to me."

Schwartz hoped the jury would see through the witness's contrived nonsense and recognize it for what it was—a failed effort to
put herself at home at 7:27 p.m. as an alibi, if the time of Betsy's
death was established as between 7 and 7:20 p.m.

"Now, when you were interviewed by the police the next morning, you told them the last time you saw Betsy, she was sitting on the
couch with her blanket on, watching television. Is that correct?"

"Yes—or she was putting a blanket on."

"Well, you said . . . Let's be accurate . . ."

Hicks objected to the form of the question and Schwartz re-
worded it without waiting for the judge to rule. "How was Betsy po-
sitioned when you last saw her?"

"She was going to get cuddled up to watch a movie on the couch
with her blanket."

"What did you tell the police two days later when you talked to
Detective Kaiser, when she came back to see you? She asked you,
'When was the last time you saw Betsy?' What did you tell her?"

"I don't remember."

"Isn't it true that you told her the last place you saw Betsy was at
the front door, waving good-bye?"

"I don't remember."

Pam rejected Schwartz's offer to read the police report. He moved
on, this time hoping the jury would catch a clue in the way she
talked about the time of Betsy's death while interviewed by the police the next day.

"Did you ask them, toward the end of your interview, 'What time
did this happen? This morning?'"

"I don't remember that," she said before rejecting yet another
offer to listen to the recording of the interview.

Schwartz cited the phone call with her brother during the police
interview. "You told your brother . . . 'My friend—something happened to her last night and I have two police officers here asking me
questions.' Do you recall telling that to your brother?"

"Yes, I do."

"So, why did you say later in the interview—why did you ask
them, 'Did this happen this morning?'"

"If I did, I just found out my good friend has been killed and, I don't know, I . . . Obviously, I did just say it . . ."

And then Pam Hupp created a new excuse for the contradictions in her statements and testimony.

"I have a little bit of a memory problem. I'm fifty-five and going through menopause. It's been two years. I can't tell you every minute of what I have said about anything, honestly."

Schwartz couldn't let this new attempt to wriggle out from under her lies go unchallenged.

"Is this memory problem the reason why you would have told the police that you didn't go inside?"

"No."

"Is this memory problem the reason you would have told . . . the police you called her when you got home?"

"No."

Schwartz aimed his last attack at putting her exactly where the bloody evidence was found. Pam agreed that Betsy had shown her the jewelry chest Russ gave her as it sat in the bedroom with a broken leg. That not only put her in the bedroom, where police found the bloody slippers and light switch, but it also put the lie to Askey's comment to the jury that the broken leg suggested there had been a struggle when Betsy was killed.

On redirect examination, Richard Hicks hoped to get a final answer to whether Pam Hupp told police she did not go into the house and then said later she did.

"Did you ever lie to them and say, 'No, I never went in'?"

"Never . . . I told them every room I was in and what we did and what we talked about and what we saw and everything. I was always up front."

That persistent lie ended Pam Hupp's testimony before the jury. But Schwartz had more questions for her in an offer of proof to the judge after the jury left the courtroom. He hoped to convince Mennemeyer to allow him to question her in front of the jury about the beneficiary change on the life insurance policy.

* * *

Under the new line of questioning, Pam agreed that Betsy had made her the beneficiary, but remarkably denied knowing who the beneficiary was before. Schwartz asked why she never told the police, the morning after the murder, that she and Betsy had gone to the post office, where she assumed Betsy mailed the form.

Pam said she didn't know why it wasn't mentioned, adding that she wasn't sure then that Betsy had mailed the form. She agreed with Schwartz that sometime after Betsy's death, she told the insurance company that she and Betsy went to the post office to mail it. She said she hadn't told police because it didn't seem relevant. She said she knew the insurance company scanned the beneficiary form into its system the day after Betsy was killed.

"Now, why did Betsy change that policy to you?"

"She said that she wanted, she just wanted to change it to me. She didn't want whoever was on it—and we had talked about Russ, I assumed it was Russ on it—any longer, and she was changing on all her policies. She had a sister as a secondary on one of the policies . . . and she was going to change another policy to her cousin that also had breast cancer."

Pam said she may have told the police in the first interview that Betsy wanted her to give some money to her daughters when they were older. But she denied telling the insurance company that Betsy's daughters would get none of the money. Schwartz said he had an affidavit from the insurance company's business records department quoting Pam as making that statement to a company official. She said she thought that was wrong, adding, "I don't know what you're talking about."

On redirect, Hicks asked who brought up the insurance policies when the police first interviewed her.

"I did. They didn't know anything about it."

He asked about the costs of changing a beneficiary compared to drawing up a trust. She said changing the beneficiary was free, but she spent $1,400 to set up a trust. He asked about the insurance money.

"I received a check for one hundred fifty thousand dollars. . . . I put one hundred thousand in a trust for the girls and the other fifty thousand dollars—my other girlfriend died of breast cancer in August and she had a twelve-year-old daughter that I'm trying to help."

"But one hundred thousand is in a trust fund for the girls?"

"Absolutely. I have the paperwork right here."

Schwartz came back immediately to ask when she created the trust.

"It was official, I think, in July . . . June or July."

Schwartz didn't argue with her, even though he knew she had not created the trust until the week before this trial in November. Instead, he commented that opening a trust fund in June or July would have been right before the trial was originally scheduled.

"I got it done when I could get it done," she said. "I have a son with cerebral palsy. My mother just died on the thirty-first of Alzheimer's, that I had been taking care of. So it's taken me a bit to get around to it. But if it was done for court, I probably would have done it the first time around."

Pam's mention of her mother's death seemingly passed without notice. It wouldn't be the last mention, however.

Pam Hupp completed her testimony and, under the umbrella of protection by Judge Mennemeyer's rulings, avoided explaining to the jury the potentially incriminating fact that she was the last person known to see Betsy Faria alive, just four days after Betsy made her beneficiary to a $150,000 life insurance policy.

Although the judge would later deny Schwartz's request to educate the jurors about that, he hoped they would find the long list of contradictions and lies he had been able to expose reason to doubt anything Pam Hupp told them and to suspect she might even be a murder suspect.

But one man in the audience couldn't believe that what he had just heard from Pam Hupp about becoming Betsy's beneficiary— just days before the murder—would not be presented to the jurors. Chris Hayes from FOX 2, the only reporter covering the trial, could barely restrain his reaction. He thought, What the hell is going on? This is astounding! Why isn't the jury hearing this testimony?

He would ask Joel Schwartz for an explanation at the next break, and Schwartz directed him to the judge's decisions prohibiting the defense from presenting evidence about the insurance or cross-examining Pam Hupp about it.

Hayes realized he had just discovered what was really at the center of the Faria case.

CHAPTER TWENTY-EIGHT

Russ Faria's call to 911 was about to be played for the jury. The defense had agreed with prosecutors that the dispatcher who took the call did not have to testify and her supervisor could introduce the recording. But when Leah Askey began questioning the Lincoln County Director of 911 Services, Margie Harrell, about Russ's behavior on the call, Nate Swanson immediately saw this testimony going off the rails.

At a sidebar with Judge Mennemeyer, he objected to Askey eliciting Harrell's opinion on Russ's demeanor on the call. An opinion from Harrell would invade the jurors' rights and duty to judge the call for themselves. Richard Hicks argued it was proper for Harrell, who had taken thousands of 911 calls in sixteen years, to describe her observations of Russ's behavior. The judge agreed and overruled the objection, adding that Swanson could object again if he believed specific questions were improper.

Askey asked Harrell if she found Russ to be hysterical and Swanson objected. But Mennemeyer overruled Swanson again and allowed Harrell to answer—just as Swanson had feared.

"Yes, ma'am, at first. . . . Normally, if we have a hysterical caller, it's very hard to derive information. . . . You're more trying to get them to breathe, to where you don't have a second patient at the scene, more than you are anything else. It's hard to get further information from them. Whereas, with this one, there was hysteria. Then it was, you would ask a question, you get an answer. It would stop. You get an answer, and then it would go back to be hysteria again."

Askey played the 911 recording and the judge allowed a transcript to be projected on a screen by the witness stand. At the defense table, Russ Faria lowered his eyes and locked them on the table as the sounds of his own wailing and sobbing filled the courtroom. It was impossible not to relive those moments. The image of Betsy crumpled on the floor ripped into his heart almost as viciously as it had that night. Joel Schwartz had advised Russ against any display of emotion in front of the jury and Russ was determined to remain stoic. Schwartz and Swanson had heard the call many times before, but it still wounded them to hear the man they had come to know so well sound so shattered and helpless. Across the room, the jurors kept their eyes glued to the transcript as it scrolled on the screen.

Swanson was ready for cross-examination and quickly guided Harrell through the protocol for dealing with a hysterical caller. She said the goal was to calm the caller by asking questions and telling the caller to breathe. That was exactly what the dispatcher on this call did, she said.

"So, when you said this is odd—that's what you said earlier—this is an odd audio?"

"I said that it's odd in reference to hysteria—when you are talking to someone to try to get them to calm down . . . to be able to get good information."

"But that's what your training requires you to do?"

"Yes."

"That's what this dispatch person did?"

"Yes."

So, Swanson thought, the 911 dispatcher got a call from a hysterical husband who had just found his wife's body and used her training to calm him down so he could answer her questions. And there was something odd or suspicious about that?

The first Lincoln County deputy sheriff who arrived at 130 Sumac Drive was now a patrol officer for the City of Troy. Officer Chris

Hollingsworth told the jury he knew immediately that Betsy had not killed herself. He was in the house less than a minute before he ushered Russ Faria to a chair on the front porch. Worried that Russ might go into shock in the cold night air, he then moved him to a warmer patrol car.

The two men talked for an hour, perhaps less, mostly about the nearby Florissant/Hazelwood area, where they both grew up, and the places where they hung out as kids. When Hollingsworth asked about an area called Bubblehead Road, Russ joked that he "used to take women there and scare the hell out of them."

"And at that time, while he was having this conversation about Bubblehead Road and scaring women, did he seem like he was hyperventilating?" Askey asked.

"No, ma'am. He was calm and we were laughing."

Askey's voice rose. "He was laughing?"

"Yes, ma'am."

"Other than at the beginning, when you were out on the porch and trying to control his breathing, was there ever a time after you got in the car that he was crying, hysterical?"

"When he had made statements regarding . . . telling his mom and the daughters about the incident."

"But other than that, he was able . . . to have normal conversation?"

"Normal conversation. Laughing."

"Jovial?"

"Yes, ma'am."

Joel Schwartz began cross-examination by having Hollingsworth repeat all the steps he had taken to try to calm the "visibly upset" Russ. And then he asked, "How much grieving had he gone through in 2009 when his wife was first diagnosed with cancer?"

"I couldn't tell you. I didn't know him in 2009."

Schwartz tried to ask Hollingsworth if he was familiar with all of the events that could have caused Russ to grieve for Betsy before that night, but Askey objected that there was no foundation for that. Schwartz tried a different approach, but the judge sustained another objection by Askey, drawing a surprised "I'm sorry?" from Schwartz.

The judge said, "Sustained as to lack of foundation."

Schwartz tried to provide a foundation. Was Hollingsworth with the Farias in Rhode Island when they got the news that her cancer had spread? Was he with them on their so-called survival cruise in November 2011? Askey objected again and the lawyers argued at the bench before the judge ruled Schwartz could ask if Hollingsworth learned any of those things while he was with Russ. But she would not allow Schwartz to ask "fifteen questions we know he doesn't know."

Schwartz had Hollingsworth confirm that he did not know how much grieving Russ had done since Betsy's fatal cancer diagnosis.

Schwartz ended his cross-examination by having Hollingsworth use photographs projected on the screen to explain that if he walked in the front door and focused on the door to the garage on the left, he wouldn't immediately see Betsy's body to the right in the living room. So much, Schwartz thought, for Askey's attempt to discredit Russ's account of putting down the dog food and taking off his jacket before he saw Betsy's body.

Betsy Faria's body was cold and stiff, and her blood was dried, when first responders arrived at her home, Lead Medic Michael "Mike" Quattrocchi told the jury—but only under cross-examination by Nate Swanson.

Prosecutor Richard Hicks had focused his direct examination on Quattrocchi's assumption that he was in a crime scene as soon as he walked in, not the scene of a "suicide by blade," as had been said by the dispatcher for the Lincoln County Ambulance District.

After Swanson drew Quattrocchi's testimony on cross that the body was cold and stiff, and the blood was dried, he asked the veteran of twenty-five years as a paramedic, "What did that suggest to you?"

"That she had been down for quite a while."

"A couple hours?"

"I'm not a medical examiner, but yeah."

Quattrocchi described the cut on Betsy's arm: "There was no blood in it or anything and it was laid open."

"And what does that suggest to you?"

"Maybe she was already . . . bled out when that one was done to her."

On redirect, Quattrocchi told Hicks that he did not get any blood on his hands or knees when he knelt down to check the body. He also testified that when people cut their wrists to commit suicide, there is always a lot of blood—another redundant attempt by the State to prove Betsy didn't commit suicide.

Under recross, Quattrocchi referred to his original report for the time he arrived at the house—9:51 p.m., just eleven minutes after Russ called 911.

Not much time for a body to get cold and stiff and for the blood to start drying.

CHAPTER TWENTY-NINE

Tuesday, November 19, 2013—
second day of trial testimony

To open the second day of the trial, the deputy commander for the Major Case Squad's investigation into Betsy Faria's murder spent a long time explaining how the MCS operates—without saying anything about the actual investigation. Lieutenant Mark Schimweg of the St. Peters Police Department described the process for local departments to request the manpower and expertise from the MCS and how detectives from member agencies respond to the call for assistance.

Leah Askey's questioning finally got around to the case at hand. Schimweg said MCS officers made an initial arrest of Russ Faria two days after the murder, but Askey had said there was insufficient evidence to issue formal charges until more investigation was completed a few days later.

Joel Schwartz began cross-examination by asking what that meant. Schimweg explained that police have limited time to get a warrant—a formal charge—from the prosecuting attorney before they have to release a suspect. Schwartz pointed out that Russ Faria had been arrested two days after Betsy's murder and asked, "You applied for warrants and they were refused at that time?"

"Yes."

"The more information you have, the less chance of making a mistake and arresting the wrong person. Correct?"

"Sure."

"And you wouldn't want to make a mistake and arrest the wrong person. Would you?"

"No."

Schimweg confirmed that several detectives interviewed Russ several times and also visited places and people—including everyone from game night—to check on his alibi. They interviewed witnesses to confirm everyone was where they said they were during the time Betsy was murdered. Schwartz wanted to know why Pam Hupp's whereabouts and the clothing she wore that night weren't similarly investigated and confirmed. Richard Hicks objected, citing the judge's prior rulings limiting questions about Hupp, and the judge sustained the objection.

Schwartz thought there was just no bottom to the prejudicial decisions this judge would make to deny Russ Faria his rights to a fair trial. And then there was immediately another one.

Askey had just started her redirect examination of Schimweg when Schwartz filed his third motion for a mistrial. She asked if the repeated interviews with the game-night players were designed to get them to take polygraphs.

Meeting in a sidebar with the judge, Schwartz objected and Hicks said the point Askey wanted to make was that the game-night players had refused to take polygraphs. Schwartz argued they weren't officially asked, but he moved right to the heart of the issue.

"It's inadmissible in court. It is incredibly prejudicial with this jury. I would ask the jury to be instructed to disregard the last question and I would ask for a mistrial based on that last question," Schwartz declared.

Hicks shook his head. "One, the mere mention of a polygraph is not error in a trial. The case law—"

Schwartz interrupted with a new threat. "We can recall Pam Hupp. We are talking about refusing to take a polygraph. That's fine if we want to go down that road."

"These are your alibi witnesses," Hicks fired back. "Anyway, the issue here is not whether they took a polygraph. It's the fact that they were not willing to." He argued that Pam Hupp couldn't be asked about not taking a polygraph because case law said that, except for a defendant, refusal by a witness to take a polygraph could not be used to impeach the witness.

Schwartz was amazed. Hicks had just argued it was appropriate to ask if some witnesses—the game-night players—had refused to take a polygraph, but it was inappropriate to ask if a different witness—Pam Hupp—had refused to take a polygraph.

As the argument continued, Askey said she would withdraw the question. That didn't satisfy Schwartz.

"I would still request a mistrial."

Judge Mennemeyer said she would instruct the jury to disregard Askey's last question and added, "The request for mistrial is denied at this point."

The bloody slippers and switch plate, the knife in Betsy's neck, and all of the photos of her body and the house—Crime Scene Technician Amy Pratt from the St. Charles County Sheriff's Department (SCCSD) said she and other technicians spent six or eight hours collecting evidence and taking photos at the Farias' house the day after the murder. She identified a photo of the white plastic switch plate and noted that there appeared to be a pattern in the blood. She said the light switch was about eight feet from the closet where the slippers were found in plain view, seemingly just "tossed" on the floor at the back by the men's clothes.

For a moment, the Farias' dog (now happily living with Russ's parents) became the focus of the trial. Pratt identified the photos she snapped while a detective took paw prints and fur samples from a scared Sicily, whom Pratt incorrectly remembered as a male. She was worried because Sicily looked like "he" was freezing on the back porch.

"He actually seemed a little sad, standing at the door watching us," Pratt said.

To explain the need for Sicily's paw prints, Askey had Pratt identify the photo she took of what the police thought was a paw print on the hip of Betsy's pants.

Nate Swanson started cross-examination by getting Pratt to agree the pattern on the switch plate appeared to be a "crosshatched pattern" that could be made by fabric.

"So someone likely touched that switch plate with a piece of fabric that had blood on it, leaving a stain?"

Askey objected that the question called for Pratt to speculate and the judge sustained it. Swanson tried twice to reframe the question, but Mennemeyer sustained Askey's objections each time.

Swanson moved to the bloody slippers. When he asked if there was any way for blood to get on the soles other than stepping in blood, Pratt said simply, "That's a good question." She didn't know how the slippers got in the closet, but she had not found any bloody footprints leading to the closet or anywhere else in the house.

Swanson showed Pratt a report on Bluestar Forensic testing of Betsy's pants and had her read the last paragraph that concluded there was no blood present. An objection from Askey fomented a long argument over who could say what about Bluestar test results.

Swanson said the judge had already prohibited the State from saying a positive reaction from tests on the kitchen floor indicated there could have been blood there, but had ruled the defense could elicit testimony that a negative reaction proved there was no blood. Schwartz added that the defense was justified in presenting testimony that tests found no blood on the alleged paw print because Askey had said in her opening statement that it was blood.

When Judge Mennemeyer decided to take a break before ruling, Schwartz protested that would allow prosecutors to confer with Pratt before her testimony continued. The judge said there was no rule prohibiting that, and Schwartz was free to ask Pratt about it. When court resumed, the judge ruled prosecutors could present evidence that Bluestar testing had produced a positive reaction, but could not say that meant blood was present.

Swanson immediately asked Pratt if she had talked to prosecutors during the break. Yes, they discussed the fact that, while she did not write the report on the testing, it accurately stated that she conducted the tests and described the results. He led Pratt on a lengthy explanation of Bluestar test results and then asked if the alleged paw print showed no reaction to Bluestar, expecting her to confirm her earlier answer.

"It did react," she said this time.

That was not what Swanson expected or wanted to hear. He responded, "It's not what the report says."

Pratt said the reference to negative results meant they had not been able to enhance the image they believed was a paw print; it did not mean there had been no reaction to a test for blood. She didn't know if there was blood because that would have been determined by a different test by someone else at the laboratory.

In short, rapid-fire questions, Swanson got Pratt to agree that she did not know if the mark was in blood, did not know how old it was, and didn't have a clue how it got on Betsy's pants. Schwartz wanted a more direct attack on Pratt's sudden change in testimony and asked Pratt to identify the test and the result.

"When we enhanced it for the paw print, it was negative as a paw print," Pratt said.

She was hedging and Schwartz couldn't let her get away with it. "That's not what you testified to earlier when Mr. Swanson was questioning you. You said you enhanced it with Bluestar luminol and that it was negative."

"To enhance it."

"So you never enhanced it for blood?"

"We did enhance it for blood."

"And that test was negative?"

Pratt seemed to be struggling to maintain her new position on the purpose of the test. "I do not . . . It was used as an enhancement tool to try to draw the paw print up. That was the whole reason for it."

"And you keep calling it a paw print, but now you are saying you enhanced it to determine if it was a paw print, and you can't even say that. Can you?"

"I can't. I can't tell you if it was a paw print."

Schwartz got Pratt to agree that the mark could have been on

Betsy's pants for a month and could have been made in mud from when the dog was outside.

Schwartz was frustrated. He could only hope that the jurors had found it suspicious that, after conferring privately with the prosecutors, Pratt changed her testimony from saying the test found no blood was present to insisting the test was to determine if the mark was a paw print. Would the jurors interpret Pratt's changing testimony as the result of the prosecutors coaching the witness?

Several of Betsy Faria's relatives left the courtroom as the next witness took the stand. They didn't want to hear Dr. Kamal Sabharwal, the medical examiner, describe the scores of wounds to their beloved Betsy—and they especially didn't want the photographs of her body to become their last visual memory of her.

But as questioning began, Schwartz objected to testimony by Sabharwal about cadaveric spasm, the much-debated theory that a part of a body that undergoes extreme strain or stress just before death could immediately enter rigor mortis—the stiffening of muscles and tissues that develops normally two to four hours after death. Schwartz knew Askey and Hicks hoped to use the cadaveric spasm theory to suggest Betsy's body could have entered rigor mortis in the ten-to-fifteen minutes between the time they said Russ killed her and first responders found her body cold and stiff.

Judge Mennemeyer had already denied Schwartz's motion asking for a special hearing to take scientific and medical testimony on whether the concept of cadaveric spasm met the legal standards for evidence in a trial. Hicks agreed now there was "no scientific measure or test that can be done to figure out if this happened" and that it was a rare phenomenon. But he said it was supported by many doctors, including Sabharwal. It was up to the jurors to determine if cadaveric spasm could explain the condition of Betsy's body. Mennemeyer rejected Schwartz's new request for a hearing, ruling prosecutors could ask about cadaveric spasms and Schwartz could make more objections then.

Dr. Sabharwal then began the litany of stabbing and cutting and slicing, describing all fifty-five mutilations by location, direction, length, and depth as the photos of the wounds came up on the screen. He said all of the entry wounds were on the left side of the head, face, and neck. The cutting and slicing wounds all over the right arm and wrist could be consistent with defensive wounds.

Hicks led the doctor on an explanation that a knife making the gash across the right forearm, more than one and a half inches deep, would have to cut through the skin, underlying soft tissue, tendons, muscles, and some blood vessels. Hicks clearly was fishing for a comment from Sabharwal that would imply the killer was more likely to be a man with the strength to inflict that kind of wound with a steak knife. But the best answer he could get was "It would take a little effort, yes."

When Hicks asked the doctor to define "cadaveric spasm," Schwartz resisted the urge to object again. Another unfavorable ruling from the judge might lead jurors to assume the defense was trying to hide something more important than this really was.

Sabharwal explained to the jurors how rigor mortis naturally occurs as muscles and tissue stiffen, usually starting two to four hours after death. He said rigor mortis could occur almost immediately if there was a lot of exertion or physical activity just before death. That could deplete adenosine triphosphate (ATP), the chemical that causes muscles to contract, and that could cause the muscles to go into spasm—or rigor mortis—faster. That was the rare event called cadaveric spasm that medical reports said had happened under certain circumstances.

Schwartz went directly on the attack.

The doctor agreed that there was no test to determine if cadaveric spasm exists or had happened in a specific case, and that some doctors accepted the theory of cadaveric spasm and some rejected it. The pathologist said he believed it could happen if extreme physical exertion depleted the ATP.

Schwartz hoped to minimize the value of this speculation as he asked, "Cadaveric spasm would not account for cooling of the body or drying of blood, would it?"

"That's correct."

Sabharwal agreed he didn't know if he had ever seen an incidence of cadaveric spasm and couldn't tell if it had happened to Betsy's body.

"Here, you have no basis to say that it did happen?"

"In this case, no."

The doctor also agreed that, since he did not know when Betsy's body was discovered, he had no way to tell when rigor mortis would have set in naturally.

Looking again at the photo of Betsy's body lying on her living-room floor, Sabharwal agreed with Schwartz that he would expect to see more blood from the seven-inch-deep wounds to her abdomen and back, as well as the gash to her right wrist, if she had been alive when they were inflicted. Schwartz asked if Sabharwal would expect, given that he said Betsy had "bled out," and there were defensive wounds to her arms and hands, that whoever stabbed her would have blood on them somewhere.

"I would think so."

Hicks came back for quick responses to some points Schwartz made on cross. Sabharwal agreed there had been significant internal bleeding from the abdominal wounds. He said the only way to tell if rigor mortis had set in would be to move the body—not simply touching it or looking at a photograph. And the doctor said the time it takes for blood to begin drying depends on the volume of blood and the thickness of the layer of blood.

Schwartz used more recross to show the doctor the photo of Betsy's body with the blood under her head and to ask how long it would take for a pool like that to dry.

"The area where there is a lot of blood—that would take longer than minutes. That would take some time to dry up or coagulate," Sabharwal said.

If it would take longer than minutes, Schwartz thought, then Russ couldn't have spilled Betsy's blood just minutes before first responders examined her body. He hoped the jurors could put those common-sense facts together.

CHAPTER THIRTY

Crime Scene Technician Tiffany Fischer had written the report that seemed to confuse the issue of whether there was blood on Betsy Faria's pants, in what may or may not have been a dog's paw print. Referring to the report Leah Askey handed her, Fischer said Bluestar was not used to test for blood, but the stain there was consistent with other stains on the pants she described as "red bloodlike stains." She used Bluestar to try to enhance the pattern, but was unable to improve it beyond what could be seen with the naked eye.

Nate Swanson had Fischer confirm again that there was no reaction to Bluestar when she applied it to the mark on the pants. She didn't know what the laboratory did with that stain or mark after that.

Swanson was only too happy to move on and have Fischer identify the photos she took of the front passenger seat of Russ's car showing the paper bag and receipt from Arby's, two bottles of Brisk iced tea, and a carton of flip-top boxes of Edgefield cigarettes. For a complete effect, Swanson had her read the receipt for two junior cheddar-melt roast beef sandwiches that was dated December 27, 2011, at 9:09 p.m.

On redirect, Askey tried to reframe the testing of the paw print by asking if a positive reaction to Bluestar indicated there could be blood present.

"There was a chemical reaction that caused the chemiluminescence, which would indicate the possible presence of blood," Fischer said.

Swanson wouldn't let that stand. "When you say 'possible,' you don't know if it's blood?"

"I do not know if it's blood."

"You don't know what it is?"

"Correct."

The first detective to arrive at the Faria house that night told the jury he immediately rejected the possibility that Betsy committed suicide because "those were not self-inflicted wounds that she had, and . . . the majority of the wounds on her hands and arms appeared to be defensive wounds."

Detective Mike Merkel also said Russ was cooperative during the initial four-hour interview at the police station. Hicks asked what Merkel observed on the remote TV broadcast while Russ was alone in the interview room.

"Well, on more than one occasion, it appeared that his demeanor was, I'll call it erratic. He would be overwhelmed with emotion at times and then what appeared to be completely emotionless and just stoic at other times."

"What about any observations you might have made about him crying? Was he sobbing or crying?"

"I think, when you say 'crying' . . . was he shedding tears? Not necessarily. He would sob, but it didn't appear as though . . . any water was coming from his eyes, any tears were coming out."

Schwartz was disgusted by the cynical attempt to suggest to the jury that Russ's heartbreaking reaction to the bloody death of his wife was anything less than genuine and sincere. Who has the right to judge the emotional response of someone who has just discovered the brutal murder of his wife? Who sets the standard for the correct way to grieve?

Merkel told the jurors Russ demonstrated how he dropped to the floor about a foot in front of Betsy's face. When Hicks asked if Merkel questioned Russ about how he could have done that without getting any blood on him, Merkel's memory was inaccurate.

"I don't think I questioned him as directly as that sounds. I more inferred that I had needed to understand if there was any trace evidence from this person that did that on him, and if we needed to collect any of that from him."

What did Russ say when asked why he didn't embrace Betsy's body?

"I don't think he really provided an answer. . . . I don't know that he was expecting that question or even knew how to answer it."

Knowing that Schwartz would attack that misleading answer, Hicks handed Merkel his own report on the interview. With his recollection refreshed, Merkel said, "According to my report, when I asked him that, he said she was already gone."

"Did he tell you what he believed had happened as far as why she was dead?"

"He stated that he thought she had killed herself."

Hicks handed Merkel his report on the search of the house on January 3, 2012, the day before Russ was arrested, when the police used Bluestar to look for evidence of blood in the kitchen, dining room, and bathroom. Schwartz objected and told the judge in a sidebar that the defense had never seen that report—written by Merkel and approved by Sergeant Ryan McCarrick on April 3, 2013, exactly fifteen long months after the search—or the photographs the police took that day.

Schwartz said Merkel should be barred from testifying about the search or the Bluestar testing. Hicks said he had just received the report and agreed it should have been provided to the defense, but added that Schwartz already knew about the Bluestar tests. Swanson responded that the defense had asked specifically for reports on forensic testing in the house and had been told no such report existed. Askey shot back that all of this had been discussed when the prosecution's witnesses were deposed. And Hicks added that none of this meant Merkel couldn't testify now that the tests showed only the possibility of blood. Schwartz relented and said he would accept Merkel's testimony, as long as he didn't say the tests were positive for blood.

Judge Mennemeyer offered a final ruling: "Everybody can say it's presumptive: could be, couldn't be." And then she said to Schwartz, "You could say it couldn't be, right?"

But before Schwartz could answer, Swanson brought up the related issue of the photographs of the tests Merkel would say produced a glow from positive results. "Those pictures would have been important to document your investigation, yet none of those pictures were developed successfully. You don't have any of those to give to anybody?" Swanson asked.

Hicks said, "I think he [Merkel] will tell you, sadly, that is the case."

It would be some time before it was known if that, indeed, was the case.

When testimony resumed, Hicks wasted no time taking Merkel to the Bluestar testing on January 3, 2012. He asked Merkel to step down from the stand and approach the screen where photos of the kitchen and dining room were being displayed for the jury. He explained the police didn't spray the entire floor, but followed a trail of positive reactions.

"It's just like, follow the trail of bread crumbs, essentially," he said. He identified spots on the kitchen floor and near the table in the dining room that reacted to Bluestar with "a positive chemical luminescence," as did the front of a drawer on a kitchen cabinet.

"Do you recall what was in that drawer?"

"If I recall, there were towels . . . hand towels."

Schwartz's cross-examination first targeted the January 3 date of the tests. Merkel didn't know if the house had been returned to Russ's control after he was released by the police on December 29, but he did not remember any police barricades around the house on January 3 and if the house been released. Merkel knew of nothing that would have prevented Russ, his family, or anyone else from cleaning up the scene before the day of the tests.

Merkel said he had reviewed the photographs taken that day and they showed "absolutely nothing . . . because of a malfunction in our camera that we have had, since then, repaired."

"There's no photographs we can see?"

"They did not produce any results because of the camera mal-function."

Police claims of malfunctioning equipment or cameras irritated Schwartz. While he had no specific examples of lying by police, claims of evidence unavailable because of some mechanical mal-function always seemed too convenient. He thought his suspicions would someday prove justified, but he didn't know then just when that day would arrive.

Schwartz drew Merkel's agreement that Bluestar testing could yield "false positive" results, but he said he wasn't aware if "com-mon household cleaning agents" could cause false positives.

Schwartz returned to Russ's behavior in the interview room, hav-ing Merkel explain the police do not inform people that they are recorded by a hidden camera. He agreed that Russ cried; repeatedly whispered, "No, no, no, no, no, no, no, no"; prayed; put his head into his hands on the table and sobbed; and fell to his knees, while whispering "no" again. Merkel couldn't remember if Russ banged his head against the wall, but he agreed after Schwartz showed him his own report.

Schwartz cast a quick glance at the jurors. My God, what else should Russ have done for his grief to be judged genuine by a cop? Would those twelve people agree with the police that he somehow had not shown enough "real" grief to avoid being tagged as the killer?

Merkel agreed that, "to the best of my knowledge," the police confirmed everything Russ told them about his activities the day and evening of the murder. Looking at a photo of Betsy's body, Merkel also agreed that there were no more than a few "droplets" of blood on the floor where Russ said he lay to look at her. Schwartz hoped that would negate any concerns by jurors over the lack of blood on Russ's clothes or body. And he followed that by asking if the video of Russ pumping gas at the Conoco station didn't show he was wearing the same clothes he was wearing when police arrived at the house—the same clothes the police seized from him in jail. Merkel said he didn't remember exactly what Russ was wearing in the video, but agreed Schwartz's description of an orange T-shirt, blue jeans, and boots sounded familiar.

Under redirect, Hicks returned to the issue of Russ's grief. Merkel agreed he had interviewed other witnesses who cried and that he had given them Kleenex tissues.

"Did you ever have to do that with Mr. Faria?"

"No, sir."

Schwartz shook his head. So Kleenex was now the standard for the appropriate level of grieving.

The next witness, Major Ray Floyd of the Troy Police Department, would surely resurrect the continuing conflict over testimony about Betsy's life insurance policies. Schwartz asked for a sidebar to object again to the judge's rulings limiting testimony about insurance to the fact that Russ told police he was beneficiary on $300,000 to $400,000 in policies on Betsy. Schwartz argued again that it was wrong to allow prosecutors to say money from life insurance was Russ's motive to kill Betsy, while preventing Schwartz from saying that money from life insurance was an equally valid motive for new beneficiary Pam Hupp to kill Betsy.

Hicks began his argument with what Schwartz thought was a profound admission. "I would agree, absolutely, that that would be motive for Pam Hupp," Hicks said. "But Pam Hupp—that's not relevant for us to bring up because there's no direct evidence of her involvement. That's the difference."

The frustration was unending for Schwartz. Pam Hupp stood to profit substantially from Betsy's death, was the last person known to see Betsy alive, and was the only person known to be at Betsy's house about the time she was killed—yet the prosecutors and the judge found no "direct evidence" linking her to Betsy's murder.

Schwartz fired back, "I would argue there's less—substantially less—direct evidence that Russell Faria was with her at the time of her death."

Schwartz thought Hicks was desperately flailing about to try to justify his position: "There is much more evidence against Mr. Faria than there is against Pam Hupp. There is a history of animus and anger and fighting between these two. There is her blood. . . . He has her blood on his slippers in the closet. There is him finding her and claiming that she committed suicide, when it's clear to everybody else that she didn't commit suicide."

And then Hicks shocked Schwartz with what seemed another admission about the State's case against Russ. "I think that, in and of itself, may not be enough direct evidence to ultimately convince a jury. I don't know. We're going to find out. But it is much more direct evidence than they have, than just her mere presence—Pam Hupp dropping her off during that time period."

Judge Mennemeyer quickly confirmed her previous decisions. Floyd could testify that Russ said he was the beneficiary on Betsy's policies.

Hicks started by having Floyd tell the jury the questioning of Russ Faria "started at roughly four o'clock in the morning and probably concluded somewhere around four o'clock in the afternoon" on December 28. The actual interrogation took up five or six of those twelve hours; the rest of the time was for breaks to get Russ cigarettes and water, for him to use the restroom, and to feed him. Schwartz hoped the jurors would remember that the twelve hours with Floyd came after almost six hours of interrogation by Detective Merkel or Russ sitting alone in the tiny interview room with his grief. Would jurors think about what it must have been like for a man who had just found his wife's butchered body to spend those hours alone in haunted disbelief interrupted by intense police questioning and accusations that he murdered her?

Hicks chose a curious place to start that story—with questions about the Farias' chow/golden retriever mix, Sicily. Asked what Russ told him about the dog, Floyd said, "He said that strangers—it would probably come at them. Friends and family, it was friendly with."

There was the implication Hicks was seeking—that Sicily would attack any threatening stranger who came into the house. Therefore, the killer must have been a family member.

Hicks also led Floyd through a series of questions designed to make jurors think Russ was adamant that Betsy had committed suicide and was trying to deceive the police. Floyd agreed that Russ said several times he believed it was suicide.

"And would keep coming back to it, right? He believed that she committed suicide?"

"He believed she committed suicide."

"But then did you ask him . . . if she committed suicide, why would she have picked this time to do it?"

"He thought it was because he was going to be away from the house at that time."

"Did he acknowledge to you in any way whether . . . there were life insurance policies on Betsy's life?"

"Yes, he did."

Schwartz chaffed at the word "acknowledge," as if Floyd had to beat that information out of a reluctant Russ, instead of him informing them in a very matter-of-fact way during what he thought then was his effort to assist the investigation.

Hicks closed his direct examination by asking about Pam Hupp. Floyd said Russ considered Pam and Betsy close friends. He thought Pam was "a nice lady," the two of them had a good relationship, and he considered her a friend, too.

Schwartz wanted to immediately put the life insurance policies and the discussion of suicide into the proper perspective for the jurors. He started cross-examination by having Floyd confirm Russ told police Betsy had a short time to live because of the new cancer diagnosis. Floyd also said Russ agreed the way Betsy died was not a typical way to commit suicide and he hoped she had not taken her own life. Russ said Betsy once left a so-called suicide note, but Floyd didn't remember Russ saying Betsy had actually tried to commit suicide once.

Schwartz returned to what he thought was abuse of Russ by the police.

"So, how long had he been up when you were talking to him?"

"Thirty-six hours."

The prosecutors knew their next witness would draw more objections from the defense, so they called for another sidebar. Hicks warned Betsy's life insurance agent, Lee Lester, would testify that Russ called him on New Year's Eve, four days after Betsy's murder, to ask about collecting on the State Farm policy. Schwartz argued that would violate the judge's limits on testimony about insurance policies.

Hicks naturally disagreed. "It's not just he knew about it, but he was concerned about it. He was interested in it just a few days after his wife's death. . . . It goes directly to motive."

The argument continued until Schwartz had almost passed his breaking point and he threw out a comment that could have raised some judges' eyebrows, if not their tempers.

"Judge, you do what you want," he said in a tone he was sure conveyed his opinion that the situation already caused by the judge's rulings was ridiculous.

Mennemeyer agreed with Hicks. "I think . . . the timing of it is probative."

But Schwartz then objected because the agent had been sitting in the courtroom all day listening to testimony. That violated the judge's order excluding witnesses except for Betsy's family. Assured earlier testimony had nothing to do with questions for Lester, the judge agreed he could testify.

Lester said Russ called him because "he wanted to get the money, he said, for her funeral. . . . I said there was going to be an investigation before that can happen. . . . He was, like, maybe, surprised by that. He was like, 'Really? An investigation?' I was like, 'Yeah, any kind of case like this gets pushed up to our special unit.'"

Schwartz asked if Russ told Lester the funeral home suggested calling the agent to get money for funeral costs.

"That's correct, I believe."

A computer analysis of Russ Faria's cell phone showed that between the four hours of 5 to 9 p.m., on December 27, 2011, there was only one call out and one call in. Captain Michael Lang of the Lincoln County Sheriff's Office, an investigator for the Major Case Squad's Technical Operations Group (TOG), testified the call from Russ's phone at 5:22 p.m. was to his mother and lasted thirteen min-

Betsy and Russ Faria danced together
as they enjoyed her "celebration of life" cruise,
a few weeks before she was murdered.

Pam Hupp became Betsy Faria's life insurance
beneficiary four days before Betsy's murder.
St. Charles County Police Department CSI Unit.

Defense attorney Joel J. Schwar■
Photo by Suzy Gorma■

Nathan Swanson, a key member
of the defense team.
Photo by Charles Bosworth Jr.

Fourteen-year-old Jonah Schwartz voiced an astute opinion as to the identity of Betsy Faria's killer after reading police reports with his father, attorney Joel Schwartz. *Photo by Joel Schwartz.*

Sergeant Ryan McCarrick suggested to Pam Hupp that she open a trust fund for Betsy Faria's daughters.

Russ and Betsy Faria shared many happy times together during their eleven-year marriage.

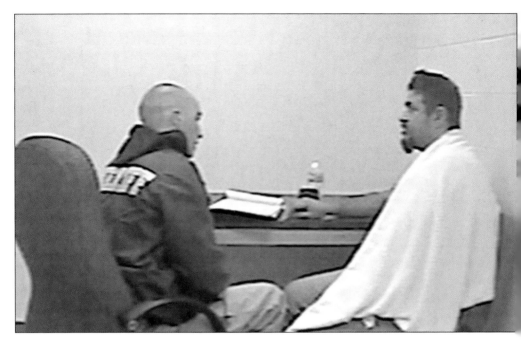

Russ Faria, huddling under a blanket for warmth, was questioned by Detective Mike Merkel barely an hour after finding his wife's body on December 27, 2011.

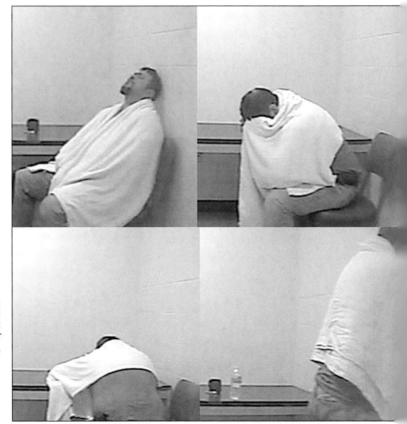

Faria cried, moaned, wailed, and banged his head against the wall in grief in the police interview room.

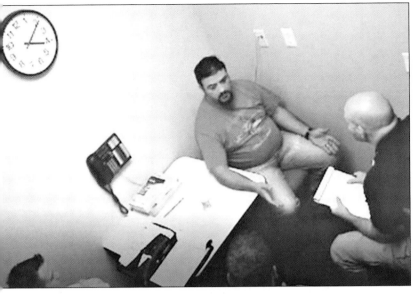

Faria swore he did not kill his wife, as his interview, led by Detective Ray Floyd, became increasingly intense.

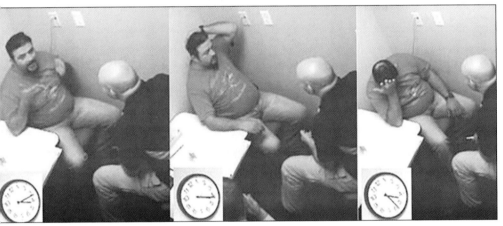

Left to right:
"I am telling the truth." — "I wasn't here." — "Oh, my God," as police told Faria his wife was stabbed "25 times and counting."

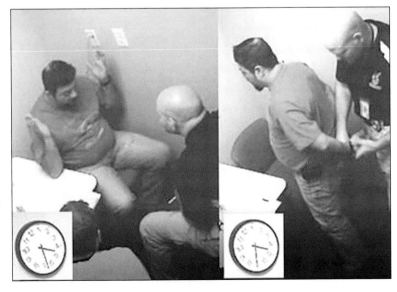

Right to left:
"I want a lawyer" and "You're under arrest."

The living room where Russ Faria
found Betsy's body on the floor
(bottom of photo).

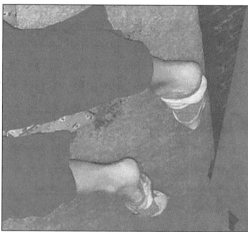

Betsy Faria's legs and feet
with her socks barely on her feet

Pam Hupp submitted to a police photo,
showing she had no injuries or marks on
the morning after Betsy was murdered.

The knife found protruding from Betsy's neck is believed to have made all 55 wounds.

Investigators found blood smeared on the light switch plate in the Farias' bedroom.

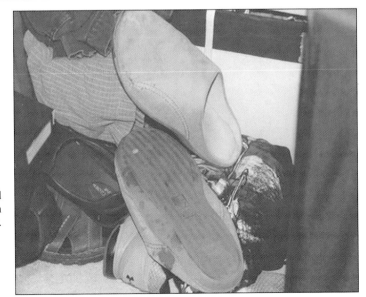

Russ Faria's blood-stained slippers were found in his bedroom closet.

The Farias' home on the corner of Sumac and Osage Drives in Troy, Missouri, near St. Louis
Photo by Charles Bosworth Jr.

Police took paw prints from the Farias' dog, Sicily, to compare them to a mark found on the hip of Betsy's pants.

The cigarettes from U-Gas, bottles of Brisk iced tea from QT, and Arby's bag that police found on the front passenger seat of Russ's car supported his account of the night of the murder.

Russ Faria's mug shot after he was arrested by the Lincoln County Sheriff's Office on January 4, 2012.

Russ Faria was interviewed in prison by *Dateline* after being sentenced to life without parole for his wife's murder. © *NBC Dateline.*

The body of Pam Hupp's mother, Shirley Neumann (covered by a purple blanket at bottom left), lay below the damaged railing on her third-floor balcony. *Courtesy of the St. Louis County Police Department.*

The railing on Shirley Neumann's balcony showed six spindles dislodged from the bottom rail and two of them missing. *Courtesy of the St. Louis County Police Department*

Lincoln County Prosecuting Attorney Leah Askey, left, interviewed Pam Hupp before Russ Faria's second trial in 2015.

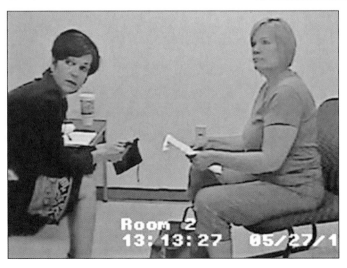

Russ Faria arrived for his second trial accompanied by his cousin, Mary Anderson, on November 2, 2015. *David Carson/Post-Dispatch/Polaris.*

uss Faria hugged his mother, Luci Faria, after his acquittal. *Chris Lee/Post-Dispatch/Polaris.*

St. Louis County Circuit Judge Steven Ohmer acquitted Russ Faria on all charges in his second trial for the murder of his wife.

Louis Gumpenberger was shot to death by Pam Hupp on August 16, 2016, in her home. She said he was trying to kidnap her to force her to go to the bank and get "Russ's money."

Detective Kevin Mountain, lead detective on the O'Fallon police investigation into the Gumpenberger murder.

Pam Hupp demonstrated for O'Fallon police detectives how she held the gun in both hands as she shot Gumpenberger.
St. Charles County Police Department CSI Unit

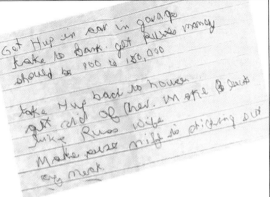

Excerpt from note, in Louis Gumpenberger's pocket, that an analyst said was written by Pam Hupp: "Get Hupp in car in garage. Take to bank. Get Russ money. Should be 100 to 150,000. Take Hupp back to house. Get rid of her. Make look like Russ wife. Make sure nife [sic] is sticking out of neck."
St. Charles County Police Department CSI Unit.

The .38-caliber, five-round pistol Pam Hupp used to shoot Louis Gumpenberger.
St. Charles County Police Department CSI Unit.

Louis Gumpenberger's body was found on the hallway floor just outside the door to Hupp's bedroom on the left.
St. Charles County Police Department CSI Unit.

Pam and Mark Hupp were seen leaving their home after she shot Gumpenberger. Police later searched the trash bags they were carrying.
Christian Gooden/Post-Dispatch/Polaris.

Carol McAfee's home surveillance video showed her approaching Pam Hupp's car as Hupp tried to lure Carol into being the victim in her new plot to frame Russ Faria. *Courtesy of Carol McAfee.*

Carol McAfee was interviewed by *NBC Dateline.*
© *NBC Dateline.*

O'Fallon Police Sergeant Jodi Weber arrested Pam Hupp on August 23, 2016, for the murder of Louis Gumpenberger. *St. Charles County Police Department CSI Unit.*

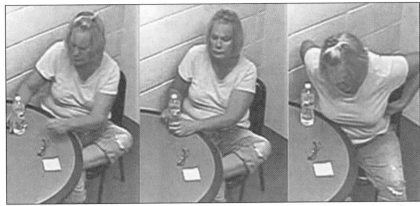

While alone in a police interview room, Pam Hupp palmed a ballpoint pen in her right hand and hid it in the back of her pants. *St. Charles County Police Department CSI Unit.*

Pam Hupp's "maxi-pad" mug shot at St. Charles County Jail in August 2016. *St. Charles County Police Department CSI Unit.*

Hupp went to the restroom, where she stabbed herself repeatedly with the ballpoint pen in the neck and wrists. *St. Charles County Police Department CSI Unit.*

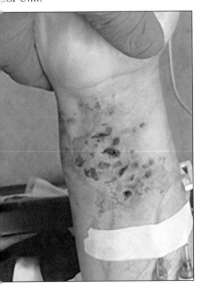

Pam Hupp's inmate photo showed her remarkable change in appearance by the time she entered Missouri state prison in August 2019. *Courtesy of Missouri Department of Corrections.*

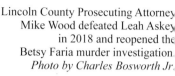

Lincoln County Prosecuting Attorney Mike Wood defeated Leah Askey in 2018 and reopened the Betsy Faria murder investigation. *Photo by Charles Bosworth Jr.*

St. Charles County Prosecuting Attorney Tim Lohmar described the case against Pam Hupp at a news conference after she pleaded guilty in June 2019 to murdering Louis Gumpenberger. *Christian Gooden/Post-Dispatch/Polaris.*

Pam Hupp — handcuffed and wearing a COVID mask — left the Lincoln County Courthouse in Troy, Missouri, on July 27, 2021, after being arraigned on charges of murdering Betsy Faria. *Photo by Charles Bosworth Jr.*

Russ Faria and Joel Schwartz at the premiere event for the two-hour *Dateline* episode "The Thing About Pam," in September 2019, at a theater in New York City. *Photo by Mary Ann Schwartz.*

utes. The call into his phone was at 8:57 p.m. from Betsy's mother and went to voice mail.

Askey asked if the records indicated that Russ listened to Meyer's voice mail.

"Yes . . . a call to the number that was listed as voice mail . . . about thirty seconds later."

Lang also testified that he was among the officers sent to arrest Russ at his mother's house on January 4, 2012. Lang said he seized handwritten notes next to the phone on the desk where Russ was seated when police arrived. There were three phone numbers with names written next to them; the names were Sergeant Ryan (McCarrick), Ryan Lance (a friend of Russ's), and Mike (Corbin). And there was a note that said "Elizabeth policy," followed by a policy number; the names Russell S. Faria, Mary Rodgers, and Deb Suchomski (Russ's aunt); and then "$150,000."

On cross, Nate Swanson had Lang confirm he did not know who wrote the notes and had not been told the funeral home advised Russ to call the insurance agent about money for Betsy's funeral.

Swanson also challenged Lang's conclusion that Russ listened to the voice mail thirty seconds after Betsy's mother called his phone. Wouldn't her call to Russ's phone still have been connected to voice mail in thirty seconds?

Lang admitted, "It could be a call to the voice mail. It just wouldn't be able to retrieve the voice mail yet."

"So there's no evidence that Russell Faria ever listened to the phone call from Janet Meyer?"

"No."

Swanson hoped the jurors would realize that Lang had just contradicted his direct testimony for Askey that Russ's phone proved he had listened to the voice mail. That wasn't what the data showed and Lang had to pull back his testimony.

Swanson referred to the texts beginning at 3:46 p.m. between Russ and Betsy, when she told him Pam Hupp had offered to drive her home: "'She offered and I accepted,'" Swanson read the 3:52 p.m. text aloud. He wanted to be sure the jury understood the arrange-

ment for Pam to drive Betsy home. Swanson asked, "[Russ] told her
he would come and get her? . . . She told him he didn't need to, that
Pam Hupp had offered, she accepted, and Pam Hupp would be
bringing her home?"

"That's correct."

Another direct and provable contradiction to Pam's false testimony that Betsy asked her to drive her home, and more evidence
that Pam was determined to be alone with Betsy, at the house, at the
time she was murdered.

Judge Mennemeyer sent the jury home for the night.

CHAPTER THIRTY-ONE

The numbers sounded impressive, but they proved very little.

The chance that the blood found on the outside and the sole of Russ Faria's right slipper belonged to someone other than Betsy Faria was one in 178 quadrillion—quadrillion being the number that comes after a trillion, which comes after a billion. So that's one in 178,000,000,000,000,000—with fifteen zeroes. And the chance that the DNA found inside the slipper was from anyone other than Russ Faria was one in 978 billion—one in 987,000,000,000.

So, Joel Schwartz thought, the jury now knew the blood at the scene of Betsy's murder was hers and Russ had at some time worn his own slippers.

The rest of the testimony by Daniel Fahnestock from the crime lab at the St. Charles County Sheriff's Department didn't prove much, either. The DNA analysis only proved that someone—no one knew who—had put Betsy's blood on Russ's slippers. And proving that Russ had worn his own slippers certainly didn't prove he killed his wife.

But Askey had Fahnestock, the crime lab's DNA technical leader, present all of his analysis, starting with his description of the blood on the slippers as "droplets," adding "they weren't smears. They didn't appear to be transfers."

"So, not like someone could pick up the slipper and rub it in the blood?"

"That's not what it appeared to be to me."

Fahnestock said the blood on the switch plate from the master bedroom was a mixture from two people. The major contributor was Betsy. The other contributor was male, but the sample was so small as to be "of no comparative value" for identification. A loose end Schwartz thought didn't cut in favor of the prosecution or the defense.

Fahnestock said the rape kit—standard in the murder of a woman—showed a mixture of material from Betsy and Russ, including eight sperm cells, in her vagina. A swab from the outside of the rectum showed a mixture of materials from Betsy and a male. But again, the sample was too small to allow identification.

Swanson used cross-examination to put the lab tests into perspective. Fahnestock had not found any blood on Russ's T-shirt, jeans, socks, belt, and wristwatch. He did not know how old the blood on Russ's slippers was or how it got there. Betsy's T-shirt showed extensive amounts of her blood, but Fahnestock never saw Betsy's pants. No blood was found on any of the cabinet doors or the floor tiles from the kitchen and dining room, including one he tested after it reacted to Bluestar/luminol. He agreed with Swanson that the reagents had a high level of false-positive results to "things like plant materials. It could be dirt, bleach. A lot cleaning supplies will give false positives."

Material from fingernail clippings from Betsy's right hand was mostly Betsy's. There was one particle of DNA called an "allele"—a tiny form of a gene located on a chromosome—from someone else. It was not from Russ, but it was too small to identify another source.

Askey immediately tried to rebut implications from Swanson's cross-examination, starting with the possibility of DNA from an unidentified third person. Fahnestock said one allele under Betsy's fingernails meant nothing and could have been deposited there during normal activities. Without referring specifically to Betsy's pants, he said he would not typically even test an article of bloody clothing from a victim unless there was a specific reason to do so. He said being unable to reproduce the reaction to Bluestar on floor tiles and cabinet and drawer fronts—because the liquid reagent just rolled off the surfaces—did not mean the glowing results when police tested them were wrong.

Swanson thought the jurors were certain to be confused by that round of questions by Askey. He asked Fahnestock if the high rate of false-positive results from Bluestar meant a reaction was not meaningful if he couldn't confirm it.

"It's not meaningful for us to continue with doing DNA analysis. It may be meaningful in the reconstruction of the crime. But for me to proceed with DNA analysis, that's only meaningful if I can confirm it's blood."

Nate referred to the lack of bloody footprints anywhere and especially on the carpet near the pooled blood around Betsy's body. "You were not able to confirm any blood here?"

"I was not."

Askey called her next witness, apologized for putting her on the stand, and asked her to identify herself.

"I'm Janet Meyer, Betsy Faria's mother," she said.

Askey had Janet explain that she had called Russ at 8:57 p.m. to check on Betsy's whereabouts after she failed to answer a call. She left a message, but Russ didn't return it, as he usually did when it concerned Betsy.

Askey ended her short examination by asking if Betsy usually showered before she went to chemotherapy or other events, a question clearly aimed at doubting the timing of the deposit of the seminal material Russ said was during sex on Christmas night.

"Yes, yes, yes. She was a very clean person."

It was clear to Schwartz that Askey did not like the inference that the seminal material was from the Farias having sex Sunday night before her death on Tuesday night. He would have to wait until closing arguments to find out why. But he addressed that in his first questions for Janet Meyer. Yes, she had heard that Betsy and Russ had sex on Christmas night. She didn't remember what Betsy was wearing when she came to her home on Monday.

Schwartz asked if Janet told police that Pam said she had not gone into Betsy's house, but that drew an objection from prosecutors and led to a lengthy debate at a sidebar. Hicks argued the only reason to pursue what Pam said about going into the house was to point the finger of guilt at her. Schwartz responded that Janet could testify about what she told police and that was proper impeachment of Pam's denial that she told Janet she had not gone into the house.

Judge Mennemeyer was obviously tiring of the arguments over Pam Hupp, but in a rare event, she still ruled for Schwartz. "You can ask her what she said, but we're not going to go over and over and over the issue."

Schwartz had Janet confirm again that Pam called her at 8:52 p.m. "And then did you also tell [police] that Pam had indicated to you she did not go into Elizabeth's residence because the house was dark and the door was unlocked?"

"I think so."

"All right. You didn't make that information up, if it says it in your report?"

"If it says it, yeah, right. It would be true, yes."

Schwartz and Betsy's mother fenced a bit about whether she told police it wasn't unusual for Russ not to return calls on his game night. Schwartz asked, "But if he didn't listen to the message, he wouldn't have known what it was pertaining to, correct?"

"I feel like he listened to it and didn't call me back. That's how I feel."

"You *feel* like he listened to it?"

"I do. . . . That's my feeling."

Schwartz decided not to ask her how she could know that. The jury might not like further challenges to the grieving mother of a murdered daughter.

As Janet Meyer left the witness stand, Judge Mennemeyer turned to Askey. "Further evidence on behalf of the State?"

"No, Your Honor," Askey said. "The State rests."

CHAPTER THIRTY-TWO

Joel Schwartz immediately made his motion for the judge to acquit Russ Faria at the end of the State's case. As he expected, Judge Mennemeyer immediately denied it. He had tried few cases where a judge's "directed verdict of acquittal" was as warranted as it was in the *People of the State of Missouri* v. *Russell Faria*. The State had failed to present a case jurors could conclude proved Russ guilty beyond a reasonable doubt. The defense team thought the State proved only that Russ was miles away from his home from five o'clock until at least nine thirty—certainly the time frame when Betsy was murdered. An objective analysis of the State's evidence should result in an overwhelming doubt—way beyond a reasonable doubt—about Russ's guilt. The judge should order Russ acquitted now. But Schwartz knew Mennemeyer would deny the motion—and she did.

Before Schwartz could call his first witness, Mennemeyer also denied his motion to reconsider her rulings limiting cross-examination of Pam Hupp. The judge agreed case law established the defense's right to cross-examine a witness on accuracy, veracity, and credibility, and that the interest of the witness in the outcome of a case is never irrelevant. But she confirmed she found no direct connection between Pam Hupp and the murder, so she was correct to prohibit Schwartz from questioning her about some points, including becoming beneficiary of Betsy's insurance—four days before she was killed. The jury had heard there were inconsistencies or contradictions in some of her statements and testimony because the defense had been allowed to cross-examine her on those points. But it was inappropriate to engage in questioning that would get into who Pam Hupp thought killed Betsy or whether she killed Betsy. Pursuing those questions "would be prejudicial and confusing," the judge said.

Schwartz had known exactly what was coming. He responded with a cool, flat, and vaguely sarcastic "Thank you, Your Honor."

And then he began presenting his case to prove that Russ not only *did not* kill Betsy, but that he *could not* have killed her.

The first defense witness was the first firefighter or EMT to examine Betsy's body. Captain Robert Shramek of the Lincoln County FPD said the body was cold to the touch when he checked for a brachial pulse on her upper arm. When he tried to move that part of her arm, her entire arm moved.

"What did that mean to you as a firefighter for thirty years?"

"That she had been there for some time and that rigor mortis had started to set in."

"Did you notice the condition of the blood?"

"It was set up. It was coagulated, I guess you would call it."

"What does that mean in layman's terms?"

"The blood was cold. It had been there for some time."

Richard Hicks's cross-examination took Shramek right to the State's major theme: He never thought Betsy committed suicide. But he also told Hicks he thought Betsy's body had entered at least the onset of rigor mortis, which could happen within a couple of hours after death.

Schwartz hoped Shramek's testimony would help the jury set a time of death close to 7:30 p.m., so his next four witnesses—the game-night players—could establish Russ's alibi for that time. He began with host Michael Corbin—a forty-one-year-old sign maker who had known Russ for fifteen years and had been playing fantasy board games since junior high school. Mike explained the details of the Rolemaster game for the jury: Players take on specific characters—a monk for Russ and an elf investigator for Mike's girlfriend, Angelia Hulion—and roll dice to move around a board that Mike utilizes to set up fantasy adventures.

Mike verified everything Russ had always said about game night. He remembered Russ's phone ringing once, with its distinctive ring—the recognizable "Imperial March" music from *Star Wars*. Russ looked at the phone and put it back in his pocket without answering it.

Was Mike "100 percent" certain no one left the house between six and nine o'clock that night? "I am positive of that. We all sat within eight feet of each other the entire evening, except if one of us got up to go to the restroom."

Prosecutor Hicks took the group's role-playing game in an odd direction, starting by having Mike explain that he served as the referee who made up the adventures and drew up the game board. Did Mike have to be imaginative to do that?

"Somewhat . . . you have to be able to think on the fly."

"Right. You are thinking on the fly. You're trying to come up with story lines, adventures. I think you used the term 'missions'?"

"Yes, that would be one way to look at them. I usually refer to them as adventures."

"'Adventures' or 'missions' where a particular character has to accomplish something?"

"Usually it's the entire group working together."

Mike said he had to write Russ's "peaceful, monk-type character" out of the game after he was arrested. The monk simply wandered off into the woods, never to be heard from again.

Hicks asked, "I thought you told me in the deposition he was a martial arts expert?"

"He did have those skills, but he didn't use any weapons—typically, tried to defuse situations in the game, so . . ."

"Then, in that same deposition . . . do you remember . . . when I asked you about *Conan the Barbarian,* your response was 'Oh, well, we don't play those types of games'?"

Mike offered a pointed answer to correct Hicks's memory. "Actually, you had asked me about missions that involved kidnapping people, and I stated, 'No, we don't have any kind of ill will in any of the games.' Typically, I run a heroic-type game, where these are good guys trying to defeat bad guys."

Are there "nonheroic-type role-playing games"?

"There are people that do that, but I think that's kind of an unhealthy thing."

"Somehow for you, that's different from just watching the movie *Conan the Barbarian?*"

"I guess watching the movie is a much more passive type of activity."

"Rather than to actually become the character?"

"Than to actually play out or act out. I mean, you know, we don't dress up or anything. This is just a board, pieces of paper, dice."

Schwartz had to shake his head. Hicks seemed to be trying to turn a harmless fantasy board game among friends into Charlie Manson's "Helter Skelter"–inspired mayhem playing out before a murder.

The second player up to bat was Marshall Bach, a twenty-nine-year-old auto mechanic who offered the same details Mike Corbin had just recounted. Again, Hicks went right to the board game in cross-examination. Marshall confirmed his character was a weapons master named Oden. Hicks asked if the players got to know each other's game characters better than they knew the players themselves. Marshall agreed, admitting he didn't know Betsy had cancer or whether Russ had children.

Hicks challenged Marshall's testimony that he and Brandon Sweeney arrived just after Russ. Hadn't Marshall said in his deposition that Russ arrived after them?

"Right. It's hard to remember a lot of this stuff. . . . He might have been there. I don't know. If any kind of time span, it's minutes, though."

Hicks also questioned Marshall's ability to remember where everyone was sitting that night. But Marshall had a reason to remember he was sitting on a dining-room chair: "I was the only one that didn't have a nice chair."

The witness confirmed again that he and Brandon, his friend since grade school and current roommate, left just after Russ, at what he remembered as exactly 9:03 p.m. by the clock in Brandon's car. They followed Russ in his car until they got to the turn to their house, just a few blocks and two or three minutes from Mike's. Brandon dropped Marshall at home and then drove to the nearby Jack in the Box to get something to eat. He agreed that the Arby's where Russ stopped was across the street from Jack in the Box.

The third gamer to the stand was Brandon Sweeney, twenty-eight and an employee of the federal Centers for Medicare and Medicaid—he simplified that as Obamacare. When Betsy was murdered, he had been a regular at game night for about a year. He had known Russ for ten years or so. Schwartz asked if Rolemaster was violent.

"Sometimes. I mean, like I said, it's kind of *Lord of the Rings*-style, so every once in a while, there would be a horde of orcs that you would have to go kill off because they were trying to raid the town and steal whatever from the town, like goods or like special gems, stuff like that. So every once in a while, yeah, it would get a little violent."

"Did you ever actually leave to conduct a mission?"

"No, sir."

Schwartz then had Brandon explain that he still had the receipt from his purchase at Jack in the Box at 9:13 p.m. He had crumpled it and thrown it into the backseat of his car. The detectives who interviewed him the next morning advised him to keep it. He even made a copy in case the ink on the original faded. Brandon pulled the receipt from his wallet and handed it to Schwartz, who entered it as evidence.

The last of the game-nighters to testify was Angelia Hulion, the forty-year-old employee of a uniform company who had lived with Mike Corbin for twenty years and was the mother of their son. She offered the same general description of Rolemaster and remembered everything else exactly as her friends. Asked how she remembered they watched a movie from the Conan the Barbarian series, she delivered a line that put the entire case—that evening, the investigation, and the trial—into perspective.

"How do I remember that? I've only talked about it, I guess, five or six different occasions now, so it's pretty stuck in my mind."

CHAPTER THIRTY-THREE

Joel Schwartz had to make at least one more attempt to get Judge Christina Kunza Mennemeyer to reverse her decision barring testimony that could establish a murder motive for Pam Hupp. With the defense's case nearly complete, Schwartz tried to demonstrate the relevance of Pam's interest in Betsy's insurance with an offer of proof with testimony from Betsy's close friend and confidante, Linda Hartmann.

"Betsy's husband is a relative of my husband and I met her through the family," Linda explained in her soft English accent. "I found out that she had breast cancer and that's when I got in touch with her, because I had just got over breast cancer, too."

When Schwartz asked about the girls' weekend in Branson just before Christmas, Linda said the Monday-to-Thursday getaway could have lasted a couple more days, but Betsy said she had to go home because she had a meeting with Pam Hupp on Friday, December 23, at 9:30 a.m.

Linda added, "And she didn't want to go to the meeting with Pam."

"She told that to you?"

"Yes."

"What did she tell you about her passing—her eventual passing?"

"She said to me, one day she just said to me, 'Linda, do you know I'm OK about passing on?' Because we had not spoken about, you know, her leaving, and I got very sort of emotional about it when she said that. And I said, 'Yes.' And she said, 'I'm OK with passing on because when I leave, I'm going to be leaving life insurance with Russ and the two girls, so it's going to be split into three.' She said, 'So I'm really, you know, pleased that I've been able to do something once I've been here.'"

"So that would be approximately—unfortunately—about a week before she died?"

"Yes, yes."

Schwartz couldn't understand how the judge could prohibit jurors from hearing what she had just heard. Linda's insight to Betsy's desire for Russ and her daughters to share her life insurance money—and her reluctance to attend the meeting with Pam to change the beneficiary—created a suspicious perspective that jurors should hear. The judge made no immediate ruling on Schwartz's request to present Linda Hartmann's testimony to jurors.

Schwartz was eager to call his next witness when the jury returned—a detective who would help confirm, if unintentionally, essential facts of Russ's alibi. Dean Frye of the O'Fallon Police Department had worked with the Major Case Squad and was assigned to check on Russ's account of his stops on the way to game night. He collected videos from the Conoco, U-Gas, and QT stations and a receipt from Greene's Country Store.

On the screen facing the jury, Schwartz projected the video snippets Frye collected. At the Conoco service station, the first of Russ's stops, Frye said, "That's him there" as he pointed to the image of Russ putting gas into his Ford Explorer. Checking his own report, he added that Russ had been at pump nine from 5:16 to 5:20 p.m.

When the video from U-Gas played, Frye identified Russ driving up to the store at 5:29 p.m., wearing the same clothes as when he was arrested. Frye identified the receipt he collected at Greene's Country Store showing that Russ paid for dog food with a credit card at 5:52 p.m. Frye next identified the video from inside Quik-Trip showing Russ entering and leaving the store.

Schwartz had Frye agree that he confirmed Russ had been to exactly the places and at the times he told police and was wearing the same clothes police seized.

To save time, Schwartz had agreed to let prosecutors question Frye about matters not discussed by Schwartz rather than forcing them to call Frye as their own witness. So, what did Hicks want Frye to talk about? He first had Frye describe the burnt marijuana smell that he and his partner identified outside and inside Corbin's mobile home about six o'clock on the morning after the murder. Frye then denied that Brandon Sweeney mentioned the receipt from Jack in the Box or retrieved it from his car at the detectives' request. Frye said he would have kept the receipt as evidence if Brandon had mentioned it.

Joel Schwartz's private investigator told the jury he bought food at the Arby's in Lake St. Louis and then drove to Russ Faria's house in Troy several times, each time taking between twenty-eight and thirty-two minutes. Schwartz wanted the jurors to hear again that Russ could not have possibly been home before 9:35 p.m., scant minutes before he called 911 at 9:40 p.m. Kurt Ponzer, a thirty-seven-year veteran investigator whose career began as what used to be called "a Pinkerton man," submitted a video he took while driving Russ's route. Ponzer made it simple for the jurors; the drive home, which Russ began at Arby's at about 9:09 p.m., takes approximately thirty minutes. Prosecutors had no questions.

Ponzer had given the jury a pretty good time frame, but Schwartz hoped his next witness would nail it down beyond any doubt.

Greg Chatten, a forensic computer analyst certified as an expert by the courts in Missouri, had charted the activity by Russ's cell phone in what is called "cellular mapping and data forensics"—a specialty that requires a license issued by the Missouri Board of Professional Regulation. He explained that cell phone towers make a record of every incoming or outgoing call, text message, and data transaction, such as connecting to the internet or receiving information from the internet. Each tower's range creates a circle around the tower that he compared to "Grandma's home-baked pie and split into thirds." The tower identifies which third a phone is in when each activity is recorded.

Using information from T-Mobile, which the defense received from Askey, Chatten created a map showing which "pie slice" of each tower Russ's phone was in every time it activated. Chatten walked up to the screen and offered the jurors an uncomplicated explanation of the data on the map. At 5:07, 5:08, and 5:10 p.m., Russ's phone was in the sector that included his home. At 5:11, 5:13, and 5:22 p.m., the phone was in the same sector as the Conoco service station. At 5:50 p.m., the phone was in the more populated, congested area close to Lake St. Louis and O'Fallon. At 7:50 p.m., the phone was in the area that included Mike Corbin's house. At 9:25 p.m., Russ's phone was in a sector at least ten miles from his home. It arrived in the same sector as his house at approximately 9:37 p.m.

When Swanson asked if Chatten had received information from AT&T, Hicks asked for another sidebar with the judge. Assuming Swanson was about to ask for the locations of Pam Hupp's phone at 7:04 and 7:27 p.m., Hicks said, "There would be no reason to do this other than to suggest that she's the one who committed this murder. And so, based upon a pretrial motion, I don't think it's relevant."

Schwartz replied that the defense was entitled to use the cell location map to impeach Pam Hupp's contradictory testimony about where she was when she called Betsy at 7:27 p.m. to say she was "at home" or "home free."

Judge Mennemeyer asked why Schwartz was trying to impeach Pam Hupp's testimony, when she admitted "home free" did not mean she was at home. Schwartz said Chatten was about to testify that Pam was still in Troy when she made the call at 7:27 p.m. Mennemeyer said Schwartz could make an offer of proof on that point later, outside of the jury's presence.

Hicks's cross-examination drove directly into "paid witness" territory. Chatten said the defense paid him $250 an hour for work in his laboratory, $350 an hour for work outside of his lab, and $1,500 a day for testimony. He couldn't say whether Hicks's estimate of a total of $3,000 to $3,500 would be accurate.

Hicks asked if Chatten testified only for the defense and he said yes, mostly because the police and prosecutors had state-operated labs that did such work for them. Had Chatten refused over the lunch hour that day to discuss his testimony with Leah Askey? Yes, because he thought she was getting into defense trial strategy, which would be improper for him to discuss.

On redirect, Swanson asked Chatten if his role as a defense witness affected the results of his cell phone analysis.

"Not at all. I'm a fact finder, whether I do cell mapping or forensics. The fact is the fact. The data is the data."

"Would your answers have been any different if you had been hired by the State?"

"No."

Hicks asked, "How would we know? You've never been hired by the State."

Chatten smiled. "You should hire me."

Schwartz ended what he thought was an effective and convincing defense of Russ Faria as he announced, "Your Honor, at this time, the defense would rest."

Leah Askey quickly moved into the State's rebuttal case by calling Detective Patrick Harney of the Lincoln County Sheriff's Office with fresh challenges to Russ's alibi. Harney said that, at Askey's request that day, he checked on the availability of Brisk iced tea and the price of a carton of Edgefield cigarettes at the Conoco station in Troy and the U-Gas station in Wentzville the day of the murder. He said cigarettes at U-Gas were only sixty cents cheaper than at Conoco, noting Russ had driven an older SUV fourteen miles to save that small change. He didn't know the price of gas on that date, but agreed with Askey that they couldn't remember a gallon costing less than $3 in a long time.

Schwartz noted that Russ had not gone into the store at the Conoco station. "My point is, Officer Harney, you have no idea if he knows what's sold at the Conoco, do you?"

"I don't know what Russ Faria knows."

"Exactly."

The State's rebuttal was complete and the judge sent the jury out of the courtroom so Schwartz could present his offer of proof about Pam Hupp's phone calls.

*　*　*

Schwartz called Greg Chatten back to the stand to explain his analysis showed Pam Hupp's cell phone was in the same cell tower sector as Betsy's house when she made the calls at 7:04 and 7:27 p.m. The second call could not have been made when she was on Highway 61, south of Troy, or at her home in O'Fallon, as she had told police previously and testified under oath.

Schwartz thought the evidence placing Pam Hupp at or near—perhaps even inside—Betsy's home at 7:27 p.m. was damning. But the judge later would refuse to allow the jurors to hear that from Chatten.

With the testimony and evidence complete, Schwartz filed another motion for an acquittal because the State failed to prove the charges beyond a reasonable doubt. Mennemeyer immediately denied the motion and sent the jury home for the night.

And first thing the next morning, Prosecuting Attorney Leah Askey delivered the most deceitful, spurious, cynical, demented fantasy of a closing argument that Joel Schwartz had ever heard or could even have imagined.

CHAPTER THIRTY-FOUR

Thursday, November 21, 2013—
fourth and last day of trial

"I'm going to tell you how I think it happened," Leah Askey told the jurors as she stood before them to begin her closing argument. She pointed at Russ Faria. "He decided that this would be the ultimate role play—the ultimate game. The ultimate way to stage. But it required all hands on deck. It required a pretty good script—one that could be committed to memory and one that could be anticipated—anticipation of every move.

"Now, I'm not suggesting that he knew all along that December twenty-seventh was going to be the day. But I am suggesting that months before—maybe years before—he had the idea and I think he brought it to his friends. I think he talked about it. 'How would we do this? How would the ultimate role play happen?'"

Oh, my God, Joel Schwartz thought. She's accusing Russ's game-night friends of being co-conspirators in a murder plot, which would open them up to murder charges, too. He looked at Russ Faria and Nate Swanson, whose wide eyes showed they were arriving at the same astounding realization.

Askey told the jurors Betsy learned her new cancer assault was terminal at the same time her marriage was getting worse. Askey suggested Betsy was asking herself, "'I'm going to just wait this out? Live in this life? Die with this man? Or am I going to take care of my kids?' What was her goal, as a mom, do you think?

"He knew she had three hundred thousand dollars in life insurance, at least. . . . I think he started this conversation. And once he realized his wife calls on December twenty-seventh and says—well, she texts, actually—and says, 'I think I'm going to come back. I'm going to be coming home tonight.' And he says, 'Here?' 'Yeah, home to Troy.' He didn't expect her."

Askey said Betsy's decision to go home that night sealed December 27 as the day she would die. Askey said a "doting husband" who knew his wife was tired and sick would have likely canceled game night and picked her up early to take her home to rest.

"No," Askey said, "he knew she was tired and he knew if he told her he had a game—which he later orchestrated the get-together—that she's not going to wait around until nine o'clock. She's tired. She's had two days, three days of Christmas, and, let's face it, folks, she's got cancer. So she says, 'You know what? I'm going to head on home. A friend is going to take me.'" Askey paused and then added, "Exactly what he wanted to happen."

Schwartz continued to be absolutely stunned by what he thought was an absolutely insane theory. He thought again about objecting and even asked Swanson what he thought; Swanson shrugged. Schwartz decided that Askey's argument was so outrageous, such an extreme departure from any reasonable interpretation of the facts, that no juror would ever find it believable. He decided to let Askey ramble on while he demonstrated to the jury that her theory was too ridiculous to warrant an objection.

Askey's voice intensified. "And so the ball starts rolling. The momentum starts gaining. He makes all of these stops so that he can establish an alibi. Not a bad idea. He goes to the Conoco station in Troy, and I thought it was interesting, and you guys probably noticed, he pumped fuel for less than three minutes in an Explorer SUV. How much gas do you think he got? Do you think he didn't have enough to get down to U-Gas, where those cigarettes were so much cheaper? Fifty-nine cents, I think he saved. Did that seem strange?

"He laid it out. Canceled dinner with his mom because he had lots of errands that he ran. . . . He got down there and he said, 'Tonight's

the night.' I don't know if any of you picked up on it when Brandon
Sweeney was on the stand. But when defense counsel said, 'When
was the last time you saw Russ Faria?' he said, 'Not since the night.'
Not 'That night. That night we played. That night we watched
Conan the Barbarian. That night we celebrated Christmas.' *The*
night. '*The* night we've been talking about for months, for years.
The night. It's here. Tonight is *the* night.'"

Schwartz was thinking that Askey was stretching a prosecutor's
right to draw reasonable inferences from the evidence so far past
"reasonable" that the whole courtroom might explode. She had just
pushed four innocent people into the center of a murder plot using
the most outrageous and unsupported accusations. And she was
nowhere near done.

"He leaves his phone [at Mike Corbin's] and he heads back to
Troy. He comes into the house. Betsy is on the couch/love seat.
She's covered with a blanket, and I submit to you that he has sex
with her. That he violates her one more time. That he controls her
just one more time. 'I'm going to humiliate you in a way that only I
can.' One more time. Knowing she's tired, that she's sick, that she's
not well. She lay there, probably disgusted with many things at that
point."

Russ Faria struggled not to react to this tawdry and demented fantasy Askey was spinning for the jurors. Russ had *violated* Betsy, had
humiliated her, before *killing* her? His relationship with the woman
he loved was being described in sadistic terms that made him want
to scream or throw up. Schwartz again withheld an objection, even
though Askey was now contradicting Fahnestock's testimony supporting Russ's account that he and Betsy last had sex two nights before the murder.

Askey was rolling. "And why doesn't he have blood on his
clothes? Because I don't think he was wearing clothes. I think he
walks past her in the kitchen. I think he goes around the refrigerator
to the butcher block, where he knows it is. I think he gets the steak
knife out in his own kitchen. I think he gets this knife out and he
comes around to where she's lying on the sofa. . . . I think he comes

around the corner and I think he's really hopeful that he's going to stab her one time in the neck and it's going to look like a suicide.

"And, folks, I'm not going to pretend that I think the stabbing in the neck is a suicide or even looks like one, and I'm sure you don't, either. But guess what? The defendant sure does. And why do we know that? Because when he called 911, he said, 'I just walked in. My wife killed herself and she had a knife sticking out of her neck.' He believed that's plausible.

"I think he stood over, [on] top of her. He stabbed her in the neck. When she moved, he stabbed her with such force in her bicep as she lay on her side that it went through her bicep and into her lung. I think she, at some point, obviously gets up. She sits up and she struggles somewhat, but not much. Luckily for her, I would imagine that she died within a minute.

"But it was personal. It was passionate. He gets her on the ground, and at some point, I think, the overall feeling is 'Oh no! This went horribly wrong.' Reality sets in. 'Now what do I do?' The killer gets careless. He starts—'I'm going to cut her arms.' Except we know that happened after she died. 'What do I do?' He goes back, takes a shower, gets any evidence off of him that he has, and then he comes out. And the killer is careless because—guess what? They have got a family dog and he forgets that a dog, by nature, is going to be inquisitive. When there's blood, they are going to be inquisitive, and, let's face it, it's the dog's owner and so the dog is kind of investigating things, and he's like, 'Oh no!' He picks the dog up. He throws it over to the kitchen and then gets it outside on the chain. He's careless."

Russ simply could not believe the increasingly unhinged and despicable fiction he was hearing from this officer of the court. He thought Askey sounded like a lunatic as she spun a ridiculous story about a psycho, naked, après-sex killer who butchers his wife and thinks he can make the police believe she committed suicide. How could even one juror believe any of this?

But Askey was just warming up. "At some point, either he goes down to Wentzville, Lake St. Louis, and picks up his phone, gets his Arby's bag, and heads back to Troy to call in the suicide—or I would submit to you that Brandon Sweeney is the one that goes to Arby's, gets the receipt, then drives across the street to Jack in the Box, just about five minutes later is the time on those receipts. Gets his receipt, because he wants to cover his own behind, and then he drives to Troy, brings the defendant his phone, and just as he's bringing the phone so that he can get the receipt in the other car, the defendant's calling—on the landline—911."

Schwartz reached an entirely new level of shock and amazement. Askey had just named Brandon as an active co-conspirator in this crazy murder plot created by contorting the facts and logic beyond all reason. She had already suggested the four game-night players were at least aware of a demented plot by Russ to kill Betsy, if not co-conspirators. But Askey had just elevated Brandon to a major player in the construction of Russ's alibi and his cover-up of murder.

Askey didn't slow down. "And he's on the phone and, ladies and gentlemen, you will be able to listen to that 911 call if you want to. I ask you to listen to things like the differences in the pitch, the differences in the echo of his voice. You can tell that he's moving when he's on that call, and I would submit to you that, while he's talking to 911, he realizes—the slippers. The killer gets careless. He's thought of everything else. It's perfectly staged, but the slippers . . . He runs back into his bedroom and the light's on. 911 is already on the phone. He knows they are dispatching. He turns the light off because he doesn't tell them he was ever in the bedroom and he quickly tosses the shoes in the closet."

Askey turned to the "doglike paw-print pattern" on the hip of Betsy's pants. The jurors could make their own comparisons that would show that the print was similar to every paw print taken from the family dog. That was important because Russ told the 911 dispatcher that the dog was chained outside when he came home. "How did he know that? He just walked in the door. How did he know where the dog was, unless he put it there?" she asked.

The reactions to Bluestar on the kitchen floor and cabinet drawer fronts could have been false positives, but also could have been reactions to cleaning agents. "And I'm OK with all of that, because I don't know anybody that just cleans one drawer facing and I don't know anybody that just cleans one path on the kitchen floor that goes from the dead body to the back door and to the one drawer that, incidentally, is not next to the sink, but the one drawer that holds the kitchen towels. So it could be a cleaning agent. It could be serological fluid. But we know that's where the Bluestar reacted."

Askey took a sideways shot at the suggestion that the semen found in Betsy's body at the autopsy on December 28 was from sex with Russ on Christmas night. "Common sense . . . reason," Askey said to imply that the semen was more likely from sex Russ forced on Betsy before he killed her.

She began wrapping up her argument by suggesting that Russ Faria's conduct throughout the investigation had been so incriminating that it already had been judged by others.

"We heard from the 911 operator. He's hysterical, and then he can answer a question; he's hysterical, and then he can answer a question. She judged him a little bit.

"We heard from Officer Hollingsworth, who said, 'Hey, this guy, I think he's going into shock. And then minutes later, he's in my car smoking cigarettes. We're laughing. He's talking about how he used to take girls down to Bubblehead Road and scare the hell out of them. Laughing it up, not even an hour after his wife is dead.' He judged him.

"Detective Merkel, Detective Floyd, Detective Harney—they judged him. He's crying, he's on his knees, he's wailing, though he never needs a Kleenex—not one time in all of those hours.

"And, ladies and gentlemen, I'll be frank. I judged him, too."

Askey told the jurors that reasonable doubt was "a doubt based upon reason—common sense." She trotted out the worn cliché to define reasonable inference: "If you go to bed at night and you wake up and there's snow on the ground, you can infer that it snowed. In this case, you need to make reasonable inferences."

Askey was parsing the difference between doubt and inference to try to convince the jurors to accept her preposterous scenario as reasonable inference from the evidence. If she considered her hallucinogenic account of the plot and execution of Betsy Faria as reasonable, Schwartz wondered how far-fetched a story would have to be for her to consider it unreasonable.

Askey closed with the standard call for a conviction. "I believe that the State has proved its case beyond a reasonable doubt. I believe that, based on the evidence, based on all of the things that I've described here, and that you've heard over the last several days, that you should be firmly convinced—and you should return a verdict of guilty on all counts. Thank you."

CHAPTER THIRTY-FIVE

Leah Askey's almost-demented flight of fancy still seemed to be echoing in Joel Schwartz's ears when the judge called on him for the defense's closing argument. Schwartz didn't even take the time for any introductory niceties before he launched into his attack on Askey's shameful fiction.

"It sounds to me that she just accused four people of being complicit in murder—Michael Corbin, Brandon Sweeney, Marshall Bach, and Angelia Hulion," he began. "They just got accused of murder by the prosecutor of Lincoln County—without one shred of evidence. . . . That's offensive."

Askey objected to personalizing the argument, but the judge shrugged it off and Schwartz didn't even slow down.

"Those people were accused of murder five minutes ago." He struck a tone of disbelief as he mocked Askey's suggested call to arms by Russ. " 'Tonight's the night'?" he said incredulously.

"Let's talk about the word 'proof.' She talked about reasonable doubt. I talked to all of you about that in voir dire. Proof! Let's not go to reasonable doubt. Let's talk about proof. All she said was 'I think. I think he came home, got undressed, and had sex—because there were eight sperm cells left inside of his wife.' Fahnestock said, if it's recent, there's thousands, and it can last for a long time. Yeah, and a smudge on the rectal area? That can last for a long time, even if you shower. . . . She's still in the same clothing from the day before. She's wrapped in that blanket, curled up on that couch. When did she have sex? He's naked and she's wrapped up cozily in that blanket? Proof?"

To counter Askey's barrage of conclusion-jumping speculation, Schwartz detailed the proof the defense presented to support everything Russ told the police, starting with the videos and receipts from his stops on the way to game night. "That's proof. We saw it. You saw it with your own eyes. You saw the time and it corresponds with his cell phone.

"Four people—one who only knew him six or eight months—Marshall Bach—he testified he was there. Angelia Hulion. Michael Corbin. Brandon Sweeney. Are those four people complicit in murder? That's proof he was there."

Schwartz reminded the jurors Russ appeared on videos or had timed receipts proving he had been exactly where he told police he was, at the times he claimed, and conducting the business he described. "That's proof beyond a reasonable doubt."

Schwartz scoffed at Askey's questioning of Russ's purchase of cigarettes at U-Gas. "Well, what does the State prove to you? That he spent sixty-seven cents less—because that's where he gets his cigarettes."

The defense had produced the photo showing the bag of dog food leaning against the door to the garage, just where Russ told police he put it when he got home. "I showed that to you—not the State," he added.

Buying Brisk iced tea at QuikTrip? They're specially priced at two-for-one there, Schwartz suggested. Russ drank one bottle on the drive home, while eating the two sandwiches he bought at Arby's. Police found the almost-empty bottle and the unopened second bottle in his car.

With a tinge of anger in his voice, Schwartz turned to Askey's unsupported suggestion of a grand conspiracy of murder and mayhem. He asked the jurors to read the texts between Russ and Betsy, and Russ and his game-night friends. Betsy reminded Russ to get dog food and asked if he had "game" that night. Russ responded, "'Yeah, I got game tonight and I'll get the dog food when I come in'. . . . He's not *setting up* something. This is what they do *every Tuesday*. . . . So, what is this plan? He's going to go pick up his wife and bring her home so she can spend the night at home on a Tuesday night. She responds, 'OK. Great, honey.' Is this a victim of domestic violence?

"What have you heard as far as domestic violence? That teenage stepdaughters, who had moved out, were having problems when he cussed. From a sister who, I think, in 2004 interfered in a domestic argument that they were having and he made a threat, five, six, seven years earlier. That's what they are using as proof? That's not proof."

He noted that Betsy texted Russ that Pam Hupp had offered to take her home. "'She offered. I accepted,'" he recounted.

Schwartz gestured toward Askey. "'Tonight's the night,' like she said? Boy, that was a pretty detailed plan. 'Hey, if the police talk to you, don't remember what I wore, because that would sound too obvious. Tell them we watched movies. Tell them we watched *Conan* and we watched *The Road*.' Nobody would say that. 'Remember where we sat.' That's crazy."

The prosecutors were unable to prove anything the game-night players said was untrue. Not a single statement during multiple interviews and recorded statements from all four had proven to be false.

Schwartz turned to more facts that contradicted Askey's magic murder theory. The medical examiner testified Betsy's killer would certainly have blood on them. "There was no blood on his hands, on his feet, on his hair, on his skin, under his fingernails . . . and it's not because he cleaned up and cleaned his fingernails and washed his hair, because Detective Merkel told you they looked at those drains. There's no blood anywhere suggesting the cleanup. None . . . Fahnestock told you . . . Not one iota. Not a scintilla of blood. And we know how detailed it can get because there was one microscopic, unable-to-see cell of somebody under her fingernails that wasn't Russ and it wasn't Betsy. I don't know where it came from. I'm not telling you it was the person who killed her, but that's how detailed this stuff can be. There was a lot of blood. There wasn't one scintilla of blood on him. He apparently got naked—but kept his slippers on—to kill his wife? That's crazy."

The police searched Russ's car and, again, found not a speck of blood anywhere. If Russ hauled off a mop or towels or anything used to clean up a bloody murder scene, there surely would have been some trace of blood left behind.

Askey's suggestion that Russ had sex with Betsy just before he killed her was absurd. Russ told police he and Betsy had sex Sunday night—less than forty-eight hours before she was killed—and vaginal tests at the autopsy on Wednesday found eight sperm cells. The medical examiner said that was consistent with sex as much as seventy-two hours earlier. Again, the evidence proved Russ's statements.

"Miss Askey's theory is now that he left his phone down there [at Mike Corbin's]. Well, there's nothing to prove that. That's conjecture. That's a guess. . . . That's jumping to a conclusion. . . . Russ jumped to a conclusion when he walked in there and saw his wife laying on the floor. He jumped to the conclusion of suicide. That was the wrong conclusion. Based upon that, the police apparently jumped to a conclusion and focused on him to the detriment of investigating this thing properly.

"But not you. You have now heard it all. The State has not proven it. Don't you jump to a conclusion."

Schwartz argued that Russ's assumption of suicide was understandable. In the shock of finding his wife dead, all he really saw was her slashed wrist and the knife in her neck. She had threatened suicide at least twice before. With those threats, a history of depression, and the recent diagnosis of terminal cancer, it was not unreasonable to jump to a conclusion of suicide. But it was absurd to suggest that the killer who inflicted fifty-five gruesome wounds to Betsy would expect the police to be misdirected by a suggestion she committed suicide.

Schwartz said the police questioned the way Russ was grieving, even though he was crying, praying, wailing, and whispering repeatedly, "No, no, no, no, no." How would the critics have reacted in Russ's circumstances? "I'm not saying how anyone would react. Nobody knows. This is grief. His wife is now deceased. Did he grieve appropriately? I don't know. He tried to be helpful. He was hysterical. You can . . . listen to the tape. You make a judgment. It's not a fair judgment, because none of us would have any idea."

What about the supposed paw print? There was no conclusive evidence the mark was a paw print; if it was in blood, mud, or some other substance; or how or when it got there. There was even disagreement between the technician and Fahnestock about whether the mark was sent to the laboratory and analyzed there.

Then Schwartz addressed the State's only physical evidence—the slippers and switch plate. The blood on the switch plate appeared to be in a pattern that clearly resembled cloth fabric, a pattern similar to the fabric of Russ's slippers. It seemed someone had been carrying the bloody slippers when they turned on the light. "If that somebody was Russ, don't you think he would have wiped this off? Don't you think he would have gotten rid of the shoes?"

He asked the jurors to look at the blood on the slippers to see it wasn't in droplets from dripping blood or blood spurting from knife wounds. It had to be from someone wiping the slippers in blood. There were no footprints in the pooled blood near Betsy's body or on the carpet nearby, and no bloody footprints leading to the closet where the slippers were found.

"Ask the State to tell you how blood gets on the bottom of those shoes without making an impression in the blood—and not someone dipping them in the blood and carrying them back, flipping on the light switch, and putting them in that closet to deflect suspicion from whoever that person is. And that person is not Russ. . . . Don't be fooled by these slippers. That's the only thing that they can present to you that links him to this—the only thing."

Schwartz noted the forensic expert for the police had no answer when asked how there could be that much blood on the soles of the slippers and not a single bloody footprint anywhere. "And if you've got a good question like that, with the only piece of evidence that potentially links him to this, that is reasonable doubt."

Schwartz also rejected Askey's conclusion about the stab wounds. They were not inflicted by a killer in a rage, but by a killer who wanted it to look like they were in a rage. Almost all of the wounds were precise and inflicted from the same direction, and that certainly didn't fit the pattern of someone in a rage. Betsy had not been moving when the knife struck again and again. She was already dead from the wounds to her neck when nearly all of the other wounds were made—including the gash to her wrist.

"Whoever did this wanted to make it look like something like passion or rage. They didn't want to make it look like suicide. And whoever did this certainly wasn't going to say it was suicide. This thing was set up."

Schwartz thought surely the jurors would see that Russ was set up, too. He reminded the jury of the sad truth hanging over this whole tragedy. If Russ's motive was to collect the insurance money, he didn't have to devise a complex conspiracy with his game-night friends and then brutally kill his wife and expose himself to life in prison or even a lethal injection. All he had to do was wait a little longer. Betsy had terminal cancer. If it was money he wanted, he knew it was coming—free and clear, sooner rather than later.

Schwartz began his final approach by asking what the State had proven. That Russ yelled at his stepdaughters and sometimes used inappropriate words? That his sister-in-law thought he could be degrading to Betsy? That a friend of Betsy's who met Russ three times thought he could be demeaning and didn't like him?

What about this bizarre murder conspiracy Askey concocted? Russ would have had to set everything in motion after 4 p.m. when he learned from Betsy that Pam Hupp was giving her a ride home. He would have to decide to make all of those stops to set up his alibi on the drive to Mike Corbin's house. Then he had to instruct the four players to cover for him when he went home to kill Betsy. He "hightailed it" on a thirty-minute drive back home to let the dog in, put on his slippers, stab Betsy fifty-five times without getting blood on himself, and remember to put his slippers back in his closet, where they could easily be found by police.

Schwartz looked at the jurors and deadpanned: "I submit to you—not any chance that anybody who did this was wearing slippers." Then Russ "hightailed it" back to Mike Corbin's to get his phone and add another instruction for his co-conspirators: "'Oh, yeah. If you happen to go to Jack in the Box, save the receipt.'" Schwartz had a two-word response to the State's allegation that Brandon Sweeney kept that receipt as part of the conspiracy, and that Brandon was the one who actually bought the sandwiches in the drive-through at Arby's before he stopped at Jack in the Box: "That's crazy."

"I don't have to prove to you that he didn't do it," Schwartz said as he faced the jurors for a final few moments. "I don't have to prove to you he wasn't there, but I think I did. They have to prove he was there. They have to prove it beyond a reasonable doubt—and they can't.

"Everything she said was, 'I think he had sex with her. I think he was naked. I think those four people are lying for him. I think he went there, left his phone, and drove home'—only because she can't possibly think anything different because I can prove his phone was there. I can prove he was there. I can prove he went . . . to those places. So, what's she got to work with within those contexts with the things I can prove?"

As the bailiff announced the end of Schwartz's time, he quickly offered a final thought. "Shame on them for judging his grief. Shame, shame, shame! Find him not guilty. Find that they did not prove their case beyond a reasonable doubt."

Askey launched her rebuttal argument with an attack on Russ's alibi by claiming the game-night players couldn't remember whether they watched one or two movies. Schwartz objected that she was mischaracterizing the evidence and asked that jurors be instructed to recall the evidence as they remembered it. Judge Mennemeyer sustained the objection and echoed Schwartz's instruction to the jurors to remember the evidence for themselves.

Askey ticked off a list of questions from Russ's alibi. Why didn't he drink his iced tea at game night when they were smoking marijuana, but claimed they didn't drink anything? Why was the only call to Russ's phone at 8:57 p.m. and not earlier, as the other players remembered it? Why did the records show that Russ listened to the voice mail from that call from his mother-in-law within thirty seconds after she left it?

Askey's sarcasm was obvious as she said, "Are we to assume that this is a ghost killer—that someone just came in and killed her and wanted to make it look like a suicide—but wait, 'Maybe I want to set him up, too, and I'm going to do a really bad job of it?' "

Why would Russ say Betsy had committed suicide? "Because at that point, it's so far gone you have to say something. He's committed himself to it. He's married himself to it and, by God, he's going to stick with it all of the way through his ten hours . . . of interrogation."

Schwartz thought that may have been the most inane explanation she had offered yet. But she topped it with comments about the slippers. Russ wasn't wearing them when he killed Betsy; he put them on after he took a shower and took them off again when he was putting the dog outside. "He's got to step out of them. That's why there's no tracks," she said in yet more baseless silliness.

She said Russ's cell phone records didn't really prove he was at Mike Corbin's between six and nine o'clock. He could have left the phone there while he went home to kill Betsy.

"What about Brandon Sweeney and his receipt? Who keeps a receipt eighteen months after they buy a sandwich at Jack in the Box? And not only keeps the receipt, but makes a copy, keeps it in their wallet on their person, and then lies and says that law enforcement told them to do that? Who does that?

"Folks, we talked about reasonable inferences and evidence. There isn't any evidence that points anywhere else."

Schwartz erupted with an objection as Askey violated the judge's order banning comments about alternate suspects—the whole point of his long and unsuccessful battle to introduce evidence against Pam Hupp. Mennemeyer sustained the objection and, as Schwartz requested, ordered Askey's statement stricken from the record and for the jury to disregard it.

Askey moved toward the moment when the jurors would begin deliberations.

"Folks, in every crime scene, the victim leaves behind a voice. In this case, Betsy Faria left her voice on the light switch in her bedroom. She left her voice on the slippers in her closet. She left her voice throughout the kitchen on those positive reactors. I would submit to you the very fact that they were able to determine that she not only had sex, but that she had sex recently—her voice. She left it through her dog, Sicily . . .

"I'm asking you to hear Betsy's voice and return a verdict of guilty."

Schwartz looked at Russ Faria next to him at the defense table. The evidence and the arguments were complete in the *People of the State of Missouri* v. *Russell Faria*, and the jurors were just minutes from beginning to deliberate on Russ's fate. Schwartz and Russ remained as optimistic as possible that the jurors would see through the State's fog of faulty conclusions, unsupported innuendo, and shamelessly fictitious scenarios. Swanson was less optimistic, but he kept that to himself. Russ was convinced that the judge's rulings—especially on offering Pam Hupp as the killer—had sent Schwartz into the battle with both hands tied behind his back. Even so, Russ thought Schwartz had provided jurors with an abundance of reasonable doubt that Russ butchered Betsy in their living room two days after Christmas. Russ was scared and nervous, but he was confident that all or at least some of the jurors would look at the ridiculous case against him and see an innocent man. He was still thinking, We've got this.

Sitting in the courtroom to hear his boss deliver the closing argument against Russ Faria, Assistant Prosecuting Attorney Mike Wood had been embarrassed. He had expected listening to Askey deliver the closing in her first murder trial would be valuable to him as a young prosecutor in her office for only ten months, mostly handling low-level criminal cases. But Askey's outrageous argument left Wood not only embarrassed for her, but also for everyone in her office, all members of law enforcement, the courts—the entire justice system. She had presented this demented closing argument without a shred of evidence to support her wild scenario accusing the game-night players as co-conspirators in a murder that, if true, would have warranted arresting all of them. She was so far beyond the ethical limits for closing arguments that Wood could only think of one word to describe how he felt at that moment—embarrassed.

In fact, Askey's performance in the closing argument was so disturbing to Wood that he left her office about a month later to become an assistant prosecuting attorney in adjacent St. Charles County. But he wasn't leaving Lincoln County's justice system permanently. He would be back.

CHAPTER THIRTY-SIX

Thursday, November 21, 2013, 11:30 a.m.

Experienced prosecutors and defense attorneys generally agree a jury that reaches a verdict in a murder case after four to five hours of deliberations will return a conviction. If jurors begin deliberations at 11:30 a.m., as they did in the Russ Faria case, a verdict returned about 4 p.m. would probably be guilty. That would be just enough time for jurors to have lunch, elect a foreperson, conduct a conversation and assessment of the evidence without any serious disagreements, and sign the forms for a guilty verdict.

The jurors took just over two hours to eat lunch and begin deliberations before they sent a written request to Judge Mennemeyer at 1:45 p.m. They wanted to see the receipts from Arby's and Jack in the Box, photos of the inside and outside of the Faria house, the medical examiner's autopsy report, the crime lab's DNA report, reports by detectives and crime scene investigators, emails, phone records, transcripts of depositions by defense witnesses, maps of cell phone locations and cell towers, and videos taken by police as they drove the routes Russ said he had traveled.

After conferring with the State and the defense, Mennemeyer sent jurors a note explaining they would get everything they requested except for the witness depositions and the written evidence reports, which had not been introduced into evidence.

Schwartz and Russ hoped the request was a good sign. The jurors were taking all of the evidence seriously and weighing it with careful consideration.

The prosecutors and defense attorneys who predict a conviction in a verdict after four to five hours will also say that the longest seconds and minutes known to man are those between the time the jury returns to the courtroom with a verdict and the time the verdict is announced.

That clock began for Russ Faria and Joel Schwartz at 4:30 p.m.—exactly five hours after the jurors began deliberating. As the jurors solemnly filed back into the jury box, Schwartz and Russ searched their faces for some clue to the verdict—and found nothing. No eye contact. No red eyes or weeping. No signs of stress or relief.

In response to Judge Mennemeyer's request for the foreperson to rise, a man identified as Juror Number 44 stood and handed the verdict forms to the bailiff, who quickly handed them to the judge. She asked the defendant to rise and Russ, Schwartz, and Swanson stood uneasily.

The judge read: "'As to Count One, we, the jury, find Russell Faria guilty of murder in the first degree . . .'"

Schwartz felt his body jerk backward, his head drop, and the bottom fall out of his stomach. He quickly turned to Russ, whose face betrayed the same shock and surprise that Schwartz felt in his gut. They could hear gasps from family and friends of the Farias and the Meyers, followed immediately by sobs and tears on both sides.

The judge continued to read the jury's verdict without reacting to growing and conflicting sounds of grief or relief rolling up from the audience. "'We assess and declare the punishment for murder in the first degree at imprisonment for life without eligibility for probation or parole. As to Count Two, we, the jury, find Russell Faria guilty of armed criminal action.'"

In less than thirty seconds, the judge delivered soul-crushing guilty verdicts that consigned Russ to the hell of a prison cell for the rest of his days.

Through rising shock and disbelief, Russ thought, I'm going to prison for the rest of my life? Someone came into my house and murdered my wife, and I'm going to prison for the rest of my life?

He had been optimistic the jury would return to the courtroom and declare his innocence. But these twelve good citizens of Lincoln County—still averting their eyes from him now as they sat in the jury box—had somehow believed Leah Askey's mind-bending tale of a killer husband's money-driven conspiracy with a coven of sinister game players to murder his terminally ill wife.

As the judge called on the jurors, one by one, to confirm their guilty verdicts, Schwartz fought through the overwhelming disbelief to take Russ by the arm and look into his face. "This isn't over," he said with as much confidence as he could muster. "I guarantee you that we'll be back and we will beat this. This isn't over."

Russ nodded. The word "guilty" seemed to still be echoing off the courtroom walls when sheriff's deputies handcuffed his wrists behind his back and began to escort him out of the courtroom for the short trip back to the Lincoln County Jail. He struggled through this new tsunami of shock and disappointment to assure himself this was a temporary setback—that Joel Schwartz would find a way to reverse this injustice and set him free. Russ clung to that hope like a drowning man to a lifeline.

In the seconds after the verdicts were announced, Schwartz glanced at the prosecutors. He thought Richard Hicks's face betrayed genuine surprise—perhaps even dismay. But Schwartz thought he saw elation in what he would always describe as a smug look on Leah Askey's face.

The calm confidence that Russ, Schwartz, and Swanson tried to maintain at the front of the courtroom contrasted with the emotional scene behind them. Russ's parents, sister, and the rest of Russ's family were crying and sobbing in disbelief. Mary Anderson struggled to catch her breath and finally threw up behind one of the benches. As Russ was led out of the courtroom, his mother collapsed in a faint. Russ tried to rush back to her, but a deputy stopped him. She had to be carried out by paramedics and taken to a hospital for brief treatment and observation.

As deputies were leading Russ out of the courtroom, Judge Mennemeyer asked if the attorneys wanted to set the date for sentencing. Schwartz couldn't help himself when he responded, "Why don't we set the date for a new trial, because I guarantee there will be another one." The judge didn't respond. Schwartz realized he had never said anything like that to a judge, and never would have believed he would.

On the other side of the courtroom, tears of relief were flowing from Betsy's family. Betsy's sister Mary Rodgers told Chris Hayes of FOX 2, "After almost two years, justice finally has been served. I just hope people remember all of the positive things about my sister." She added that seeing her former brother-in-law convicted for killing Betsy left the family painfully conflicted. "We cared for the man. He was part of our family. So it's hard."

Leah Askey said she believed the jurors had heard Betsy's voice, as she had asked them in her closing argument. She told Hayes, "They were out for four and a half hours and they deliberated a long time. . . . I was pleased with the outcome and think that justice was served."

Joel Schwartz's shock and anger were obvious when he said to Hayes, "Ridiculous, absolutely ridiculous. There's not one shred of evidence—not one."

Hayes said it looked as if Schwartz almost jumped out of his shoes when Askey accused the four game players of being co-conspirators in a murder plot in her closing argument.

Schwartz nodded. "I was outraged. These were four innocent people who were not guilty of anything. They were accused of murder in that courtroom."

Hayes asked, "So, what's next?"

Schwartz hardened the tone of his voice. "We file the appeal and we'll do this again—I guarantee it."

And then Schwartz began setting the stage for his appeal—and his case against Pam Hupp—with a short and simple declaration. "There was evidence pointing toward another, but the court kept that out."

Schwartz clenched his teeth and thought, The case against Pam Hupp begins now.

* * *

At 7:33 p.m., Schwartz was still seething, and trying to find a way to deal with the verdict, when his phone chimed with a text message—from Leah Askey.

> I'm not sure what has happened as I thought we had a fairly good relationship prior to the verdict—obviously not feeling that way now.

Schwartz fired back without taking too long to think about it.

> I think your closing argument was irresponsible and unethical. And wholly unsupported by any evidence. Additionally, you threw in the insurance in several instances (knowing better). I . . . am very angry. NO DOUBT in my mind, an innocent man was convicted of murder . . . of a woman he did love. By the way, the alibi witnesses will all take polygraphs and are not very happy. They didn't understand why they were even involved assuming whatever happened was after Russell left their house.

Askey responded to Schwartz's candid outpouring.

> We have separate opinions—closing argument is just that "argument"—insurance was always fair game—I didn't go public with any accusations or insinuations or evidence that my professional rules of conduct prohibit—I have a job to do as do u—at any rate—until now it's been a pleasure.

Schwartz couldn't let her comment stand unchallenged—or uncorrected.

> Closing argument cannot deviate from "reasonable inferences" based on the evidence presented. You made up a story. I don't take it personally . . . but I have to do my job.

In twenty-three years as a defense attorney, often trying the most difficult and challenging cases, Joel Schwartz rarely lost sleep over a verdict.

He would lose sleep this night.

*   *   *

In the days and weeks ahead, reporters tracking down members of the jury would reach a few of them to capture some surprising comments. The first vote was evenly divided at six to six, but those voting for acquittal soon were convinced to vote guilty. One man said the game-night alibi witnesses sounded so rehearsed that they did not help Russ at all.

The jurors said Askey's timeline seemed more logical than Russ's alibi and his claim he could not have been there when Betsy was killed. One man thought Russ had enough time to kill Betsy after he arrived home and before he called 911. Another scoffed at the idea that someone had dipped Russ's slippers in blood to try to frame him. They also thought the crime scene probably was cleaned up and believed the suggestion that the killer knew which drawer held the kitchen towels.

The jurors had indeed discussed Pam Hupp as a suspect because it was clear to them that was what Schwartz was implying. One man had written in his notes, *They're trying to pin this on Pam Hupp.* But the jurors said they knew of no motive for her to kill Betsy—unaware until after the trial that the judge had suppressed evidence about Pam becoming Betsy's beneficiary. And one of the jurors said Pam was so disabled with a back injury that she would have been physically unable to overpower and stab Betsy.

One man admitted he wasn't sure he would have voted to convict if he had known everything the jurors learned after the trial. While he was still comfortable with the conviction, he was glad there was an appeal process to review the jury's decision.

CHAPTER THIRTY-SEVEN

Friday, November 22, 2012—
the day after Russ Faria's conviction

The TV reporter got it, even if the judge didn't.

"You're about to hear evidence kept from a jury in a high-profile murder case," Chris Hayes of FOX 2 News in St. Louis told viewers the day after Russ Faria was convicted. "Arguably, some of the most intriguing facts in this Troy, Missouri, case were suppressed by the judge. This is evidence that came out in open court during the murder trial of Russell Faria, but after the judge ordered the jury to take a recess."

Hayes explained Betsy's friend Pam Hupp may have been the last person to see her alive, had admitted to being in the house where Betsy was murdered, and had become beneficiary to Betsy's life insurance—just days before the murder. He told viewers Betsy had failed to answer prearranged calls from her daughter in the minutes before 7:30 p.m. And he said Pam, at first, told police she called Betsy from home in O'Fallon at 7:27 p.m., but cell phone records showed she was still in the vicinity of Betsy's house then. That was all evidence the judge kept the jury from hearing.

In about ninety seconds, Hayes presented viewers with the essence of the murder case against Pam Hupp in simple language that any reasonable person could agree should have been heard by jurors before they decided to convict Russ Faria. Surely, a reasonable inference from this TV news report would be that there was another person with ample motive and opportunity to kill Betsy Faria—another person who should have been subjected to the same level of scrutiny the cops and prosecutors applied to Russ Faria.

It was the first in a long, continuous series of reports by the only reporter who covered Russ's trial gavel-to-gavel and who had immediately grasped not only the incredible prejudice and unfairness in the rulings by Judge Mennemeyer, but also the identity of a more culpable suspect.

Hayes also was the first to report on what surely was one of the most remarkable postconviction motions ever filed by a defense attorney in Missouri. On December 13, 2013—just ten days before Russ was scheduled to be sentenced to life without parole—Joel Schwartz filed a bombastic eleven-page motion entitled "Defendant's motion for judgment of acquittal notwithstanding the verdict or, in the alternative, motion for new trial." In plain but scathing language, Schwartz laid out eleven points that were either errors by Judge Christina Kunza Mennemeyer or misconduct by Leah Askey—errors and misconduct so contrary to established trial law and so prejudicial to Russ's rights to a fair trial that overturning the verdict or granting a new trial were the only remedies. And the motion left no doubt that the defense believed Pam Hupp was really Betsy's killer.

The motion opened with a direct attack on one of Judge Mennemeyer's rulings with a statement that was also a broadside at Askey and her case: *The evidence presented in no way established Defendant's culpability for the crimes for which he was accused. Despite the State's arguments at closing, the inappropriateness of which will be discussed in depth below, the evidence did not establish that Defendant was at his home or in the area during the time at which the crime occurred, much less that he personally committed the crime.*

Regarding Mennemeyer's denial of his motion for an acquittal at the end of the State's case, Schwartz said: *[It denied Faria's] right to equal protection, due process, and a fair and impartial jury as guaranteed by the Fifth, Fourteenth, and Sixth Amendments of the*

United States Constitution and Article I, Sections 2, 10, and 18(a) of the Missouri Constitution.

Most of the motion focused on the defining issue in this case: Judge Mennemeyer was wrong to grant Askey's motion barring Schwartz from presenting evidence and arguing "someone else committed this crime"—the SODDI defense: some other dude did it. Schwartz listed twelve items of evidence Mennemeyer's errors kept him from presenting to portray Pam Hupp as the likely killer. They included Betsy's reluctance to meet with Pam on the day she filled out the beneficiary form; Pam Hupp's "consistently inconsistent" accounts of her actions the day of the murder; and her persistence in being alone with Betsy about the time she was murdered.

Schwartz also argued Judge Mennemeyer's ruling preventing detailed cross-examination of Pam Hupp violated Russ Faria's constitutional right to confront witnesses against him. Mennemeyer misinterpreted the direct connection rule to ban the effort to implicate Pam Hupp by finding that there was no direct evidence connecting her to Betsy's murder. While direct connection should not have been the controlling factor, Schwartz argued she was directly connected by her inconsistent statements, cell phone location data, and the presence of unidentified DNA under Betsy's fingernail. That should have been enough to make Pam Hupp a suspect.

Schwartz said there was a different and controlling legal issue that should have allowed him to implicate her. Every appellate court ruling on the direct connection rule involved cases where the alternative suspect had not testified in the trial. Schwartz said Pam Hupp's testimony came under the Missouri Supreme Court ruling that a witness who had a stake in the outcome of a trial—such as helping convict someone else of the murder, while remaining beneficiary to the victim's life insurance—could be cross-examined on any issue that showed an interest or bias of the witness. Schwartz quoted the supreme court's language: *[It was a] reversible error for a trial court to refuse to allow cross-examination of a prosecution witness suspected of committing the crime for which the defendant is on trial regarding the witness's motive for testifying against the defendant.*

That ruling by Mennemeyer also deprived Russ of the right to argue essential elements of his defense. His defense consisted not only of the argument that he had an alibi and did not kill Betsy, but also that Pam Hupp was the last person to see Betsy alive, and by her own admission was present in the house during the time when prosecutors conceded Betsy could have been murdered. Schwartz should have been allowed to argue there was a reasonable inference from those factors that she was the killer or, at least, had knowledge about the crime.

Judge Mennemeyer also erred by denying Schwartz's motions for a mistrial based on Askey's statement to the jury that the case was about greed and collecting on the insurance, as well as her question to a detective if the game-night players had refused to take polygraphs.

Schwartz struck hard at Askey's manic, over-the-top closing argument, calling it improper and citing her inappropriate allegations about matters not in evidence—specifically, her unsupported claims that Russ and the game-night players had been planning Betsy's murder for some time, even years, and that Brandon Sweeney made the purchase at Arby's and then drove to Russ's house to deliver the food and return his cell phone just before Russ called 911. Schwartz also cited the outrageous speculation that a naked Russ had sex with his wife first and cleaned up the scene after he had killed her.

Schwartz created a long list of Mennemeyer's errors: Allowing testimony about cadaveric spasm, alleged "previous bad acts" by the defendant unrelated to Betsy's murder, and allegations that Russ directed foul language at Betsy's daughters and made "ill-conceived statements" years earlier; allowing testimony from a witness who had been sitting in the courtroom while other witnesses testified; allowing the supervisor from Lincoln County 911 service to offer her opinion about Russ's conduct on the 911 call; and denying Schwartz's motion for the prosecutors to provide a bill of particulars—a list of specifics of the crime, such as date, time, and theory of how the crime was committed.

Schwartz used Chris Hayes's story on the motion to make some pithy comments:

"In twenty-five years, I've never seen a prosecution like this. . . . It's clear in the State's case and the closing argument of the State that everything still remains a guess . . . because it's virtually impossible for him to have done this. . . . One hundred percent, in my mind, the wrong person is in jail."

Mary Anderson's husband, Steve, had been encouraging her for months to contact the NBC *Dateline* program to see if they would be interested in a show on the mistaken prosecution of Russ Faria for the gruesome murder of his wife. The theory was that a *Dateline* episode could put the case—and the police and prosecutor—under the powerful microscope of intense national attention and create a groundswell of support for Russ.

Mary agreed the story seemed perfect for *Dateline*. A popular, outgoing woman already stricken with terminal cancer stabbed fifty-five times in her home in a quiet Midwest town on a holiday night. A husband arrested despite a seemingly ironclad alibi that put him thirty miles away. A good friend who became the life insurance beneficiary days before the murder and was the last one to see the victim alive. A handsome hotshot defense attorney challenging an inexperienced, eager prosecutor in a trial before an inexperienced, in-over-her-head judge.

Who couldn't hear reporter Keith Morrison's ominous baritone timbre telling that story?

Mary Anderson had run the idea past Joel Schwartz and he had recommended waiting to learn the outcome of Russ's trial. He wasn't sure the national media attention *Dateline* could bring would be beneficial before the trial. But now that the story had taken such a catastrophic turn with a guilty verdict, combined with Chris Hayes of FOX 2 pursuing heavy news coverage, Mary was free to enlist *Dateline* as potentially another voice of support. Immediately after the verdict, she sent a long email to the *Dateline* producers and rounded up family members to do the same. *Dateline* responded quickly, and not long after Thanksgiving, a producer named Cathy Singer began setting up interviews with Keith Morrison after the Christmas holidays. And Singer said she would be in the courtroom when Russ was sentenced just before Christmas.

The *Dateline* episode entitled "The House on Sumac Drive" would air on March 14, 2014, and present an intriguing look at the case from all angles. But that show was only the first in what would become *Dateline*'s longest series of episodes covering one case—and nearly as highly rated as their episodes on O.J. Simpson and JonBenét Ramsey. And *Dateline* would even find itself pulled into the case later in a typically, unexpectedly, Pam Hupp way.

CHAPTER THIRTY-EIGHT

Monday, December 23, 2013—*a month*
after Russ Faria's conviction

Two days before Christmas Day, 2013, Russ Faria stood in a Lincoln County courtroom to be sentenced to life in prison for the murder of his wife, two days after Christmas Day, 2011.

Joel Schwartz had prepared Russ for the grim event, but cast it as a necessary step on the way to an appeal to overturn the conviction. Russ thought the hearing was a ridiculous formality altogether. It seemed especially cruel, redundant, and gratuitous.

Judge Christina Kunza Mennemeyer opened the hearing by noting the sentence for first-degree murder was mandated by state law as life in prison without parole. Evidence or discussion at the hearing would, therefore, relate only to the sentence for armed criminal action.

The first order of business was almost as difficult for Russ to withstand as being sentenced. He had to listen as someone he had considered family for a dozen years—Betsy's sister Julie Swaney—read a victim impact statement. It's an opportunity for survivors of a crime to describe, in their own words for the court record, how it has affected their lives. More often than not, such statements in murder cases were fueled by righteous, emotional calls for the offender's sentence to include eternity burning in the most merciless fires of hell.

Julie Swaney's statement was moderate—perhaps even restrained—by most standards, but still painful for Russ. She opened by assessing the loss by those who loved the woman she described as "positive, upbeat, a shining light, strong-willed, charitable, and music-loving." She read aloud, "'Losing Betsy at the young age of forty-two has been devastating to our family, all of Betsy's friends, and her two young daughters.'" The family thought Betsy had been uncharacteristically low key at Christmas parties because "'she knew something bad was about to happen.'"

With all due respect to Betsy's family, and with sincere sympathy for their loss, Schwartz thought that kind of emotional hindsight was so simple, but usually without foundation or value.

Speaking from prepared comments, Julie said some of Betsy's friends reported she had been discussing plans to replace Russ as beneficiary on her insurance policies. When a friend asked why she didn't trust Russ, "'Betsy responded that she loved Russ, but she felt he might mismanage the money and she wanted her girls taken care of.'"

And then Julie delivered a motive. Betsy had already replaced Russ as beneficiary on one policy and said she had accidentally left paperwork replacing him on another policy on the kitchen counter when she went to her mother's the day before her death. With absolutely no proof there ever was such paperwork, Julie theorized that Russ found it and that "'led him to the level of anger that it took for him to plan and execute this murder. There was anger building in Russ even prior to this.'"

Julie repeated Bobbi Wann's claim that Betsy had confirmed Pam's account of Russ holding a pillow over Betsy's face and saying, "'This is what it would feel like to die.'" Julie turned to the "gruesome details" of Betsy's death and put the knife in Russ's hand. "'The number of stab wounds, the sheer strength and force it took to commit such a violent, heinous, and cowardly act, is still incomprehensible for my family. Her arms were almost severed off. This is the work of a disturbed man who should never be allowed the opportunity of freedom.'"

And then she crossed the final bridge. "'Even though Russ has not admitted his guilt in public, he knows what he did. The evidence showed what he did, from the bloody slippers to the neatly-placed gloves behind Betsy's body, to the bloody paw print. Betsy knows what he did. God knows what he did.'"

Schwartz was torn between allowing the grieving relatives to have their say and a desire to correct Julie's mistakes and unsupported allegations that were now part of the court record. He swallowed hard and asked Judge Mennemeyer for permission to question Julie, even though that was not his usual policy. Askey objected to that as inappropriate and the judge agreed. Schwartz demurred without protest.

Richard Hicks reminded the judge that before she could impose the sentence, she had to hear the attorneys' arguments on Schwartz's motion to acquit Russ Faria or grant him a new trial. Schwartz wasted no time getting to the point.

"Your Honor, if the court chooses to sentence Mr. Faria today to any sentence whatsoever, it would be sentencing an innocent man. It would be sentencing a victim as big as Ms. Meyer or Ms. Swaney. . . . This trial was like what Ms. Swaney just testified to. Everything she said was based on nothing other than conjecture."

Echoing his written motion that Mennemeyer had in front of her, Schwartz again criticized her rulings that prohibited him from discussing another suspect—even though the definition of an alibi defense is that someone else did it—or mentioning the insurance policy and Pam Hupp's sudden inheritance.

He cast Judge Mennemeyer's rulings in the light they deserved. "I have to admit, initially, we didn't take that seriously because the case law and the state law is absolutely certain and it all says that any witness's bias or interest is never irrelevant. The State relied on the direct connection rule. After the court ruled on this, I actually congratulated Mr. Hicks on his creative lawyering. His response was he never imagined the court would actually go for that. Well, the court did—and that precluded Mr. Faria from getting a fair trial."

Citing the preposterous, unreal assumptions Askey made in closing arguments, Schwartz cracked, "I would argue the State created a bad Stephen King novel. . . . And the entire argument from the State was 'I believe this. I believe that. I believe that Russ Faria came home, had sex with his wife, took off all of his clothes, took a shower, got out of the shower, stepped into his slippers, somehow got blood on the bottom of those slippers by just stepping into the blood, swooping up the dog, and carrying the dog outside.' Not only does that defy logic, it defies any shred of evidence. There was not one single iota—a piece—of proof that came into the court regarding any of those things that were argued to that jury. . . . That closing argument by the State was irresponsible and, frankly, unethical. Based on that alone, the court should overturn the verdict."

Leah Askey clearly was stung by Schwartz's attack and she quickly made her response personal. She noted that twelve people had listened to the evidence and took just four hours to agree with her that Russ Faria was guilty.

"Mr. Schwartz and all of his experience—which he was proud to tell me I was out of my league—he knows that four hours is pretty darn quick on a murder trial. And he didn't expect that coming out here to Lincoln County. I understand and I feel his pain a little bit, I guess. I understand that's not what he really thought he was going to get when he got here."

She defended proposing her own scenario to the jurors. "Closing argument is just that—argument. The State never accused anyone. I think exactly what I said was 'I wish I could tell you exactly what happened, but I don't know. I wasn't there. Neither were they, except for the defendant and the victim. I wish I could tell you. This is what I think could have happened; in the alternative, this could have happened. I don't know.'"

She took another swipe at Schwartz for questioning the jury's verdict. "When we talk about unethical and irresponsible—which Mr. Schwartz had been really good at throwing around for the last few weeks—I think he probably needs to look at what he is doing right now."

She defended the direct connection rule, which kept Schwartz from naming Pam Hupp as a suspect, as preventing attorneys from painting almost anyone in a defendant's circle as a suspect.

Askey also insisted that the four game-night players had refused to take polygraphs. And she added that, on Schwartz's advice, they had refused to provide buccal swabs for DNA tests.

She ended with more personal attacks. "In every case, one side or the other is not going to win and, unfortunately, ethics, responsibility, all of those things, evidently at times, get checked at the door because it becomes all about the win, about how you win with grace or how you lose with grace—not about throwing people's name around and not about acting like you got completely [run] over because your client lost. And that is what this is all about. As far as I'm concerned, that is what it has been about since the day the jury returned a verdict and that is what it will be about until the court of appeals makes a ruling.

"It is about a big-city lawyer coming out to little Lincoln County against a prosecutor who is new and 'out of her league.' Mr. Schwartz can say it is not, but I think we all know differently.

"The State would argue against a new trial."

Schwartz responded sharply and directly. First, he was not the game-night players' lawyer and never advised them on anything. Second, he never said anyone was out of anyone's league. "Ms. Askey continued to repeat that *she* felt she was out of her league," he said. And, again, the police and prosecutors never asked game-night players to take a polygraph, despite their offers to do so. The defense never opposed introducing evidence on the change of beneficiary on the insurance. That was what the defense wanted all along, believing it was a direct connection between Pam Hupp and Betsy's murder.

"I leave that to everybody at the court of appeals," he said, ending his comments with, "There is clearly direct evidence that Pam Hupp was involved at that house at the time of the murder."

Judge Mennemeyer leaned forward with a quick defense of her decisions and the ruling Schwartz expected. "The court ruled in accordance with what it believed the status of the law to be and, in sitting through the jury trial, did not find that the jury could not have found as it did. . . . The defendant's motion for judgment of acquittal notwithstanding the verdict or motion for a new trial is denied."

The judge then took less than thirty seconds to impose a sentence of life without parole or probation for first-degree murder and thirty years for armed criminal action.

Russ Faria offered no reaction to officially being ordered to spend the rest of his life in prison. Although he had prepared himself, it was still shattering to hear.

Schwartz immediately asked the judge to set bond so Russ could await the results of an appeal at home, instead of in prison. Askey said an appeal bond was not appropriate on a conviction for first-degree murder and the judge agreed. Russ would go back to his cell at the county jail to await the next step.

That came within days, as Russ found himself in a cell in the Jefferson City Correctional Center (JCCC), the state capital's penitentiary. He wasted no time beginning to make friends with the older "cons," as he had in the Lincoln County Jail. He hoped he would be able to navigate the dangerous whirlpools of state prison as well—and as safely—as he had in the county jail for almost two years. But he was warned soon after his arrival that the prison was a place where a carton of cigarettes could cost your life—a warning to be heeded. He was glad to be in a one-man cell and, reluctantly facing an untold number of Missouri summers in that cell, he was relieved the prison was air-conditioned. Perhaps that could make the cell feel a little less like hell.

CHAPTER THIRTY-NINE

The anonymous calls to Joel Schwartz began not long after his most famous client had been sentenced to life in prison. While the callers didn't offer direct information about Betsy Faria's murder, they did open an entirely new, shocking chapter in the story of Schwartz's prime suspect, Pam Hupp.

The callers clearly had followed Russ Faria's trial and the growing publicity that followed the guilty verdict that was now being questioned by the media and many in the public. Chris Hayes from FOX 2 was delivering a relentless barrage of stories focusing on Pam Hupp as a bona fide suspect, Leah Askey's conduct in the trial, and the evidence that Judge Mennemeyer kept the jurors from hearing.

In an unusual arrangement, Hayes and FOX 2 partnered with the *St. Louis Post-Dispatch* and reporter Robert Patrick to produce investigative stories questioning the evidence against Russ, Pam Hupp's involvement in the case, the conduct of his trial, and his conviction. There would be a comprehensive front-page account and analysis of the case in a Sunday edition under the headline DID RUSS FARIA KILL HIS WIFE? It was matched by reports on FOX 2 news. Hayes and Patrick would interview Russ in prison, giving him the chance to proclaim his innocence before a wider audience than ever before. Joel Schwartz became a regular on TV and in print attacking the case and the trial and decrying Russ Faria's imprisonment as an innocent man. A special FOX 2 report on the case by Hayes and Patrick won an Emmy Award.

While all of that was building, the callers to Schwartz focused on a report from the trial they said was mistaken or an outright lie. When Pam Hupp testified outside the presence of the jury but still under oath, she said her mother had died of Alzheimer's almost three weeks before—on October 31, 2013—Halloween, no less. That was one of the many stressful matters she said she had been dealing with as she tried to decide whether to provide any of the $150,000 from Betsy's life insurance policy to her daughters. But the callers kept telling Schwartz that her testimony was a lie and he should look into the death of her mother.

The headline on the story in the *Post-Dispatch* on November 1, 2013, said: WOMAN, 77, DIES AFTER FALLING FROM THIRD-FLOOR BALCONY OF FENTON-AREA RETIREMENT HOME. It appeared that Shirley Neumann had broken *through* the metal railing on her balcony and plunged three stories to her death. Her body was found about 2:30 p.m. the day before on the ground below her balcony. And the last person known to see her alive was her daughter—Pam Hupp.

Schwartz rocked back in his chair and stared wide-eyed at the story on the computer screen. A second person whose death meant a big inheritance for Pam Hupp had died under suspicious circumstances—and she had lied again about what happened. Her seventy-seven-year-old mother—a photo with the story showed a bright-eyed, silver-haired, stylishly-dressed woman—had not died of Alzheimer's, as Pam had testified under oath. She died of injuries from a fall through a metal railing on a third-story balcony. This was the same woman whom Pam Hupp had so shockingly volunteered to Sergeant Ryan McCarrick in June 2012 as a much more vulnerable murder-for-profit victim than the younger and stronger Betsy Faria.

"And if I really—hate to say—wanted money, my mom's worth a half a million that I get when she dies," she had said cavalierly to McCarrick. "But if I really wanted money, there was an easier way than trying to combat somebody that's physically stronger than me. I'm just saying."

Pam Hupp had said that in June 2012 and her mother had died violently sixteen months later. Was Shirley Neumann actually her second victim, in her second plot to inherit hundreds of thousands of dollars?

The newspaper quoted the St. Louis County Police saying there was damage to several of the vertical spindles in the metal railing on her mother's balcony, which they believed was caused by her fall into and through those bars. Oddly, the top and bottom horizontal bars were undamaged. Schwartz wasn't an expert, but it seemed an unlikely scenario for an elderly woman to fall into a metal railing with such force that two of the uprights were broken out of the railing and found next to her body on the ground, and four others were bent and dislodged at the bottom, presumably allowing her body to break through the railing and free-fall to the ground below.

The police said they were investigating Shirley Neumann's fall as an accident, but Schwartz thought even the scant information he had read suggested something more sinister. Especially with Pam Hupp standing to inherit hundreds of thousands of dollars. Especially with Pam Hupp callously weighing the challenge of murdering her mother against that of murdering Betsy Faria. Especially with Pam Hupp brazenly lying under oath about the way her mother died.

An autopsy showed that Shirley Neumann's system contained more than eight times the normal dose of Ambien—a sleep-inducing drug in the class called sedative hypnotics. But the St. Louis County Medical Examiner's Office agreed with the police investigation and listed her death as an accident and the cause of death as blunt trauma to the chest.

News stories later would report that the police reviewed their investigation into Shirley Neumann's death in November, the month after she died, based on an anonymous note alerting them that the victim's daughter had been investigated in Betsy Faria's murder. The police learned Pam Hupp had, once again, been the last person known to have seen the victim alive. Employees at the Lakeview Park Independent Senior Living community, just outside of Fenton, another St. Louis suburb, said Pam Hupp had taken her mother to the hospital on October 29 after staff found her incoherent on her bed. Shirley spent that night at her daughter's home and Pam brought her back to the care center about 5 p.m. on October 30.

Pam told the staff that her mother would not be coming to the dining room for supper because she had already eaten. She would miss breakfast the next morning as well, but probably would eat lunch. After she did not show for lunch on October 31, a housekeeper went to her apartment and found the front door open, water running in a sink, the white metal storm door to the balcony open, and the railing damaged. She looked over the railing and saw the body on the ground below.

One of Shirley Neumann's two sons—Pam's brothers—told police his mother suffered from memory problems and arthritis. And he had no concerns about foul play in her death. The police closed their review again without finding an indication of a crime—and again without interviewing Pam Hupp, the last person to see her mother alive.

Joel Schwartz was baffled. For the second time, Pam Hupp stood at the center of a suspicious, violent death that would put hundreds of thousands of dollars in her pocket—and walked away virtually unscathed.

The likelihood that a seventy-seven-year-old woman, even one weighing 218 pounds, could break through the metal spindles of an aluminum railing in a fall was rejected flatly by experts consulted in separate interviews and experiments by Chris Hayes from FOX 2 and Keith Morrison from *Dateline*.

The report by Hayes featured a structural engineer who tested a similar railing by the same manufacturer by building a pendulum with a 218-pound weight—essentially a battering ram—and slamming it into a railing to determine what kind of force would be required to dislodge or bend the spindles enough for a person to fall through it. Releasing the pendulum to slam into the railing—at what the engineer said would be the likely force exerted in a fall by a woman like Shirley Neumann—failed to damage the railing or dislodge any spindles.

Only when the engineer had the pendulum pulled as far back as possible—some sixty-five inches from the railing—and released to strike the railing at nine miles per hour did it dislodge any spindles and bend the bottom rail. The expert said it would take an NFL linebacker charging full-speed at the railing to damage it the way it was when Shirley Neumann was killed. He also noted the damaged spindles were bent exactly the same way they bent when he kicked them hard enough to dislodge them.

Dateline hired a structural engineer, who estimated a fall into the railing by a woman of Shirley Neumann's size who tripped over the threshold onto the balcony from the apartment would exert 425 pounds of force against the railing. He laid a section of railing with slightly thinner spindles flat and stacked eight 94-pound bags of concrete mix—a total of 752 pounds—on the spindles—without any damage. The engineer estimated it would take two thousand pounds of force to damage the railing. He concluded that the damage to the balcony railing could not have been done by Shirley Neumann accidentally falling into it.

One of Pam Hupp's brothers would sue the railing manufacturer and the retirement center, but he would later dismiss the suit.

CHAPTER FORTY

Getting a phone call from David Butsch in the summer of 2014 was intriguing. Joel Schwartz knew Butsch as a fellow attorney also practicing in Clayton, the legal center and St. Louis County seat. Their sons attended the same school. The two attorneys and fathers would sometimes run into each other at school events or while doing business at the county courthouse near their offices. Butsch had gone to law school with Joel's wife, Mary Ann, and their wives knew each other quite well.

But Schwartz also knew Butsch had filed a suit against Pam Hupp on behalf of Betsy Faria's daughters to recover the $150,000 from Betsy's insurance. As Butsch was preparing to take her deposition on July 21, he consulted with Schwartz about his experience with her. And it was that deposition, Butsch said now, that was the reason for his call. Butsch had experienced the same frustrating, infuriating reaction that Schwartz had described in trying to get a truthful or even sensible answer from the woman. Butsch's first impression of her as a dimwit had evolved during the deposition—he now saw her as a manipulative psychopath.

But it was a couple of surprising disclosures by Pam Hupp that Butsch wanted to pass along to Schwartz. She had testified that, shortly after Russ Faria was convicted, she revoked the trust she set up for Leah and Mariah Day and withdrew all but $300 of the $100,000 she had deposited. She put the money in the personal checking account she shared with her husband and used to pay their bills and invest in real estate. Butsch thought there was ample evidence that she had used some of the insurance money to buy a new house in the weeks before the deposition. The suit Butsch filed for the Day sisters claimed she had violated the agreement with Betsy that was grounds for making her the beneficiary—that she would give the money to the girls when they got older.

But there was more. Pam Hupp had testified she opened the trust because of pressure from Sergeant Ryan McCarrick and implied pressure from Leah Askey. McCarrick had told her that setting up a trust for the girls would make the murder case against Russ Faria look better at trial.

Schwartz hung up the phone and took a deep breath. This new information directly from Pam Hupp's mouth was dynamite. Revoking the trust put the lie to her many statements that Betsy wanted her to give it to the girls when they were older. And keeping the money for herself confirmed she was motivated by her own greed—motivated enough to make her a prime suspect in Betsy's murder.

Schwartz knew applying these incriminating admissions to Russ's effort to win a new trial would be a challenge. The date was long past for asking the trial court in Lincoln County for a new trial based on evidence that was recently discovered. The only other obvious option—making it part of Russ's formal appeal to the Court of Appeals for the Eastern District of Missouri—was a long shot because the court was restricted to considering only evidence that had been introduced at trial. Schwartz decided he had no choice. When he filed the seventy-page appeal on December 1, 2014, the new revelations were included in a section titled "Newly Discovered Evidence." The appeal argued the jury might have acquitted Russ Faria if it had heard Pam Hupp's admission that she set up the trust only because of pressure from the police and prosecutor to improve their case against Russ. And revoking the trust after the conviction also called her motive into question.

The rest of the appeal cited the litany of errors by Judge Mennemeyer and misconduct by Askey that Schwartz had listed in his motion for a new trial that Mennemeyer denied a year earlier. Schwartz argued that Mennemeyer and Askey failed to conform to the law as established in almost seventy court cases, violating Russ's rights to a fair trial under the constitutions of Missouri and the United States.

Knowing that the appellate court could refuse to consider the new evidence, Joel Schwartz and Nate Swanson continued to look for a better way to get it in front of the court. Hannah Zhao, Schwartz's associate who had assembled the appeal, found the answer in a little-known case she remembered. In the *State of Missouri* v. *Mooney* (a criminal case from adjacent St. Charles County that was decided thirty years earlier by the same appellate court hearing Russ's appeal), the court ruled it had the inherent right to remand a case to the trial court for consideration of a motion for a new trial if evidence discovered after the trial could have resulted in an acquittal. In *Mooney*, the defense learned the alleged victim who testified that the defendant molested him made a taped statement after the trial admitting he lied on the witness stand and made up the entire story. The appellate court ruled that it had the authority and discretion to prevent a miscarriage of justice and to send the case back to the trial court, even though the evidence was not part of the trial and the time for asking the trial court for a new trial had lapsed.

On February 4, 2015, Schwartz filed a rare *Mooney* motion, citing the appellate court's decision as grounds to send the Faria case back to the court in Lincoln County to decide if the new evidence justified a new trial. He charged that McCarrick and Askey pressured a witness to take an action specifically designed to assist the prosecution and violate the defendant's rights, knew the witness lied about that in testimony before a judge in an offer of proof, and then filed motions with the judge designed to protect that witness from scrutiny by the defense.

Schwartz's research showed that successful *Mooney* motions were rare, indeed. They had been granted only three times in Missouri history. It seemed to him that the *State of Missouri* v. *Faria* absolutely had to be the fourth.

And it was.

In an unusually swift response, Chief Appellate Judge Angela T.

Quigless gave Russ and his attorneys their first new hope for the justice they had been seeking for more than three years. Just twenty days after Schwartz filed the *Mooney* motion—and without getting a response from Askey—Judge Quigless ordered Russ's case sent back to the trial court to decide if he should get a new trial. Her order said the appellate court does not usually remand a case before an appeal is concluded, but it stated: *[The court] has the inherent power to prevent a miscarriage of justice or manifest injustice by remanding a case to the trial court for consideration of newly discovered evidence presented for the first time on appeal.* She ruled that this case met the four requirements for such an order: The evidence came to the defense's knowledge after the trial; the lack of knowledge of the evidence was not the defense's fault; the evidence is likely to produce a different result in a new trial; the evidence is not just cumulative or of an impeaching nature.

Quigless gave Schwartz two weeks to file a motion for a new trial and ordered the trial court to hold a hearing and issue a ruling within ninety days of Schwartz's motion. In what Schwartz hoped was a veiled indication of what the judge believed the decision should be, she wrote, *If the motion for new trial is denied, the denial may be alleged as error in the pending appeal.*

The media climbed all over the story that Russ Faria might get a new trial. When reporters asked Schwartz about the new evidence, he couldn't resist the opportunity for a quip about the State's handling of the case. "A murder trial has turned into a soap opera," he said.

As soon as Judge Quigless's order was filed, Schwartz made an excited call to Russ Faria in prison in Jefferson City. By the time Schwartz could get Russ on a phone, the early-evening news in St. Louis had already carried the story.

"Russ, did you see the news tonight?"

"Yeah, I watched it."

"What did you see?"

"Joel, remember, we get different news in Jefferson City than you get in St. Louis."

"Oh, that's right," Schwartz said with a chuckle before he added,

"We get a hearing on a new trial. The appellate court sent the case back to Lincoln County for a hearing on a new trial."

Russ felt the smile spread across his face as he said, "Joel, that's great. That's great. It's about time we got a good decision."

By the time that first glimmer of hope arrived, Russ Faria had spent fourteen months in state prison—fourteen months that followed two years in the Lincoln County Jail. Prison was a living hell, especially for an innocent man, but Russ struggled to make the best of this god-awful situation. He knew to avoid most of the younger prisoners—the ones more likely to cause trouble. He focused on making friends who were between fifty and seventy years old because they were calmer and more willing to help educate him about prison life and survival.

One of the prisoners he befriended worked in the kitchen and helped get Russ a job there. He washed dishes until he moved up to preparing meals for prisoners who had special religious diets. He worked seven days a week, not because he wanted the $30 a month paid to working inmates, but just to spend as much time out of his cell as possible. Even with the small television he was allowed to have in the cell, the time spent there was agonizing and boring. Except when they were working, prisoners were locked in their cells twenty-three hours a day, with one hour for a shower or exercise in the gym or outside. He mostly bought food from the commissary and cooked it in his cell using an electric "stinger" that could heat up soup and coffee.

Russ got involved with the prison chapter of the Toastmasters International, the nonprofit educational organization that teaches public speaking and leadership skills. It was a good way to associate with prisoners working to better themselves while learning valuable skills that could serve them well later—on the outside.

Joel Schwartz filed the motion for a new trial on March 11, focusing on Pam Hupp's self-incriminating lies and Askey and McCarrick pressuring her to take action to buttress the State's case and improve her credibility as a witness.Schwartz accused Askey of "deliberate silence," even though she knew the witness perjured herself on the stand by denying she set up the trust specifically to strengthen the State's case against Russ Faria.

Five days after Schwartz filed the motion, Judge Christina Kunza Mennemeyer recused herself from the Faria case. The order she placed in the file said only: *Upon review of the Motion for New Trial filed by Defendant, this Court now has a known conflict and must recuse.* She offered no more explanation when contacted by reporters.

Two days after that, the Missouri Supreme Court appointed a circuit judge from the Hannibal area, north of Lincoln County, to hear the motion. Schwartz thought the judge was too inexperienced and he exercised his right to request a different judge. A month later, the supreme court appointed St. Louis circuit judge Steven R. Ohmer, a highly-rated judge on the bench for twenty-one years, including two years serving as presiding judge. He began his career in 1979 as an assistant circuit attorney in the City of St. Louis, a job he held for eleven years. He also had been in private practice. Schwartz thought Ohmer was exactly the kind of judge needed to handle this convoluted case.

By the time Ohmer scheduled a hearing on the motion for a new trial on June 5, hostilities between Schwartz and Askey were approaching open warfare. The hearing was contentious and marked by more squabbles between the attorneys. But by the end of the day, Judge Ohmer was ready to return his decision in open court. He said he had reviewed all the evidence, including transcripts of Pam Hupp's testimony in Russ Faria's trial and in the deposition with David Butsch. He concluded that the new evidence from her testimony met the requirements set by the appellate court for granting a new trial, including that the evidence was "so material that it is likely to produce a different result at a new trial." And, he said, her testimony proved that, as a person with opportunity or motive to commit the murder, she had committed an act that directly connected her to the crime—a decision that rebutted Judge Mennemeyer's insistence that there was no "direct connection" between Pam and the murder of Betsy.

All of that meant the motion for a new trial due to newly discovered evidence was granted. Russ Faria's conviction was overturned and Ohmer set the new trial for November 2, 2015.

Schwartz, Russ, and Swanson shared a special smile, and Schwartz said, "I told you we'd be back and do this again."

Russ returned the smile and said, "Yes, you did. I never doubted it."

Askey stood and announced she was prepared to try Russ again.

Outside, Mary Anderson told the media that all they had ever wanted was a second chance to prove Russ's innocence. Mike Corbin predicted a new trial would mean, "The whole world will see he didn't kill his wife."

Joel Schwartz tried to maintain a professional reserve as he said, "We look forward to our day in court—with *all* of the evidence coming in—and we expect justice to prevail."

Six days later, Russ Faria was told to pack up his gear from his prison cell. Judge Ohmer had ordered him transferred back to Lincoln County Jail in Troy to await trial in November. Stepping down from maximum security at the state prison to detention in the county jail was good news. But it didn't compare to the change a few days later on June 16, when Mary Anderson courageously and compassionately posted her home as security for Russ's $500,000 bond and paid $17,000 in cash to a bail bondsman to win his release from jail. He was greeted outside the building by a crowd of family and friends who took him to a favorite restaurant for a celebration. He was surprised that his driver's license was still good and his sister let him drive to his father's office for a special visit on the way to the party.

Russ returned to his parents' house in O'Fallon and began enjoying freedom after three and a half years in jail. He told Chris Hayes of FOX 2 that one of his great joys had been getting up in the mornings and frying an egg—something he hadn't been able to do for years. Within a week of being released, Russ also had begun an IT job telecommuting with a friend's business in Phoenix, Arizona. He just wanted to enjoy some sense of normalcy while he waited for his next opportunity to prove his innocence.

Shortly after Russ was released from jail, more tragedy struck the family. On July 3, Mary Anderson's husband, Steve, unexpectedly died of a heart attack at age fifty-one—sitting in a chair in their walk-in closet just after Mary had left to pick up Russ and attend a St. Louis Cardinals baseball game. A friend of Steve's found his body and called the O'Fallon police. Two detectives who participated in the investigation into Betsy's death refused to let Mary see her husband's body as it sat in the closet for some seven hours while they investigated to make sure Steve died of natural causes.

CHAPTER FORTY-ONE

"No, she's not really going to say *that*. Even Pam Hupp wouldn't say *that*. Wait, she is going to say . . . Oh, my God! She said it. What the fu . . . ?"

Nate Swanson's eyes widened and his mouth fell open like a trap-door. Listening to the recording of a new police interview with Pam Hupp from June 17, 2015, he had just heard her say the most re-markable thing she had said yet—and she had set a very high bar.

Pam Hupp had told police that she and Betsy Faria were lovers.

Until that moment, Swanson didn't think anything Pam could say would surprise him. But this almost made his head explode.

Pam Hupp told Detectives Mike Merkel and Patrick Harney that Betsy had come to depend on her for an intimate level of emotional support she didn't get from Russ or anyone else. What she described as Betsy's "mad crush" on her grew into something more.

"She really, really, really loved me," she said. "As her marriage started deteriorating, I would help . . . step in and help her even more, almost kind of like, I guess in her mind, a boyfriend, a care-taker."

Merkel was eager to help her explain. "You were filling the voids that she felt in her marriage?"

"Yeah, of what she wanted out of a relationship."

"Right," Merkel said without a hint of disbelief.

One time, Pam said, she set up Betsy and her daughters in a leased house and provided financial support for them when Betsy and Russ were separated.

"At that point, she started indicating that she wanted more from me than just, you know, a friend," Pam said. At first, she resisted a more physical turn in their relationship, but eventually entered a sexual affair with Betsy. "It was a progression more on her part, because I loved Betsy—I'm not in love with her. Never was in love with her. She was in love with me . . . and at that point, when I knew what was happening with her . . . I just let that go because it was a small, small thing to give her."

Pam said Betsy was still having sex with others—including husband Russ and former husband Ron—but sex for Betsy was generally a physical act that did not involve emotion. She said their physical relationship was different.

"Ours wasn't about sex. It was about emotional . . . It's not a huge thing for me. Like I said, I'm not attracted to women. So it's not like I've ever been with anybody but Betsy. It's not the same. Never will probably again. It's just a weird circumstance. . . . It's honestly a relationship with two women who really aren't attracted to women. I don't know how to explain that. It's not—I'm attracted to men— love everything about them. Can't wait till *Magic Mike XL* (the movie) comes out. But she is the same way. It's not like she was a lesbian or anything. It wasn't like that. It was such an evolution of emotional trauma for her," Pam said.

She claimed Russ was furious when he found out about the sex between Betsy and her, and that led to what she had said was a violent threat to kill her when she was at Betsy's house not long before the murder.

Joel Schwartz was just as stunned as Swanson when he heard the latest flight of bizarre fantasy. But Russ was outraged. "That's just a total lie—total bullshit," he said. "That never happened. Betsy would never do that."

Schwartz and Swanson found still more to be disturbed about deeper into that interview when Detective Patrick Harney took a totally inappropriate run at getting Pam to change her statements and sworn testimony over the last four years by saying she saw Russ at the house when she brought Betsy home that night.

"Here's what I'm going to offer you," Harney said to her. "Like Detective Merkel and I have said, we have—we were the first detectives at the house. And we have spoken in theory before about what we believe may have happened—and what we believe may have happened is that . . . that Russ was not there when you and Betsy got there. And that prior to you leaving, somehow or another Russ knew that you were there, either by a phone call or just the sheer presence of your car—or that he walked in and saw you there and that, that . . . it was that particular moment . . . motivating factor for you to leave, was him coming into the house. That is what we have discussed amongst ourselves. So now I'm going to hand that to you and ask— is any part of that correct, and it is, in fact, did you see Russ that night in that house?"

She responded with a flat "No . . . I did not see Russ in that house. . . . Did not see a soul. Didn't see anybody."

Harney's proposition would have been just an inappropriate and possibly illegal attempt to influence a witness or to get a witness to lie, until the defense team listened to the recording of another interview she gave Harney and Detective Harry Belcher four months later, on October 6. Harney's theory seemed to have planted a suggestive seed in her mind. She dramatically disclosed that she now had a recovered memory that she had seen Russ and another man in a car parked on the street near the Faria house when she and Betsy arrived that night. And when she left the house later, she saw Russ still sitting behind the steering wheel, but the other man was gone. She said Russ ducked his head when she drove by.

She said she had walked the street near Betsy's former house the morning of the interview in an attempt to stimulate her memory and put herself back in the moments when she arrived and when she left. That's when it came to her that there was a light-colored, possibly silver, car with two men parked on Sumac Drive before she got to Betsy's house.

Harney asked, "And you think you recognized one of those men?"

"I do, yes."

She said repeatedly she did not take a long look inside the car il-luminated only by a streetlight or get a good look at the man behind the wheel. But she also repeated it was her strong impression and memory that it was Russ Faria.

Harney later asked again, "And you believe one of the persons in the car was Russ?"

"I do. I do. And the more I keep going over it in my head, I do. And I don't know if I'm talking myself into it. I don't believe I am."

Pam Hupp had reached an entirely new level of outrageously ab-surd and unbalanced deception. And the cops continued to eagerly buy into her insane ramblings as if they were written on stone tablets she had brought down from Mount Sinai. Or worse, they were feed-ing into her demented ability to lie without restraint by suggesting new fields for her to mine. They didn't even flinch when she backed up her conveniently recovered memory with another diatribe about how head injuries from three car accidents in three years had left her with "huge lapses of memory" made worse by regular doses of Am-bien (yes, the same drug found at overdosed levels in her dead mother's blood). She couldn't make the missing memories return, she explained, but she could "guide" them by talking about events and trying to visualize them.

When she lamented, "And I know everybody is going to say I'm nuts and stuff like that," Harney leaped to her support.

"No, let me tell . . ." he began as he described a friend who suf-fered a concussion that left him with similar memory issues.

As they were about to end the interview, she said, "I wouldn't want to accuse anybody of anything"—an absurdly outrageous statement in itself. "I want to say what I think I saw. I could very well be wrong, but I don't think so."

Harney said, "OK. I don't have any reason to think you're wrong."

Of course he didn't; it was his idea.

The new interviews with police came after Pam Hupp met with Leah Askey in May 2015 to discuss Hupp's likely testimony at a hearing for a new trial for Russ Faria. Their conversation centered on her denial that she ever promised Betsy Faria to give any of the insurance money to her daughters, that she felt pressured from all sides to set up the trust fund before Russ's first trial, and that she revoked the fund because of the daughters' criticism of her since then.

"So, what are our chances of making the judge believe us?" she asked.

"I feel comfortable. The law is on our side," Askey replied. "I'll be happy to take them on again. . . . I don't worry about trying the case again." And Askey reaffirmed her confidence that Russ Faria was guilty. "There's not a moment that I've lost sleep because Russ Faria's in prison. I feel very comfortable in that decision."

Much of the conversation focused on the women's complaints about being mistreated by the media in false or misleading stories. Pam lamented that she had been accused of killing her mother, had been harassed and condemned in social media by Russ's supporters, and had even been subjected to death threats in phone calls under investigation by the police.

Askey called the defense team's efforts "half-assed" and dismissed Schwartz's *Mooney* motion by saying, "My four-year-old . . . could write something better."

Schwartz chuckled as he watched the video of the prosecutor and her witness confirming their paranoid beliefs that he was coordinating and manipulating all of the media coverage by reporters participating in his massive conspiracy to win an acquittal for Russ Faria. What Leah Askey and Pam Hupp clearly didn't understand was that the media, mostly following the lead of Chris Hayes of FOX 2, were recognizing that the investigation and prosecution of Russ Faria was an unmitigated and unjust disaster of incompetence and legal prejudice that had to be exposed to the public.

In the video, Askey advised Pam to ignore the media and those who listen to or read the news. Askey said she had done some reporting and news writing before she went to law school and learned the general rule was to write news on a sixth-grade level. She said that meant, "Most of the people that are paying attention [to the media] are derelicts."

Pam took this opportunity to educate Askey on her memory issues. "When I say off-the-wall stuff, it's not because I'm lying. It's because, for some reason, that popped into my head," she said. She cited as an example her contradictory statements that Betsy was lying on the couch when she left on the night of the murder and that Betsy was waving good-bye to her from the front door. "My mind works different," she added.

Joel Schwartz thought that might have been the understatement of the century.

CHAPTER FORTY-TWO

October 1, 2015—a month before
Russ Faria's second trial

By the time Judge Steven Ohmer held a hearing on pretrial motions on October 1, 2015, Joel Schwartz had made a risky decision—so risky, in fact, that almost every colleague and friend he had discussed it with warned him not to do it. More than one of them told him he would be crazy to do it.

So far, Judge Ohmer's decisions on motions had been correct on the law and unfailingly fair, especially his ruling that Schwartz could present evidence and argument that Pam Hupp was a legitimate suspect in Betsy Faria's murder. In fact, Judge Ohmer had reinforced his ruling that very day, denying Leah Askey's motion for him to reconsider because there was no evidence directly connecting her to the murder. Schwartz countered there was ample evidence of a direct link and listed several factors again. Ohmer affirmed his decision that there was enough of a direct connection between Pam Hupp and the killing for the defense to treat her as a suspect.

Ohmer had been fair to the prosecution as well. Askey said she should be allowed to present a "complete picture" of the facts by arguing that Russ could have been motivated to kill Betsy because of her plan to change beneficiaries on other insurance policies. Ohmer agreed and assured her, "The facts are going to come in."

The animus between Schwartz and Askey was still spilling into their exchanges in the courtroom, reaching the point where Judge

Ohmer had to admonish them several times and encourage them to cooperate better. He finally asked them if he was going to have to put them in the corner.

So, with all of the contentious legal points and contradictory evidence—and Schwartz's lack of trust in the integrity of the prosecution and police—he decided to file a surprising document at the hearing.

Russ Faria would waive his right to a jury trial. He would let Judge Ohmer hear the evidence and return a verdict.

Schwartz decided that a bench trial—a verdict by a judge—made more sense than putting Russ's future in the hands of jurors from the same juror pool, in the same county, that had convicted him the first time. The judge was applying a keen legal sense and understanding to the evidence and clearly was dedicated to a fair trial. This seemed like the perfect case for a judge to decide.

Unlike the opposition by most of the people Schwartz had confided in, Russ Faria listened to his attorney's explanation and agreed. "Let's do it," he said.

Sunday, November 1, 2015—*the day*
before Russ Faria's second trial

Joel Schwartz and Nate Swanson arrived on Sunday, November 1, at their hotel near the Lincoln County Courthouse in time for some final preparations for the start of the trial the next day. They ate dinner at the adjacent Panda Express restaurant. Schwartz cracked open his fortune cookie and stared in amazement at the little slip of paper before handing it to Swanson with a smile. It read: *All of your hard work will soon be rewarded.* They looked at each other and grinned.

To avoid the chance of getting a less promising prediction, they didn't eat at the restaurant again.

CHAPTER FORTY-THREE

Monday, November 2, 2015—*first
day of Russ Faria's second trial*

A police officer found several water droplets on the floor of Russ
Faria's shower just minutes into the search of his house on the night
of December 27, 2011. The cop on the witness stand didn't have to
explain how important those few drops could be as the only evidence supporting Prosecuting Attorney Leah Askey's theory that
Russ had showered to wash off his wife's blood after stabbing her to
death and before calling 911.

At the defense table, Russ Faria and his attorneys, Joel Schwartz
and Nate Swanson, were incredulous at the first report of these
water droplets in nearly four years of investigation, dozens of court
hearings, and the first trial. Schwartz's instincts, sharpened in more
than twenty-five years as a defense attorney, told him this convenient, new testimony for the prosecution simply wasn't true.

But Sergeant Mike Pirtle of the Lincoln County Sheriff's Office
had just sworn under oath that he saw the droplets during a preliminary search of the Faria house. He mentioned them to an investigator, but never checked to see if that information made it into any
reports. He found out they were never reported a few months before
this second trial.

Askey had been careful not to overplay the news of the water
droplets. She mentioned them briefly in her opening statement to
Judge Steven Ohmer, noting that Russ told police he had not show-

ered that day. And now she called Pirtle as her ninth witness on the first day of trial and had him explain he had immediately assessed the situation as a murder as soon as he arrived at the Faria house. He ordered everyone out so he could conduct a "protective sweep" to ensure no one else was in the house. He found nothing notable in the living area, the bedrooms, and the guest bathroom.

Askey asked if he had noticed anything in the shower in the master bathroom.

"Yes," he said, "I observed some water drops." He informed investigating officers, but did not write a separate report. Since he was not a member of the Major Case Squad, he returned to his regular patrol duties that night. He had nothing more to do with the Faria investigation and was not aware until recently that the water droplets had not been reported.

Joel Schwartz was shocked, but not surprised. This was not the first piece of evidence Askey had failed to produce for the defense, and he wasn't about to let this new revelation go unchallenged. He cross-examined Pirtle with rapid-fire questions.

Schwartz gestured toward the stacks of documents, reports, and statements surrounding the defense table. "So, just so we're clear, you noticing some water droplets is not in a report—anywhere—with all of this documentation. Correct?"

"That's correct."

"How did you learn that?"

"I believe I was talking to one of the investigators."

Pirtle said he had met with Askey over the summer to tell her. He agreed he was not claiming someone took a shower, just reporting the droplets. There were more than two or three, but he couldn't say how many. He saw nothing else, such as wet walls or drains. After Pirtle said he told Askey, Schwartz put a fine point on his last question. "So you thought it would help her theory in what she was going to present to the court. Right?"

Pirtle didn't bite. "I didn't know what her theory was."

The questions by Schwartz and Askey didn't satisfy the man who would decide Russ Faria's fate. In a rare step, Judge Ohmer leaned forward and began asking his own questions.

"Sergeant, would you describe these water droplets for me?"

"It was water droplets inside of the bathtub that would be quite common with, at one point, there being water in the tub."

"And whereabouts in the tub?"

"About mid tub."

"How big were these droplets?"

"Normal size."

"I don't know what that means."

"Less than a dime size."

Pirtle said there was no pattern to the droplets and he didn't remember if there were any near the drain.

"But that didn't appear in any report or any of the investigations after that?" the judge asked.

"That's correct."

Although Schwartz was aggravated by this dubious new report, he didn't think it would substantially advance Askey's otherwise unsupported theory that Russ had taken a shower. Schwartz thought the testimony about the water droplets, all in all, was a wash.

Although Schwartz had little experience taking a case to a second trial, he knew not to expect an instant replay of the first. Both sides had gone to school on the first one and would try to correct mistakes or misjudgments and prepare responses to the opposition's strong points. But the major pieces of evidence, the critical testimony from essential witnesses, and the basic facts would remain much the same.

Schwartz thought it was telling that Askey never mentioned Pam Hupp in her opening statement, saying only that a friend had driven Betsy home that night. In addition to recounting the familiar allegations against Russ, she offered a couple of new ones. First, the police had recently found the letter Pam said Betsy wrote on her computer describing Russ's increasingly abusive and threatening behavior and her fear of him. The letter was written shortly before Betsy removed Russ as her insurance beneficiary—which Askey recalled without mentioning Pam Hupp was the new beneficiary.

The prosecutor also added a new twist in her attack on the game-night players, accusing them of lying about the sequence of events that evening. Askey now insisted that all four had, at first, told police they played a board game before watching two movies. In Askey's disjointed style, she said, "It's not until the second time that these individuals are interviewed that they all abort the mission that there was any game played at all—and everyone surmises that the detectives got it wrong. . . . Maybe that is through mistake. Maybe it's by design. Maybe it's because they smoked too much dope the night before."

Askey made more questionable comments in personal attacks against Russ. She told the judge that Russ had a mistress since Betsy was first diagnosed with cancer in 2009, the affair continued until the day she died in 2011, and the mistress was pregnant with his child when Betsy died. Schwartz sighed again. Russ had acknowledged a brief relationship with a woman in 2010, but the rest of Askey's allegations were false. And Russ had to stifle his anger at being falsely accused of fathering a child out of wedlock while his wife was dying of cancer.

Schwartz opened his statement to the judge by drawing a sharp contrast between the presentations by the defense and the prosecution. "Judge," he said calmly, "our case will be based on evidence—not theories."

He immediately pulled Pam Hupp into the center of Betsy's murder. She was the only person who knew all about this letter that was recently discovered; and although she said she had never seen it, she knew exactly what was in it. It was written the day before Betsy changed her beneficiary to Pam—and this case came down to that change. Betsy had the policy since 2001, the year after she and Russ married, and Russ remained the beneficiary through their infidelities and separations, through the difficulties with Betsy's daughters, through her initial illness, through her supposed recovery, and then through the diagnosis of recurrent and terminal cancer. But four days after Pam Hupp suddenly became the beneficiary, in what Schwartz described as "an unorthodox fashion," Betsy was murdered.

Schwartz also explained that while police investigated Russ's account of the night in great detail—and proved it to be true—neither the police nor the prosecutors had made any attempt to confirm

Pam's version of her activities. They didn't get an independent account from her husband of when she returned home, what she was wearing, or what she said. They didn't use cell towers to locate her phone during critical times. They didn't conduct a forensic examination of her car. They didn't talk to her neighbors.

"They didn't talk to a soul to confirm anything whatsoever that she said," Schwartz said.

He asked the judge for a verdict of not guilty based on evidence and not on "theory or innuendo."

Askey drew no dramatic new testimony from her first few witnesses. Mariah Day, now twenty-one, and Leah Day, now twenty-five, offered the familiar descriptions of "rocky" family relationships, angry shouting by Russ and Betsy, and Russ's swearing. On cross-examination, Schwartz had Mariah confirm she had found a suicide note written by her mother, which she gave to Russ, and her mother had been hospitalized for a while after that. She agreed she first assumed suicide when she heard her mother was dead.

On redirect, Askey drew Mariah's agreement that Betsy had told one of her sisters that the suicide note was really designed to try to make Mariah feel bad about moving out of the Farias' home in Troy.

Just as she had in the first trial, Askey called a pair of Betsy's sisters as her next witnesses—Pamela Welker and Mary Rodgers. Pamela described an unusually reserved Betsy at Welker's Christmas party the night before Betsy was killed; she assumed her sister was tired and not feeling good.

Schwartz focused on the issue so important to the prosecution. "Mrs. Welker, when the police first spoke to you, your first impression was that Betsy must have committed suicide?"

"Yes . . . she had a lifelong challenge with thinking about that, so it didn't have anything to do with the cancer. She had always struggled with a bit of depression and thinking about the loss of her own life."

Schwartz asked if she had any indication that Betsy was thinking about divorcing Russ.

"I knew they were extremely unhappy. Betsy was trying hard to make her marriage work. She had done some . . . like a counseling session. She was working very hard to try to make the marriage work."

Pamela said she was surprised when Pam Hupp told Betsy's family the morning after the murder that Betsy made Pam the beneficiary. Pam said she would give the money to Leah and Mariah, but Pamela never talked to her again.

Betsy's oldest sister, Mary Rodgers, described the incident in 2004 when she called the police after she claimed Russ pushed Betsy amid a loud, emotional argument among them, Leah, and Mariah. Mary said she heard Russ say "something about cutting her up into bits and pieces and burying her in the backyard."

She agreed with Schwartz that the incident was a long time ago and confirmed she told the police something like she thought Betsy and Russ had worked through their issues and loved each other very much. She also told the police Russ had come a long way since that incident. She was proud of him for earning his college degree. She believed he was now loving and caring for Betsy and they were getting along well.

Mary offered a similar account to Pamela's that Pam Hupp told them she was Betsy's beneficiary, and Betsy wanted the money to go to Leah and Mariah.

Schwartz was surprised when Mary answered his question about being close to Betsy by saying, "We had our ups and downs. Her and I fought the most of any of us."

"You and your sister fought. . . . You and Betsy?"

"Yeah, she got under my skin."

Schwartz had Mary confirm Leah and Mariah had filed a suit against Pam to recover the insurance money. "Because we feel it should be in the family," she explained.

"Well, didn't Betsy assign it to Pam Hupp?"

Mary's voice betrayed frustration as she said, "Well, I don't know what to say about that."

And then Askey set off a minor tremor in the courtroom with a line of redirect questioning that took Schwartz by surprise.

"Mary, the rocky relationship you had with your sister was fairly warranted. Is that fair to say?"

"Yes."

"The defendant had no love for your husband. Is that right?"

Schwartz didn't know where Askey was going, but objected that the questions were beyond the scope of his cross-examination and called for speculation. The judge allowed Askey to try to lay a foundation.

Askey went directly to the heart of her inquiry. "Did your sister admit to you that she had a relationship with your husband?"

"Yes."

Schwartz was taken aback. This was the first he had heard of that. Sitting beside him, however, Russ Faria offered no reaction, exactly as Schwartz had told him to do.

Askey moved ahead. "Did the defendant know about it?"

"Yes."

"And was the defendant furious about it?"

"I think so. . . . The defendant and I never talked about it."

"But you spoke to your sister about it?"

"Yes."

Mary Rodgers had just given Askey another issue she could argue could outrage a husband—one that, in theory, could fester for years and enflame a new anger if the husband also learned he had been removed as a beneficiary to his wife's insurance.

It was always dangerous to cross-examine a witness if he didn't already know the facts, but Schwartz couldn't let Mary Rodgers's testimony stand as it was.

He asked when this relationship happened, and Mary thought it was about 2005, at a time when Betsy and Russ were already separating.

"So, how did you take it?"

"Oh, not real well," she said with a hint of understatement.

"I'm guessing you were pretty darn angry?"

"Yes."

"And I'm guessing Russ was pretty darn angry, too?"

"I'm assuming so, with his temper. Yes."

Mary said she didn't know how Askey found out about it, but she had first questioned her about it within the last month.

"I am assuming you had a few unkind words for your husband?"

"Yes."

"Did you lose your temper?"

"We were already split up at the time."

"OK. That doesn't justify what he did."

"Exactly. I'm not saying that he was right. He's the one that brought it to my attention. He told me of the affair."

"But as far as you knew, Russ and Betsy had worked through that, and as you told the police, they loved each other very much?"

"At least I thought so."

As Askey called Bobbi Wann to the stand, Schwartz was glad she had no more questions for Mary Rodgers. He didn't think the judge would see an affair by Betsy, even with her former brother-in-law, as motive for Russ to kill Betsy. But it was still a fact in the Betsy Faria murder book he hadn't expected.

Bobbi Wann was a somewhat frail-looking eighty-year-old woman who had traveled back to St. Louis from her home in Windsor, California, where she had moved from Texas, to testify. She explained she had known Betsy, Janet Meyer, and their family since they became neighbors in Lake St. Louis in 1969—the year Betsy was born.

Bobbi had been visiting Janet for almost two weeks, on December 27, 2011, when she accompanied Betsy to the chemotherapy session where Pam Hupp said Russ had held a pillow over Betsy's face. Bobbi said Betsy verified that, but didn't provide details. Betsy said Russ was verbally abusive. Betsy also said she had changed the beneficiary on one insurance policy to Pam and wanted to remove Russ as beneficiary on another one: "She wanted to be sure the girls got the money, and Pam Hupp said the money was definitely for the girls and they would get the money." Bobbi said Betsy told her she had filled out the form to change the beneficiary on a second policy, but left it on the counter at home.

Schwartz knew he had to walk a very thin tightrope while facing this delicate witness. He had to challenge the memory of an elderly woman without insulting her or coming off as a bully. The judge might be more understanding of the defense attorney's predicament and tactics than jurors would be. But there was still a risk that he could come off as rude or heavy-handed. Schwartz was certain Bobbi's memory was faulty and there had been no discussion at the chemo session about this alleged incident with the pillow or change in beneficiaries. He was convinced those memories had been planted in discussions with none other than Pam Hupp after the police interviews and while Betsy's family and friends were together before the funeral.

Schwartz's first step onto the tightrope was slow and cautious as he said, "Ms. Wann, you seem like a very nice lady."

"Thank you," she said politely.

In the same soft voice, he added, "And I'm sure you're doing everything and testifying to everything to the best of your recollection. Would you agree with that?"

"Yes." She nodded.

Schwartz had her confirm that Pam Hupp showed up at the chemo session, even though Betsy had told Pam not to come.

"And you were quite surprised?"

"I wasn't as surprised as Betsy was . . . by the look on her face."

"She was uninvited. Correct?"

"She had been told not to come."

She agreed she told the police in her first interview that Betsy was in a great mood and good spirits the day before. She described in some detail the conversation between her, Betsy, and Pam about buying Janet Meyer's former house as a home for the extended family.

And then Schwartz tried to gently approach his concerns about her testimony. Still using a soft and friendly tone, he said, "When you spoke to the police that morning, the next day on the twenty-eighth, you said nothing about insurance?"

"I told you, I was in a state of shock," she said with a slight edge of indignity. "It never occurred to me to say anything about insurance."

"And you also didn't tell them anything about a pillow over the face, did you?"

"I don't recall."

She agreed she found no mention of the pillow incident when she recently read the police reports from her interview. She contradicted herself again when she said she had mentioned the idea about the Farias buying Janet Meyer's house "because that's what brought her death." She then had to admit that she didn't know if Betsy had told Russ about that.

"Between the time you made that initial statement and your second statement, you had seen Pam Hupp? She came to the house?"

"Yes."

"Now, is that when you learned about the insurance?"

"What do you mean, when I 'learned about the insurance'?"

Schwartz swallowed hard and decided it was time to challenge Bobbi Wann's memory. But he stumbled right out of the gate.

"Ms. Hupp, I don't mean to pry. Now, how old are you?"

"My name is *not* Ms. Hupp," she snapped.

Schwartz nodded in embarrassment. "Believe me, I know that. I am *so* sorry if I just called you Ms. Hupp."

Bobbi snapped again on the second half of the perceived insult. "And what does my age have to do with it?"

There was no way to diplomatically handle his concern about her age and memory now, so he retreated. "Well, let's go back. You made a written statement on December thirtieth. Now, we're three days after Betsy had been deceased. Correct?"

Bobbi was in no mood to be cooperative. "If you say so," she answered.

Schwartz asked again if she told police, in either of the two interviews, that Betsy said she had left a policy on the counter or that Russ had held a pillow over Betsy's face?

No, Bobbi admitted.

If she thought they were important enough to mention now, why hadn't she told Betsy's family right after Betsy was murdered and before Pam Hupp told them?

"I don't know."

Schwartz echoed, "You 'don't know,' do you?"

*   *   *

Askey tried to rehabilitate Bobbi Wann's tortured testimony and memory. She agreed there was no way she could have written down or repeated for police everything that Betsy said over the two busy days of December 26 and 27. And the pillow and insurance issues weren't raised by the police to make them seem like essential points to mention.

Plus, Bobbi said, she had never been involved in a police investigation before, especially the murder of an old friend.

"I have never . . . been involved in anything so evil," she said.

Schwartz had to admit that he completely agreed with that appraisal of the murder of Betsy Faria.

CHAPTER FORTY-FOUR

Is the caller the killer?

Dispatchers for 911 call centers are trained to consider the possibility that the caller reporting a homicide may, in fact, be the killer, Margie Harrell, director of communications for Lincoln County 911, told the judge. Questioned by Leah Askey, Harrell dropped a surprising, if unconfirmed, statistic: Data showed that of the twenty-five thousand calls reporting homicides nationally in 2015, 30 percent were placed by the killer. Harrell said dispatchers are trained to analyze how a caller handles factors that can place them on a scale rating the probability that they are actually the killer—called 911 Considering Offender Probability and Statements (COPS).

Harrell said she was trained in applying the scale by weighing specific factors, including whether the caller includes a plea for help, whether there is a sense of urgency, whether the caller asks for help for himself or the victim, whether the caller is providing extraneous information that does not relate directly to the emergency, and how much the caller's voice modulates.

Nate Swanson knew Askey was taking a different tack with this witness than she had in the first trial, when Judge Mennemeyer allowed Harrell to testify that Russ's behavior on the call was out of the norm and therefore suspicious. This time, Askey was clearly leading Harrell to a conclusion that Russ's conduct on the call could put him among the 30 percent of callers who were actually the killers. Swanson would be prepared for that.

Harrell said dispatchers are trained to use "repetitive persistence" in repeatedly asking questions designed to help calm the caller, who may be hysterical, and repeatedly telling the caller to take deep breaths. Dispatchers are trained to handle what is called the "refreak"—renewed hysteria by someone who had calmed down.

Askey then played the recording of Russ's 911 call for the judge. When it ended, she asked Harrell, "Is that what refreak sounds like?"

Swanson immediately objected that Askey was trying to get Harrell to evaluate Russ's call, which the judge had prohibited in pretrial motions. Ohmer sustained the objection.

Askey began a series of questions clearly designed to allow Harrell to compare Russ's comments on the call with the list she said could be made by the actual killer. Swanson's repeated objections were sustained by the judge, shutting down Askey's tactic. When she ended her questioning, Swanson minimized the importance of Harrell's testimony by not asking a single question.

The last witness for the first day of Russ Faria's second trial was Amy Buettner, the crime scene investigator from St. Charles. She had married since she testified in the first trial as Amy Pratt. She estimated she had taken seven hundred photographs inside and outside of the Faria house after she arrived about six o'clock on the morning after the murder. Her search of bathtubs and sinks found no water droplets or other evidence that they had recently been used. When the investigators tested drains in the kitchen and bathrooms for evidence, they were so dry that investigators had to wet the swabs to collect samples.

Nate Swanson began cross-examination by having Buettner agree there was no indication on December 27 and 28 that anyone had tried to clean up evidence in the kitchen or that the bathrooms, showers, or sinks had been used recently. They were dry, as were the towels and shower curtains. No trace of blood was found on any of them.

Buettner said she had refused to conduct luminol tests on the crime scene the morning after the murder, as requested by either Detective Patrick Harney or another detective. She would only apply luminol if there was evidence a body had been moved or a crime scene had been cleaned up—clearly, not the case here. The scene had been "extremely contaminated" by other investigators by the time she arrived, and, she added, it would have been even more contaminated by the time police applied luminol on January 3, 2012.

Before Askey asked her to take Sicily's prints, Buettner said she had never taken a dog's paw prints. She noted the dog—described as "aggressive" by Pam Hupp—was scared, timid, and quiet as Buettner took her paw prints and photographed each paw. She found no visible blood anywhere on the dog and wanted to take tests for blood that might not be visible, but was told not to by Detective Harney.

Swanson questioned Buettner extensively about the State's only two pieces of physical evidence—the blood-marked slippers and the bloodstained switch plate. She said the blood on the switch plate contained two patterns—one a crisscross pattern, which seemed to have been made by a piece of cloth, and the second, "more wavy" one, but she called it indistinguishable. She also said she did not find any bloody footprints except for one that was made accidentally by an officer from Lincoln County. She agreed with Swanson that the bloodstains on the slippers appeared to have been made from someone swiping them in blood rather than someone stepping in blood.

Swanson asked, "This was a very bloody crime scene?"

"Around the victim, it was, yes."

"That blood would have gotten on the assailant. Correct?"

"Yes."

"It would be almost impossible for someone to commit the crime and have no blood on them?"

"It would be impossible."

CHAPTER FORTY-FIVE

Tuesday, November 3, 2015—*second day of Russ Faria's second trial*

Less than three weeks before Russ Faria's new trial started, Detective Mike Merkel had been one of the most unrepentantly obstinate and blatantly obnoxious cops Nate Swanson had ever tried to depose. But testifying in a trial is a completely different experience and Joel Schwartz had been looking forward to cross-examining Merkel on the witness stand.

On the second day of the trial, Schwartz waited patiently as Askey had Merkel describe arriving at the scene, concluding the victim had been murdered, and observing that her face and arms were covered in blood and nearby bags of Christmas presents were marked by blood spatter.

Was the blood wet?

"I can't say it was wet," he said. "It appeared to be. It didn't . . . Some of it appeared to be wet, and some of it appeared to have been drying."

Askey asked Merkel to describe Russ's displays of emotion during four and a half hours of interviews.

"There was a certain amount of effect to it. It seemed as though his emotions came to light more so when he was by himself in the room and there was seemingly no one around. I mean, and it was . . . it seemed to be over the top. It seemed to be very exaggerated and put on, so to speak."

Schwartz thought it was another absurdity by the authorities to believe that Russ was faking or exaggerating his grief to look innocent when there was no one in the room with him to witness the display. Another allegation by the cops that made no sense.

Merkel described the application of Bluestar in several rooms to test for blood residue on January 3, 2012, and said the police camera malfunctioned, affecting the way the photos came out. But he said his report showed that the Bluestar glowed as a positive indication of the possible presence of blood on a number of floor tiles in the kitchen and dining room and on some of the kitchen cabinet faces.

After the lunch break, Schwartz warmed up Merkel for cross-examination with a few pointed questions about his activities over the last ninety minutes. Merkel's responses suggested that he didn't intend to be any more cooperative than he was at the deposition.

"Officer Merkel, before I start, did you spend the lunch break talking to anybody about what I might ask you?"

"Talked about the case a little bit."

"With who?"

"A couple of people. I mean—"

"Who?" Schwartz asked more insistently. He wasn't surprised when Merkel still dodged a straight answer.

"There was a lunchroom sitting there—I'm not really sure who—asking me how things were going, and that was about it."

"You didn't talk with Ms. Askey about the case?"

"We talked about a couple of things briefly."

"What did you talk about?"

"I can't recall the specifics of it. Just—"

"You can't recall, like an hour ago?"

"Just this case in general."

Schwartz decided to let the judge draw his own conclusion about Merkel's attitude. Judges instruct jurors that when they assess a witness's credibility that they can take into consideration a witness's demeanor while testifying. Schwartz was certain Ohmer would follow that advice himself.

But Schwartz was surprised when Merkel was more responsive

and direct during a detailed series of questions about his interview with Russ. Often referring to his own reports, Merkel agreed Russ gave him exactly the account of his activities that he had given everyone all along. Merkel said it would have been obvious to almost anyone seeing Betsy's body that she had not committed suicide. But he also agreed that he did not know then about Betsy's suicidal threats, lifelong depression, and recent death sentence from cancer.

Schwartz led Merkel through accounts of the emotional breakdowns Russ suffered while alone in the interview room. Russ didn't know his every move and sound were recorded by a video camera hidden in the wall and a microphone in the ceiling. Schwartz thought that made any allegation that Russ was faking his grief for the benefit of the police ridiculous.

Plus, Merkel said he used techniques he learned in training to calm Russ so he could answer questions. That didn't sound like Russ was faking it, either.

And then Schwartz started the line of questioning he had been anticipating for some time. Reading from a transcript of the first trial, Schwartz reminded Merkel that he had testified that the photos of Bluestar application at the Farias' house showed "absolutely nothing."

Schwartz said, "And then I asked, 'Why,' and you said, 'Because of a malfunction in our camera, which has since been repaired.' Is that correct?"

"Yes, sir."

"So there were no pictures that were developed that day?"

"I don't believe so. No, sir."

Schwartz handed Merkel a manila envelope containing a thick stack of documents and asked him to identify them. Merkel quickly glanced at them and said, "It would be the photographs from that day."

Schwartz also handed copies of the photos to Askey, who asked quietly, "Where did you get these?"

He ignored the question. He could almost hear the steel jaws of a trap springing shut, snaring the cop in a lie and the prosecution in an unethical failure to disclose evidence to the defense. They didn't know a computer disc with those photographs had been delivered anonymously to Schwartz's office.

Using Merkel's own words against him, Schwartz asked if the photos in Merkel's hands showed "absolutely nothing."

Merkel tried to hedge. "As far as chemical luminescence, no, sir, it does not."

"Well, that's not what I asked you back in November of 2013, was it?"

"It is open for interpretation, but yes, sir."

Schwartz pointed at the images in the photographs as his voice rose in surprise. "That's 'open for interpretation'? Your answer was 'absolutely nothing.' There's how many . . . Do you know how many pictures are there?"

"There's a lot."

"There's about one hundred thirty of them, aren't there? Actually, one hundred thirty-two, if my count was correct."

Looking at the envelope, Merkel said, "I believe that's what it says here, yes, sir."

Schwartz pointed at the photographs and said, "And there is not any of those that show 'absolutely nothing,' is there?"

"No, sir," Merkel said.

Schwartz asked Merkel to pick a photograph randomly and describe what it showed. Merkel took one he said appeared to be the "returned inventory," without explaining what that meant.

"All right. So that shows something. It is not 'absolutely nothing,' is it?"

"No, sir, it is not."

Merkel described another photo as being a "general view" and another as showing a sink drain.

"When you testified under oath in trial that there was 'absolutely nothing' that developed from those pictures—is that 'absolutely nothing'?"

"No, sir, it is not," Merkel said again.

Askey tried to limit the damage by objecting that Schwartz was mischaracterizing the testimony from the first trial. The judge overruled her, adding, "It is cross-examination."

Schwartz handed Merkel more photos of that sink drain that also showed nearby drawer fronts that had been removed, a view under the sink, parts of the floor in the kitchen and dining room with placards marking spots that had glowed, and pieces of linoleum tile that had been removed. For each photo, Schwartz had Merkel agree it did not show "absolutely nothing." Asked what the lab tests of those items showed, Merkel said he didn't know for sure, but had been told there was no blood on any of them.

Schwartz suspected he had made his point with the judge, and any more questioning about the photos might be overload. But he wanted to ring the bell one more time.

"When you testified in 2013 . . . the picture showed 'absolutely nothing' . . . you just saw approximately one hundred thirty pictures of something?"

"Yes, sir."

"And this is *not* 'absolutely nothing'?"

"Correct."

Askey quickly tried to rehabilitate Merkel's testimony by having him explain that what he actually meant when he said "absolutely nothing" was "We were unable to capture the luminescence in the photographs." She showed him several of the photos again and asked, "Did you mean that all of these photographs . . . that you couldn't see anything?"

"No, ma'am, I did not mean that."

Schwartz came back for more cross-examination. What did a murder involving fifty-five stab wounds indicate in light of Merkel's training and experience?

"It's usually a crime of passion—extreme emotion. . . . There's a close personal relationship. It's an act that's fueled by emotion."

Schwartz asked if Betsy's murder could have been staged to look like a crime of passion and rage. Merkel said that would be speculation and setting up Betsy's murder to look like passion and rage would have been "a whole lot of work." He agreed with Schwartz that Russ Faria had no blood on him anywhere, which Schwartz saw as evidence that Russ had not done that "whole lot of work" to stage Betsy's murder to look like a crime of passion.

*   *   *

When Major Ray Floyd spent almost two hours accusing Russ Faria of killing his wife, the cop didn't know that Pam Hupp had just days before become the beneficiary to Betsy's life insurance. He knew she was the last person known to see Betsy alive, but he didn't know that Betsy failed to answer three arranged phone calls from her daughter in the twenty-five minutes after Pam had driven her home. He didn't know that Pam placed a call to Betsy's cell phone barely twenty minutes after they arrived at Betsy's house. He didn't know she told the police that she did not go into the house with Betsy and then later said she did. He knew four of Russ's friends said he was with them thirty minutes from the scene of Betsy's murder until nine o'clock at night. And Floyd also told Schwartz under cross-examination that, by the time he interviewed Russ, he and other members of the Major Case Squad had already concluded that he had killed Betsy.

"Your belief is he got home that night, murdered Betsy, and then somehow, in that short period of time, cleaned up and got rid of all the evidence. Is that your belief?"

"That's a possibility," Floyd said in what seemed a disgracefully weak defense of the police investigation.

"Do you know if anybody ever, if you know, talked to Pam Hupp's husband?"

"That I don't know."

"Neighbors?"

"That I don't know."

"Friends?"

"That I don't know."

"Even though she was the last one with her and got the life insurance policy, you have no information . . ."

"Once again, I was assigned the leads and I followed the leads I was assigned," said the cop who had told Russ Faria that the police investigation pointed only at him as the killer.

He had told Russ that other witnesses reported his relationship with Betsy as "rocky," adding, without naming Pam Hupp, "This is coming from a friend that she's confided in."

Floyd had told Russ he was the only one with a motive: "Money. It's the oldest motive in the world."

And he was the one who discounted Russ's insistence that Betsy was dead when he got home by saying, "She hadn't been dead hardly at all when the police got there—less than an hour."

And now he was defending his role in charging an innocent man with murder by defining his job as a homicide detective as just following the leads he was assigned.

Schwartz thought all of that was a miserable excuse for police work.

CHAPTER FORTY-SIX

Just touching a body does not provide an accurate assessment of whether rigor mortis has set in or what the temperature of the body is.

Dr. Kamal Sabharwal, the medical examiner for St. Louis County, had described the fifty-five wounds Betsy Faria suffered and now was supporting Leah Askey's argument that Betsy could have been killed shortly before the police arrived. Askey didn't mention the reports from first responders who said Betsy's body was cold and stiff, but the doctor said just touching a body would not provide much useful information.

Determining the state of rigor mortis required manipulation of the arms and legs and even the jaw. Different parts of the body also would feel different to the touch. And while the skin may feel cool, the inner parts of the body may still be much warmer.

Askey asked, "On a typical situation, would you ever, in a matter of two and a half hours, expect a body to be cold and stiff?"

"No," he said, adding there are many factors—room temperature, a cold floor, a blowing fan—that could contribute to the rate at which a body cools and when rigor mortis sets in.

Joel Schwartz asked if rigor mortis could set in faster in someone undergoing chemotherapy. That was possible, the doctor said, and individual body chemistry and the circumstances of death could cause varying rates for rigor mortis to occur.

Despite the doctor's explanations, Schwartz thought it was absurd to suggest Betsy was killed after 9:30 p.m. and her body was already cold and stiff to the touch twenty minutes or so later. That theory—with its lack of evidence—simply defied common sense.

"Detective McCarrick, one of the big questions is," Askey began, "why the heck didn't anyone investigate Pam Hupp? Certain leads weren't assigned to get information from her. So you get that, why we're here?"

"Yes," McCarrick said in his first testimony in a trial of Russ Faria.

"Why would that be, that certain leads wouldn't be assigned that the defense would have liked to have happened back in 2011?"

"At this point in the investigation, we didn't find any reason that Pam Hupp needed to be investigated any further than she was."

"It's fair to say Major Case isn't above making mistakes?"

"Correct."

"And that probably happens in every case?"

"It sure does."

"Hindsight's twenty/twenty?"

"It is—and we're human."

Schwartz was mildly surprised by this turn in Askey's questioning of the lead detective. Drawing McCarrick's testimony that he found no reason to investigate Pam Hupp was expected, but adding an implication that the only-human detectives of the Major Case Squad could have been wrong not to investigate her seemed a dangerous admission that she could have been a viable suspect then and, therefore, still could be one now.

Askey had McCarrick confirm that Pam Hupp consented to everything the police asked her to do.

"Did she ever show any sign of deception?"

"No."

Schwartz couldn't believe he had heard that correctly. "What was that question?" he inquired. "I didn't hear the question."

Askey repeated, "I said, 'Did she ever show any sign of deception?'"

Schwartz nodded. He had heard correctly—and he thought the prosecutor and the detective had just admitted not recognizing or, worse, ignoring the long list of suspicious contradictions and outrageous lies that were at the very core of everything Pam Hupp said about Betsy Faria's life and death.

Askey wanted more support for Pam Hupp. "So, when the detectives came back, they didn't report to the Major Case Squad command post, 'We think this gal is lying. We need to go back and do something different'?"

"Correct."

Askey moved to McCarrick's discussion with Pam about opening a trust for Betsy's daughters before the first trial. Schwartz thought McCarrick was rewriting history as he answered, "I told her I didn't care what she did with it, as long as she made a decision so that everybody knew what her intentions were. I told her that the family was obviously upset because they had no idea what she was going to do with it."

Before using cross-examination to challenge McCarrick's exculpatory conclusions about Pam Hupp, Schwartz addressed what he believed was grievous misconduct by the detective. McCarrick agreed that even though he knew Russ Faria had invoked his right to remain silent and was represented by a lawyer, he had Russ brought to an interview room from his jail cell to show him the letter from State Farm Insurance, which McCarrick had opened. It informed Russ that he had been removed as beneficiary on Betsy's policy—the first time Russ had heard that. McCarrick asked Russ if there was anything he wanted to say in light of the letter.

"So, what was your purpose in reading him the letter? You just wanted to see him?"

"I wanted to make sure he knew about it."

"Why? You're just a caring guy?"

McCarrick ignored the sarcasm. "It is my job as a policeman to make sure everybody is aware of what is going on." He said he didn't ask Russ any "guilt-seeking questions," so he didn't do anything wrong by meeting with a defendant without his lawyer present.

Schwartz then moved to McCarrick's revised history—his pressure on Pam Hupp to set up a trust for Betsy's daughters. McCarrick said he interviewed her on June 25, 2012, to clear up differences in her statements to police and prepare her for questions he expected Schwartz to ask when she testified.

Had McCarrick repeatedly urged her to set up a trust fund before the first trial so it would look good?

Yes, and he added, "Wanted it to look good for whatever was going to be the purpose of it." He didn't know how many times he asked her in what he said was a five-minute conversation about it. But she told him her intention was to give the money to the girls and she promised to set up the trust before the trial.

Did he know she withdrew almost all of the money from the trust within days after Russ was convicted?

He had heard that.

McCarrick denied asking Betsy's family not to sue Pam Hupp over the money until after the trial or calling Betsy's friend Rita Wolf and asking her not to pressure the family to sue Pam.

Schwartz cited some of the differences in Pam's statements to police.

"You don't call those lies, though? They're 'differences'?" Schwartz asked.

"Correct."

McCarrick confirmed that he never checked cell tower records to determine where Pam Hupp was when she called Betsy at 7:27 p.m. He did not know whether Russ's cell phone records would contradict Askey's allegation that Russ listened to the voice mail left by Janet Meyer while he was at game night. He agreed that the only pieces of evidence regarding Pam's whereabouts after she left Betsy's house were her location when she called Betsy at 7:27 p.m. and what her husband told police the next morning. But he agreed Mark Hupp never told police what time his wife arrived at home.

"Nobody followed up and went to talk to him to do an actual, real interview, did they?"

"If they've done it since I've left, I don't know that."

"Nobody ever checked or seized his cell phone to see where that was. . . . Nobody checked with the neighbors to see when Pam got home, right?"

"Not to my knowledge, no."

"Can you say where she was when Betsy was killed?"

"No."

"Is there anybody that can say where she was when Betsy was killed?"

"No."

"What did she gain when Betsy died?"

"One hundred fifty thousand dollars."

"And that one hundred fifty thousand dollars had been in a policy directed to Russ Faria since 2001. Correct?"

"Correct."

Schwartz thought McCarrick had just documented an inexcusable failure by the authorities to recognize an obvious suspect and to make even the most basic inquiries about her activities—all while accepting at face value a series of outrageous lies and inexplicable contradictions in almost everything she said.

Schwartz turned back to the insurance and McCarrick confirmed he had told State Farm about two weeks after the murders that they could release the funds to Pam Hupp because she was not a suspect. Schwartz brought up the beneficiary form and McCarrick agreed that, even though Betsy lived in Troy and Pam lived in O'Fallon, the form incorrectly listed Betsy's residence as O'Fallon, with the zip code for O'Fallon.

Schwartz wished commenting on the evidence was allowed in court. He would love to have noted that seemed like extremely unlikely errors for Betsy to have made if she filled out the form. Did those errors weigh against Betsy being the one who completed the beneficiary change form?

Askey had no redirect questions for McCarrick, but Schwartz knew that wouldn't end the cop's participation in the trial; he would be back.

* * *

Askey's next witness was Lauren Manganelli, the librarian who had reluctantly signed as witness on the beneficiary form. She identified a photo of Betsy as the woman who asked her to sign the form that already had been filled out and had a signature that said Elizabeth Faria.

While the librarian was signing as a witness, the woman explained her intent: "She said that she was just changing her beneficiary because she was getting a divorce and she wanted to make sure her children could be on the form someday."

Manganelli agreed with Schwartz that she had no idea if that statement was true.

For almost four years, Joel Schwartz had argued that the only physical evidence the State could say linked Russ to Betsy's murder—Russ's house slippers and the switch plate—didn't prove a damned thing, and, in fact, both of them could well be seen as proof he was being framed. But he had listened again as Daniel Fahnestock, the technician from the St. Charles County Sheriff's Department Crime Lab, repeated his conclusions.

DNA in the blood on the outside of the slippers proved it was Betsy's. DNA samples inside both slippers were mixtures from two people; Russ was the major contributor, the second contributor could not be positively identified, and Betsy could not be ruled out. The blood on the switch plate also was a mixture of DNA from two people. Betsy was the major contributor and the other was a male, but that sample was too small to identify.

Fahnestock said only one kitchen tile showed a reaction to luminol, indicating the possible presence of blood, but additional tests found no blood. A stain on Betsy's pants was human blood, but couldn't be linked to a source. When Askey asked if that was the stain that resembled a paw print, the judge sustained Swanson's objection that the question assumed facts not in evidence.

Nate Swanson quickly dispatched the physical evidence by having Fahnestock confirm there was no blood found on the floor tiles, the kitchen cabinet doors or drawer fronts, in the drains and pipes, inside Russ's slippers, or on any of the clothes Russ was wearing that night.

*   *   *

Cross-examining Janet Meyer was not as delicate as questioning Bobbi Wann, but Schwartz still had to be careful. Janet testified for Askey that it was unusual for Russ not to return a call to her when it concerned Betsy, as did her call to him at 8:57 p.m. while he was at game night. Janet said she always called him from her home phone, so he should have recognized her number.

Schwartz focused on more important issues. Janet agreed that she had told police Betsy and Russ had a great relationship, but Betsy's relationship with her daughters was "a bit rocky." Moving quickly to the change in insurance beneficiaries, Schwartz asked if Betsy would cut her daughters out of their inheritance.

"No, no. She wanted the money for them."

"Right. As a matter of fact, a month or so before her death, Betsy had been . . . telling you specifically that you, Russ, and the girls would be well taken care of with her insurance. Correct?"

"That's what she said, yes."

And then he moved to Pam Hupp. Janet agreed she had categorized her as Betsy's "tenth or twentieth best friend." And she agreed that she referred to her, as Schwartz put it, as a "moneygrubbing not-a-nice-word"—deciding to omit the witness's earlier spelled-out description as a "B.I.T.C.H."

Janet followed suit as she explained, "I said she was not a murderess, but she was a moneygrubbing . . ."

"But you don't know if she is a murderess, do you?"

"I believe she is not. That's my opinion."

Janet changed her position from the first trial and insisted the police made a mistake when they quoted her as saying Pam said she had not gone into the house. "Pam Hupp told me she went into the house after Betsy went in and turned the lights on," she said.

Schwartz thought that was another example of a memory altered during four years of conversations with family and friends.

Schwartz also thought Betsy's mother had hardened her feelings toward Russ over the years. She suggested that with a comment to Askey in redirect examination that she thought Russ had gotten "meaner and nastier verbally" in the month before Betsy's death.

"And I told him one time, 'Russ, you're really scaring me talking like this.' He just changed. Got worse. More violent in his talk."

As uncomfortable as it would be, Schwartz decided he had to question Janet's memories of Russ. He reminded her they had talked about all of that when he took her deposition more than two years ago. "Now, I asked you about Russ and Betsy's relationship and your and Russ's relationship."

"Russ and I had a really good relationship most of the marriage."

"You said you were close?"

"Yeah, we were. Hurts like heck, what happened."

"And I asked you about Russ and Betsy's relationship and you never said anything about it had gotten worse, did you?"

"No, but it did—I guess."

"You said Russ respected you?"

"Yes, I think he did. Yes, he did."

"And you said he was good to your daughter?"

"He was good to me."

"And he was good to your daughter?"

"Yes and no."

Schwartz left it there. It wouldn't serve anyone to try any harder to shake her memories.

Rita Wolf didn't mince words: Detective Ryan McCarrick lied when he testified that he never spoke to her about not pushing Betsy's family to sue Pam Hupp to recover the insurance money before Russ Faria's first trial. Rita, a friend of Betsy's since they were high-school freshmen in 1983, told Askey she didn't think McCarrick would intentionally lie about it and must have forgotten their phone conversation. But just seconds later, she told Nate Swanson, "It is a lie."

Swanson asked, "You were in here when Detective McCarrick said he'd never spoken with you. Correct?"

"Yes."

"That's not true?"

"That is correct. It's a lie."

"Not just a difference? It's a lie?" Swanson asked as if to define the difference for McCarrick and his view of the many "differences" in the stories told by Pam Hupp.

"Yes. It's incorrect."

"He had an extensive conversation with you. Correct?"

"Correct."

She agreed Swanson was repeating McCarrick's exact words when he asked if McCarrick told her this was *not* his "first rodeo," he wanted her to "lay off" the family about suing Pam Hupp until after Russ's trial, and it would be better for the trial if she did.

Rita said she had a lengthy phone conversation with McCarrick while she was driving home from a work-related trip. "He was wanting me to quit forcing the issue of them suing at that time. He wanted them to wait until after the trial," she said.

Rita had talked to Betsy's sister Mary Rodgers several times about suing Pam Hupp immediately. She told Mary, "I think Pam will spend that money so fast and the girls will never see it. And I was adamant about it because I knew what Betsy's wishes were."

Rita and Betsy had talked "quite a few times" about the best way to make sure her daughters were taken care of financially after her death. Betsy was worried that Russ might mismanage the insurance money and even asked Rita if she and her husband would serve as beneficiaries on a policy. Rita replied it was more appropriate to choose a beneficiary from Betsy's sisters.

Rita urged Betsy to write notarized instructions for how the money should be distributed to the girls. Betsy had set amounts to go to the girls when they reached educational, vocational, or career mileposts or got married. The last time they discussed it, Betsy had decided to make another sister, Julie Swaney, the beneficiary to "help make sure the money went to the appropriate daughter at the right time."

Swanson asked Rita why Betsy thought Russ might spend all of the money.

"Well, the impression I got was, out of grief, he would spend it all."

"Your impression was that she was fine with the beneficiaries on the other policies, correct?"

"Yes."

"And that would have been Mr. Faria, correct?"

"I would assume. I mean, I didn't know. She never really talked about that at all."

"In the year or so leading up to her death, did Betsy ever talk to you about divorcing Russ?"

"Never."

"Did she talk to you about being scared of Russ?"

"No."

"Did she talk to you about being threatened by Russ?"

"No."

Rita recalled that she and Russ once "butted heads" during a Super Bowl party because they were both strong-willed people who didn't always see eye to eye. But she said she had never observed "outrage and yelling" by Russ, adding, "I have never seen him verbally abuse Betsy."

The mysterious letter that Pam Hupp said Betsy wrote describing Russ's troubling behavior days before her death—the letter no one but Pam knew about—had been found. Detective Robert O'Neal of the St. Charles City Police Department, currently detached to the St. Charles County Cyber Crime Task Force, said he found it during a deep search of Betsy's laptop. His analysis of the computer's metadata showed it was opened with Betsy's profile and password on December 22, 2011, and the letter was written in fifteen minutes between 11:55 a.m. and 12:10 p.m. that day. Titled "P.doc," it was saved to the hard drive as soon as it was completed. It was opened again at 2:10 p.m. that day, one minute before an Outlook email program was opened. Just before it was written, O'Neal told Askey, there had been a search of "stationery templates"—different types of backgrounds and designs for a document. "Love, Betsy" had been typed three times in three different fonts.

When Askey asked for a copy of the letter to be admitted as evidence, Swanson objected that it had not been authenticated. Judge Ohmer overruled the objection and the following became evidence, with all of its misspellings, typos, and grammatical issues left uncorrected:

Pam,

I know we talked about this yesterday, but I feel I really need you to believe me. I really do feel that Russ is going to do something to me. Last night (Wednesday), he asked me why I came home instead of staying at my moms. I told him I had things to do. He was very angry with me for being in the house. I couldn't figure out why. Then I caught him with my lap top. He was reading my emails. When I asked him about it he said he could do what he wants. He said I won't be around much longer, so what do I care. He continued to tell me how much money he would make after I die. He has been talking about this for months. He wants me to stay at my moms, he likes the house to himself. He tells me it's his house and I'm just a guest. Right now I stay at my moms, linda's or a friends for most of the week. I was home last night and have to go back on Friday for the weekend. My mom has a friend staying with her from out of town, so Idont have a bed to sleep in. Last night was the worst. I fell a sleep on the couch watching tv. I woke up to Russ holding a pillow over my face. I didn't know what was going on. He said that he wanted me to know what dying feels like. I need to change my life insurance policy out of his name, but can't let him know that I have taken him off as beneficiary. I need your help with this. I cant give it to my girls because they will blow it. Do you think I could put it in your name and you could help my daughters when they need it? I really need to talk to you about this. I am so tired from the cancer. I am so afraid of staying in Troy alone with Russ. If something happens to me would you please show this to the police

O'Neal testified there was no way to verify the origin of the document, who used Betsy's profile and password to open the computer, who wrote the document, who might have seen it, whether the content was truthful, where the laptop was when it was written, whether the document was typed or "cut and pasted" from another document, or even if there was an Outlook email account on the laptop. O'Neal said he couldn't tell if the letter had been emailed to anyone.

"You're not aware that Betsy Faria used Web mail exclusively and did not use Outlook?" Swanson asked.

"I did not know that," O'Neal replied.

Swanson and Schwartz thought the letter screamed that Pam Hupp had written it to support her effort to frame Russ Faria and had planted it on Betsy's laptop for the police to find. And they weren't surprised that the police and Askey happily bought Pam's story about it as more incriminating evidence against Russ.

Leah Askey wanted State Farm Insurance agent Kathy Peterson to testify that she called police after getting an angry and threatening phone call from someone claiming to be Russ Faria's sister inquiring about Betsy's life insurance. Schwartz and Swanson objected that there was no proof of who actually made the call, the caller did not use the correct name for Russ's sister, and any account of what the caller said would be inadmissible hearsay. Judge Ohmer ruled that Peterson could not repeat the content of the call, but could testify about her own actions. Askey was restricted to having Peterson say she got the call on January 5, 2012, the day after Russ was arrested, and she immediately called the police.

Schwartz then turned Askey's witness to the defense's favor. Peterson testified she knew Pam Hupp and believed she had been fired by State Farm for what Schwartz called "alleged forgery."

Askey tried to blunt that by having Peterson agree that the police brought Pam and Mark Hupp to Peterson's office to say they did not place the call Peterson had received.

Schwartz explained that he had not meant to imply that Pam Hupp made the call. "But you do know Pam Hupp and you do know that she was fired for allegedly forging documents. Correct?"

"That is my understanding."

Schwartz had just been able to use a prosecution witness who added nothing to the State's case to confirm reports that Pam Hupp was fired for engaging in illegal activity related to insurance policies in the past. That was a clear win for the defense.

CHAPTER FORTY-SEVEN

Thursday, November 5, 2015—*fourth day of Russ Faria's second trial*

Russ Faria's old friend Jimmy Crenshaw took the witness stand and immediately became every prosecutor's worst nightmare. He testified he never said what the police wrote in their reports and denied making other statements—even after Leah Askey warned him she had him on video. He never said he saw an altercation involving Russ at Betsy's funeral, but did tell police he had heard about it.

Did he tell police that Russ said the last time he saw Betsy, she was on the couch?

"No, I did not."

Askey had to resort to the old cliché. "Sir, do you realize that perjury is a crime?"

"Yes, I do. He did not tell me that."

For the first time, Askey put the name of the woman she called Russ's mistress on the record, even though she didn't explain the reference when she asked if Jimmy knew Darlene Fuller. He said they had known each other since they were sixteen and had dated "for about three days."

All Schwartz needed from him was a quick recollection about Fuller.

"Has Darlene Fuller ever lied to you about trying to cause problems in your relationship?"

"She tried when my first wife and I got together. But that was, like I said, when we were seventeen."

"So she's lied and tried to cause problems for you?"

"Oh, yeah."

The next witness said Jimmy Crenshaw had indeed told police he saw a woman slap Russ so hard she knocked him out of his chair at the funeral home. Harry Belcher, a retired police officer who now worked as an investigator for Askey's office, said Jimmy made that statement when he and Detective Patrick Harney were interviewing him. Askey wanted to know if Jimmy had relayed what the woman who slapped Russ said to him, but the question clearly caught the judge's attention.

Belcher started to reply, "She said . . ." and the judge interrupted, asking, "Who? Wait a minute. Who said—"

Nate Swanson jumped in with a hearsay objection, but the judge was already digging in.

"*She* said?" the judge asked.

Askey responded, "This person who slapped him."

The judge was not having any part of that question. "Wait. Sustained." He turned to Askey and said, "You're asking for what this witness, Crenshaw, said. Now you're getting into double hearsay. You're trying to impeach Crenshaw. You can't do it with double hearsay. Sustained."

Askey asked Belcher if, at her request, he had looked into rumors and allegations in the media about Pam Hupp being fired from an insurance office for fraud. He said state records showed her license as an insurance agent remained in good standing until it recently expired.

Belcher also testified that he had concluded that the bloody pattern on the switch plate matched the design of the soles of Russ's slippers. Photo transparencies of the two patterns were adjusted so they were the same size, and while the match was not 100 percent perfect, he could say the sole "sure looks like that's the pattern that made that pattern on the light switch."

And he offered the same kind of conclusion about the mark on Betsy's pants: "It appears to me that pattern was made by the dog paw print."

Schwartz didn't think Belcher's conclusions had much credibility. Schwartz produced the photos showing the pattern on the slipper sole and on the switch plate.

"It's actually not the same pattern, is it?"

"I believe it is."

"You have no training in this area?"

"As far as . . . what type of training are you referring to?"

Schwartz thought that nonanswer was answer enough. "And you don't know if this was made by some sort of cloth. Do you?"

"I can . . . The only thing I can say is it appears to be made by that shoe pattern."

"That's only because you can find nothing else in the house that could have made this pattern." Schwartz didn't wait for a response as he pointed to different areas in the photo of the switch plate. "There's actually two patterns on here. Correct?"

Belcher seemed surprised. "Oh?"

As Schwartz indicated the two areas, Belcher said, "There's one definite pattern. The other part that I think you're referring to just looks like, you know, some blood."

"You have no idea what deposited that there. Do you?"

"I can't say one hundred percent for sure what deposited it there, but I can say it looks like it was from that shoe."

Schwartz thought Belcher's untrained opinion was just another prosecution theory. It certainly wasn't evidence and lacked the credibility to be taken seriously.

Darlene Fuller grew up with Russ Faria and dated him when she was thirteen or fourteen. And, she told Askey, they dated briefly in 2010, while Betsy was undergoing her first round of chemotherapy. Darlene denied telling police that she and Russ would meet for sex after he dropped Betsy off for chemo. She said they met on her lunch hour a couple of times for a drink and conversation before he would go to meet Betsy when her chemotherapy started at one o'clock. They took a camping trip together—"as friends," she said—on Memorial Day weekend in 2010.

Darlene said she wrote to Russ after he went to prison.

"Did you tell him that you had his baby?"

"Yeah, yeah . . . I lied."

Askey had Darlene confirm that she sent photos of a baby to Russ and commented on how much the baby looked like him. Implying that she told Russ she had given up the child for adoption, Darlene agreed that she told him she wanted to get the baby back.

"Yeah. I lied," she said again. She didn't know if Russ believed he was the father.

Clearly frustrated by noncommittal answers from the witness, Askey said she could play the recordings of calls between Darlene and Russ in prison to refresh her memory.

Judge Ohmer didn't like the prosecutor's threat. "You know, counsel, it is your trial. You try the case. I will make the ruling."

"Well, I'm—"

The judge interrupted her. "Don't suggest or comment. That's improper, counsel, and I don't appreciate it. You proceed and we'll go from there. I don't like you asking, 'Well, I could do this, or I could that.' Do what you want to do, and I'll rule."

Good for you, Your Honor, Schwartz thought. It was good to see Askey held to the rules.

Schwartz used a short, rapid-fire cross-examination to confirm that Darlene Fuller's brief relationship with Russ ended in September 2010 and she never told Russ in the fifteen months between then and Betsy's death that she was pregnant, that she had a baby, or that she gave up a baby for adoption. She agreed she told Russ all of those lies in 2014 after he was in prison.

Detective Sergeant Patrick Harney of the Lincoln County Sheriff's Office was Leah Askey's cleanup hitter—and her last witness.

He testified first that he and Investigator Harry Belcher worked together to compare transparencies of the soles of the house slippers to the bloody pattern on the switch plate. Harney agreed with Belcher's conclusion, saying, "It appears that the shoe print is consistent with the marks left on the light switch."

Schwartz knew this detective's role in the Faria investigation was more pivotal than Askey's brief questioning suggested—and his cross-examination would not be so quick or painless. Harney participated in several interviews of Pam Hupp, and Schwartz was about to use him to catalogue her suspicious litany of always-changing, contradictory stories and outrageous new allegations.

With quick, point-by-point questions, Schwartz went through a long list of statements by Pam Hupp that Harney agreed she had made directly to him, that he had read in other detectives' reports, or that, if he didn't remember them, he would accept as accurate, since Schwartz was reading from other police reports. Harney didn't dispute Schwartz's count of thirteen police interviews with Pam Hupp.

Harney agreed that the first time Pam Hupp ever alleged she and Betsy Faria had a sexual relationship was in June 2015, three and a half years after the murder, and just five months before this trial. She said the sex began in 2006 and that Betsy "really, really, really loved" her and "she was in love with me." She said Russ had caught her and Betsy together and threatened to kill Pam. Just weeks before the murder, Russ shoved Pam against a wall, put his arm across her neck, called her and Betsy "effing muff bumpers," and warned that if he ever caught them again, he would stab Pam and bury her in the backyard.

Schwartz thought the entire story Pam had just told was pure fiction—just more lies—perhaps even copied from the story Mary Rodgers had told about Russ threatening her.

Schwartz asked what seemed like a logical question a detective would ask after hearing that account of violent threats by their murder suspect against an important witness. "Did you ever say, 'Why haven't you told this to anybody before?'"

"I don't believe I said that."

Harney told Schwartz he accepted as accurate police reports that quoted Pam saying Russ was a nice guy, who was nice to her in the three times she had met him, and "'I don't really know him that much. . . . Though he's always been very nice to me, I don't know the hard-core stuff he's said to her (Betsy).'"

So she had said Russ was always nice to her *and* he threatened to kill her. Another logical question from Schwartz: "One of those is not true, right? . . . They can't both be true, can they?"

"I wouldn't think so."

Harney agreed he reported Pam told him she had no immediate need for money because she had no large debts, that money makes people do "crazy, crazy things," and "Money, it doesn't matter. People want it. You got it—they are going to try to do what they have to do to get it." She also said $150,000 was not a lot of money to her. But Harney told Schwartz he was not aware that at the same time she was telling police how financially secure she was, she could not afford health insurance.

Harney agreed that it was not his job to suggest to witnesses what they might have seen, but he confirmed he had offered her the theory from him and Detective Mike Merkel that Russ arrived at the house after Betsy and Pam were there and that was why she left. He had asked her if she saw Russ in the house that night or his car in the neighborhood.

"Yes, I did say that," Harney said, "and I said we had spoken in theory before about what we believed."

"Right. And you suggested that she saw Russ that night, right?"

"I told her what I believed."

That's called coaching a witness and perhaps suborning perjury, Schwartz thought, and it contaminates any effort by the police to find the truth.

Schwartz asked if she changed her story in another interview with Harney a few weeks before this trial when she said she saw Russ and someone else sitting in a car outside the house. To Schwartz's surprise, Judge Ohmer sustained Askey's objection to hearsay testimony.

Schwartz tried to explain to the judge, "I'm impeaching the earlier statement."

But the judge didn't see it that way. "Impeaching who? Sustained."

Schwartz tried again to get at Harney's role in changing Pam Hupp's story, but the judge sustained Askey's hearsay objection again.

Schwartz knew he had hit the judicial wall with that line of questions, so he moved on to Harney's discussion with her about the letter she said Betsy had written. But again, the judge sustained a hearsay objection from Askey.

Schwartz responded that Askey had opened the door to questions about hearsay documents, like Harney's reports, and the judge had previously ruled such questions were proper under the "direct interaction rule," which allows questioning about a witness's direct interaction with another person.

The judge said simply, "Sustained."

Schwartz said, "Nothing further at this time, then, Judge."

And then, for the second time, Leah Askey rested the prosecution's case against Russ Faria.

CHAPTER FORTY-EIGHT

Joel Schwartz felt a certain satisfaction in calling Sergeant Ryan McCarrick as his first witness. But his appearance led to a few unexpected chuckles among him, Schwartz, and Judge Ohmer as he was taking the stand. The judge thought he should explain the humorous exchange to the rest of the courtroom.

"It's always good to have a little levity in trials," Judge Ohmer said to the courtroom through a smile. "Mr. Schwartz thought he misplaced his eyeglasses, and the detective had the eyeglasses. So I don't know what we should make of that."

McCarrick smiled as he cracked, "Goes to my integrity, sir."

Ohmer chuckled and said, "All right. I was accused of having them first, so I don't . . ."

Schwartz smiled and adopted an apologetic tone as he said to Ohmer, "No accusations. I said I lost them—" he nodded toward McCarrick—"and wasn't accusing him, either."

As McCarrick settled in, Schwartz said, "Detective McCarrick, you . . ." He stopped and chuckled again, adding, "It's been a long week."

He only had one topic for the detective this time. McCarrick agreed that Pam Hupp had told him in June 2012 that she and Betsy had been at Betsy's tennis club the week before she was killed. Betsy said she had written her an email, but was unable to send it to her. Schwartz asked if she had said the email was written while they were at the tennis club.

McCarrick said his memory was that Pam said only that they had discussed it there. McCarrick agreed, however, that the transcript of an interview with other detectives suggested she said Betsy wrote the letter at the tennis club.

Schwartz and Swanson called several witnesses in short order to get very specific information from each of them. First, Sergeant Perry Smith of the Missouri Highway Patrol testified he helped conduct the first interview of Pam Hupp after the murder. He checked her cell phone to confirm she had called her husband at 7:04 p.m. after arriving at Betsy's house. He also confirmed that she first said her call to Betsy at 7:27 p.m. was to tell Betsy she was home, and then changed to say "almost home." She never said she made that call while parked in a fork in the road north of Troy.

Pam said she had never seen what she called a "document" or a "form" that Betsy had written to her. However, she knew it discussed Betsy making her the beneficiary, Betsy's desire not to be alone with Russ in Troy, and Russ's recent holding of a pillow over his wife's face.

Smith also confirmed that her cell phone showed the text exchange when Betsy told her she didn't want her to come to the chemotherapy session so Betsy could have some time alone with Bobbi Wann. Pam texted a simple reply: Bummer.

Detective Paul Barish of the St. Peters Police Department described for Schwartz all of the steps he took to confirm alibis for the time of the murder offered by several witnesses, including interviewing other people they said they had been with during that time. Schwartz hoped Barish's testimony would serve as a seminar on how to investigate witness alibis with additional review and careful follow-up—as opposed to the almost total lack of effort by detectives who seemed to just accept Pam Hupp's statements with little or no additional verification.

Patrol Officer Kory Gresco, also of the St. Peters Police Department, told Swanson he had pulled over Betsy Faria for a standard stop-sign violation on January 19, 2010. She got out of her car and approached him.

He asked why she hadn't stopped and she responded, "I just found out I got breast cancer and I want to kill myself."

He took her comment seriously and asked how he could help.

She replied, "I need a gun to kill myself."

Gresco said he took her to a nearby hospital and filed an affidavit used to hold her for evaluation.

Rhonda Graham's testimony turned the defense case away from the police investigation and toward the personal story of Betsy and Russ Faria. She and Betsy immediately connected when they met in 2008 at a Bible study at the Morning Star United Methodist Church and spent hours sharing all of the things they had in common, including what she called "teenage daughter issues." Rhonda spent a lot of time with Betsy at various church functions. They talked on the phone and texted each other regularly, went to lunch together, hung out at each other's homes, and went on an annual "girls' trip" to Branson.

Rhonda and her husband got to know Betsy and Russ during a lot of couples' activities and went on the "celebration of life" cruise with the Farias in November 2011. Betsy was not depressed on the cruise and never said anything about divorcing Russ or being afraid of him. Betsy and Russ had a great time and seemed very close on the cruise, obviously wanting to spend as much time together as possible. Swanson asked how Rhonda would characterize the Farias' relationship.

"When we met them, we were doing a marriage study and they were trying to rekindle their relationship," she said. "And I didn't know them before 2008, but they were always trying to be close the whole time I knew them. After she got sick, it was even a stronger bond."

Askey wanted to demonstrate Graham didn't know about the dark side of the Farias' marriage. Graham said Betsy never mentioned removing Russ as her beneficiary or that she and Russ both had engaged in extramarital affairs.

The next witness also provided a rosy view of the Faria marriage, while casting doubt on the depth of Betsy's relationship with Pam

Hupp. Linda Hartmann said she was related by marriage to Russ and became close to Betsy during her treatment for breast cancer. Linda was a breast cancer survivor and offered Betsy her support. They became good friends and spent time together at activities such as swimming, camping, and girls' weekends in Branson. Linda even helped Betsy on some of her DJ gigs.

She had spent a lot of time with Russ, too—New Year's Eves, couples' weekends in Branson, and family events. She and her husband were on the cruise in November 2011 and remembered the Farias having a wonderful time together. "It seemed like they were honeymooning. . . . She was having a lot of fun with Russ. . . . She told me she was really happy, you know, with Russ."

As Linda had testified in the first trial, Betsy had surprised her with comments about her life insurance just after her cancer recurred and before the cruise. Betsy said she was OK with dying because she was leaving the money from the insurance to Russ and her daughters. "She said to me, 'I have done really well in being here because I have left the insurance with Russ and the two girls. So I feel that they are going to be well, you know, when I am gone.'"

Swanson asked, "'Be well' financially—they would be taken care of. . . . She said the insurance was for Russ and it was for the girls?"

"Yes, you know, she was really positive . . . that she was going to leave this. . . . She wasn't going away without giving them something."

Swanson asked about the time in Branson with Betsy and Ashley Frost, Linda's daughter, the week before Betsy was murdered. Linda said what really stood out was Betsy's depressed conversation about having to go home a day or two earlier than planned because of a meeting with Pam Hupp.

"She said, 'I have to go back. I have to meet Pam.' I said, 'Call and cancel with her. Just tell her you are going to stay another day.' She said, 'No, I really do . . . I have to meet Pam—and I don't want to meet Pam.' She was very tense about that."

Linda told Askey she and Betsy never discussed leaving their husbands that weekend.

Ashley Frost immediately took the stand to deny that as well. Ashley said Betsy was her usual upbeat and happy self that weekend. Betsy did not seem afraid of Russ and kept talking about how happy she was that Russ and her daughter Mariah had a good, close relationship.

Swanson asked if the women talked about leaving their husbands and moving to Branson.

"That was a joke," Ashley said. "There's a school down there where you can, like, work on a farm and get free college tuition. And my mom and Betsy said, 'Oh, we're all going to run away, and we're going to work on this farm, and we're going to go to school and hang out here.' But it was . . . it was a big joke."

Askey tried to take Ashley to the dark side. Hadn't she told police that Russ was very controlling?

No, she had told them that Russ was a leader, such as the time he took over getting everyone seated at her mother's birthday party.

Schwartz and Swanson thought the testimony by Rhonda Graham, Linda Hartmann, and Ashley Frost should help rebut some of the negative gossip about Russ and the Farias' marriage from people who had an ax to grind with Russ—the people who decided long ago that he killed Betsy regardless of the evidence pointing away from him and toward Pam Hupp.

CHAPTER FORTY-NINE

Joel Schwartz and Nate Swanson rushed to Judge Steven Ohmer's chambers over the lunch break to request a meeting with him and the prosecutors to discuss a situation unlike any they had ever experienced in the middle of a trial. Just fifteen minutes earlier, the defense attorneys had been approached by a lawyer who gave them information that could be relevant to Russ Faria's trial. Prosecuting Attorney Leah Askey hadn't returned from lunch yet, so her second chair in the trial, Assistant Prosecuting Attorney George Gundy, met with the defense team and the judge.

Schwartz and Swanson said an attorney representing the manufacturer of the balcony railing that Pam Hupp's mother supposedly fell through to her death in October 2013 had just told them about evidence in a suit by one of Pam's brothers against the manufacturer. The lawyer emailed Swanson copies of the police reports from the investigation into the death of Shirley Neumann in the three-story fall from the balcony at her apartment in a retirement center. The circumstances of her death could be relevant to Russ's trial, Schwartz said. When Pam denied killing Betsy in a police interview with McCarrick in June 2012, she also said she could have collected more money, more easily, by killing her own mother.

Swanson said the police reports in Shirley Neumann's death revealed Pam was the last person to see her mother alive. She had taken her to the hospital, and after they returned to Shirley's apartment, Pam told the staff her mother wouldn't be coming to dinner that night or breakfast the next morning. Her body was found on the ground below her balcony when staff checked on her the next afternoon. The manufacturer's attorney suggested the railing had been tampered with and noted that her daughter had inherited money from her mother.

Swanson made the obvious connection for the judge. "It is kind of interesting Ms. Hupp would now be the last person to be with two people right before they died—and got money for it."

Schwartz asked the judge for a three-day delay in Russ's trial so he could try to locate employees from Shirley Neumann's retirement center. With Askey still unavailable, APA Gundy spoke on the record for the first time to oppose the defense team's motion. "I guess my first feeling is that nobody has even called Ms. Hupp to testify. She's here if they want to call her. They are scared to death to call her. She can testify as to any of this stuff." And then he delivered a succinct statement of opposition to bringing Shirley Neumann's death into Russ Faria's trial: "I think one murder case at a time is probably plenty."

Judge Ohmer quickly agreed with Gundy, calling the defenders' request irrelevant and "a fishing expedition." He said, "This has no connection here whatsoever. . . . No . . . we're not going to try a second murder case, which is really what you are wanting to do, to show that she has this propensity to kill somebody for their money—her close relatives." But then he offered an aside that proved he understood the defense attorneys' argument: "I'm glad I'm not closely related somehow. . . . It is very interesting."

The letter that Pam Hupp said Betsy had written to her was the only document on Betsy's computer that listed the author as "unknown," computer expert and private investigator Greg Chatten told the judge as Russ's defense resumed. All of the other documents—a list long enough to fill several pages—were created under the user names of Betsy Faria, her ex-husband, or a couple of other people. Chatten said the only way a document would show "unknown" as the author was if it was created on a different computer, or if it was created on Betsy's computer and someone changed the author to unknown.

If the document was created on Betsy's computer, it would show her as the author, unless someone changed it. Chatten also said the document was created in a Word '97 program, but Betsy's computer used Word 2003. Word '97 was not installed on it.

Swanson asked, "Would it be impossible for that file to have been created on that computer, on that particular computer?"

"In this particular case, yes."

Chatten said the last time the document was saved on the computer was December 22, 2011, about the same time the computer had been connected to a wireless network called "The Club." That was the day, Pam told police, she had been at Betsy's tennis club with her and they had tried to find the letter. Saving the document while connected to "The Club" Wi-Fi certainly suggested to Swanson and Schwartz that the document was written at the tennis club, not earlier as Pam had suggested.

Chatten said that although a Microsoft Outlook email program had been run at least once on the computer, and there were several draft emails, no email software was installed. It could not send or receive emails.

Chatten then turned his expertise to cell phone calls placed by Pam Hupp on the night Betsy died. While an exact location of a phone when a call is placed can't be pinpointed, Chatten could say her calls at 7:04 and 7:27 that evening were made from inside the same cell tower sector where the Farias' house was located. Pam was near or perhaps even at Betsy's house when she made both of those calls. That sector did not cover the highway intersection at Troy or Pam's home in O'Fallon, two locations Pam variously claimed she had been at when she made the call at 7:27 p.m.

An analysis of traffic on Russ's cell phone showed he was traveling through the cell tower sectors matching his route to and from game night at the times he said he was there. His phone was in the same sector as Mike Corbin's house in O'Fallon—twenty-four miles from Russ's home, according to Google maps—when the call came in at 8:57 p.m. from his mother-in-law. Within seconds, Russ's phone showed an outgoing call to an 805 number—the number his cell service automatically called to record the voice mail from his mother-in-law.

Chatten said the 805 call could not have been Russ checking his voice mail because Janet Meyer had not even left her message by then. The call to the 805 number was her call being sent to voice mail, not Russ checking his voice mail.

So, Schwartz thought, another of Askey's unsupported theories shot down by facts.

Joel Schwartz closed the case in defense of Russ Faria with testimony from the four game-night players—the indisputable alibi testimony that should have closed the investigation of Russ Faria the morning after Betsy's murder. Mike Corbin, Angelia Hulion, Brandon Sweeney, and Marshall Bach gave the same accounts of that night that they had repeated so many times. And they all disputed Askey's account that they told the police they played a board game before watching movies.

Mike said he even told Askey in his deposition that those police reports were wrong about that. He said the police weren't taking notes during the interview, so he understood how they could make that mistake. The gamers also said the police got it wrong when they quoted them as saying they had played a game called Lord of the Rings; they didn't even know if there was such a game. The gamers had compared Rolemaster to the more familiar Dungeons and Dragons, and the police must have confused that with *Lord of the Rings*. And, they said again, no one ever dressed up as their game characters, wielded swords, or participated in any kind of violent play action or outside missions, as Askey suggested again in her cross-examinations, and as she had stated in her outrageous closing arguments in the first trial.

Marshall told Schwartz that detectives had come to his place of work the week before the trial and offered him immunity from prosecution if he changed his testimony about Russ by five o'clock that afternoon. He felt threatened by the cops.

"Did you need immunity for anything?" Schwartz asked.

"No," Marshall said, "I didn't do anything wrong."

Askey spent cross-examination picking at nits in the gamers' testimony and memories. Yes, Marshall recalled the color of Russ's vehicle wrong. Yes, he once said Russ left after he did, but then remembered Russ left first because he followed his taillights down the street. Explaining how the gamers remembered what Russ was wearing, but didn't remember their own clothes, was simple: They had been talking to police about Russ's clothes—and every other detail of that night—for the last four years.

Askey drilled Brandon about offering the receipt from his visit to Jack in the Box to the police to document his location and the time. Brandon couldn't explain why the police denied seeing the receipt or telling him to hang on to it, but that was what happened.

Schwartz thought Askey's attacks on the gamers were weak and ineffective. Sure, there may have been an occasional blip in their memories, but none of that was related to the real issue. They established an unshakeable alibi for Russ Faria almost thirty miles from his home between six and nine o'clock. Combined with the other airtight evidence collected along Russ's route, the gamers proved he couldn't have been at home to murder Betsy between five o'clock and nine thirty on December 27, 2011.

CHAPTER FIFTY

Pam Hupp's bank records betrayed her motive for murder, her attempt to cover up her true intentions, and her continuing deception of all of the authorities trying to solve the killing of Betsy Faria. As the last day of Russ Faria's second trial opened, Joel Schwartz asked Judge Steven Ohmer to admit into evidence the bank records detailing how Pam opened a revocable trust with $100,000 in the names of Betsy's daughters, just four days before Russ's first trial, and then, after testifying in the trial that she was planning to give the money to the girls, as Betsy requested, withdrew all but $300 and revoked the trust, just three weeks after Russ was convicted. The evidence in this trial, Schwartz added, had shown Sergeant Ryan McCarrick pressured her to set up the trust before the trial to make the prosecution look better and improve her credibility as a witness.

So what? That was essentially the response by Assistant Prosecuting Attorney George Gundy. The bank records of someone who wasn't even a witness in the trial were irrelevant. "There's been a lot of . . . opinions and hearsay, but there is not one shred of evidence involving her in the case. We object."

Without explanation, the judge admitted the records, as well as a deed filed with Lincoln County showing that Betsy's name was listed with Russ's as owners of the Faria home at 130 Sumac Drive.

Swanson said it was relevant because the mysterious letter Pam Hupp claimed was written by Betsy included a complaint that her name was not on the deed and Russ had said he was the only owner.

With those documents admitted, Joel Schwartz announced that the defense would rest its case.

Askey immediately called three rebuttal witnesses. The first was a computer and cell phone expert who took issue with defense expert Greg Chatten's testimony that cell tower records showed Russ's phone was in all the places he told police he was all evening. Askey's expert also said the records showed that twenty-three seconds after Janet Meyer's call to Russ at 8:57 p.m., someone made a call on his phone to the 805 number to listen to her message.

Under Swanson's cross-examination, however, the expert's testimony wilted. He essentially agreed Chatten's analysis was accurate, and the pattern and timing of calls made it unlikely Russ had listened to the message from Meyer.

Askey called Robert O'Neal, the computer analyst from the St. Charles City Police Department, back to the stand to testify that data on Betsy's laptop did not prove "The Club" was the last network it was connected to on December 22, 2011. And he said the fact that the letter was marked as created with Word '97 could mean that the program had been on the computer previously, not necessarily that the letter had been created on a different computer and then saved on Betsy's.

Swanson got O'Neal to agree that the letter was the only document on Betsy's computer that listed the author as unknown and that he was not offering any opinion on who wrote that letter.

As the last witness in the trial, Detective Dean Frye of the O'Fallon Police Department testified he had not been mistaken when he quoted all four gamers saying they played a game called Lord of the Rings before watching two movies. He said he knew nothing about role-playing games, but had quoted the gamers accurately in his report. He also denied that Brandon Sweeney showed him a receipt from Jack in the Box; he said he would have seized the receipt if Brandon had produced it.

Swanson asked Frye if it was possible the gamers said their usual game was based on *Lord of the Rings*. Frye said they may have said that, but he insisted they told him the game was called Lord of the Rings. Asked if the police ever made mistakes, Frye said, "They do, but I didn't."

And that was it. The evidence in Russ Faria's second effort to prove his innocence was complete.

CHAPTER FIFTY-ONE

Pam Hupp sat quietly and alone in the back of the courtroom to listen to closing arguments at 11:30 a.m. She would be painted as either a valued witness to a murderous plot by Russ Faria, or the cold, calculating killer responsible for the death of her best friend for money. Although the prosecution and defense had both subpoenaed her, neither had called her to the witness stand. Joel Schwartz decided other witnesses had put all of her maddening lies and twisted stories into the record, and putting this disturbed, unpredictable woman on the stand was not only unnecessary—but also not worth the risk.

Pam managed a final taunt to the defense after she was told she would not be called as a witness. Before court opened that morning, she texted a message to Nate Swanson: What's the matter? Did Schwartz lose his balls?

Schwartz, Russ, and Swanson had to admit that was pretty funny coming from Pam Hupp.

For her second closing argument in a trial of Russ Faria, Leah Askey abandoned her delusional attack on the game-night players as co-conspirators in a plot to murder Russ's wife. A good decision, Joel Schwartz thought as he listened to her new effort to portray an innocent man as a killer. Askey's outrageous scenario may have found some traction with jurors in the first trial, but she surely realized that trying to sell such a wild theory to Judge Steven Ohmer was not a wise strategy. Schwartz was surprised, however, that Askey didn't even mention the game-nighters this time.

Askey opened her argument to the judge with an ominous quote from the letter Pam Hupp said Betsy wrote just days before her death. "'If something happens to me, please show this to the police,'" Askey recited before adding, "These are Betsy Faria's last words. Perhaps, a dying declaration."

Quoting the letter, as if it had been proven that Betsy wrote it, Askey also read, "'I have to change my insurance policies and get them out of his name, but he can't know about it. He had held a pillow over my face and told me, "This is what dying feels like." I'm growing increasingly scared to be here. He wants me out of the house. He's been looking through my computer.'"

She cited some of the evidence she believed incriminated Russ. There were no blood or DNA samples at the scene from anyone but Betsy and Russ. Their DNA was all that was found inside his slippers stained with her blood. The bloody smudge on the switch plate was her blood and a male DNA sample too small to identify. The presence of human blood was found under Russ's fingernails and on his feet (she neglected to add that it was Russ's blood). A stain identified as blood on a bath towel contained both Betsy's and Russ's DNA. And there was the new report from an officer who saw several water droplets in the shower.

The prosecutor implied Russ learned Betsy removed him as beneficiary on the State Farm policy because that was the only company he called about getting the money. He knew he was still the beneficiary on the Mutual of Omaha policy, because he found the change form Betsy said she left on the kitchen counter the morning of the murder. Schwartz thought again, Just more theory and no evidence.

To try to rebut the first responders' testimony that they found Betsy's body cold and stiff, Askey quoted the medical examiner saying there was no way to determine that simply by touching it, and a body was not likely to be cold and stiff within two or two and a half hours after death.

Askey turned Russ's call to 911 against him again. He cried to stall the dispatcher when she asked questions he didn't like, but was calm and collected when he wanted to talk. He talked about where he had been, and where Betsy had been, instead of begging the dispatcher to hurry and send help. He described two wounds to her left arm, which he couldn't have seen because of the position of her body.

Askey trotted out another theory based on what she said was a paw print on Betsy's pants. The dog had been in the house long enough to touch Betsy's body before Russ put her outside on the chain. A killer other than Russ wouldn't have bothered to put the dog on the chain.

Russ told police he and Betsy had rekindled their marriage, Askey said, but didn't tell them he had an affair with Darlene Fuller. And Askey contradicted Darlene's testimony by insisting Russ had been meeting her after dropping off Betsy for chemotherapy.

Askey ended with another summary of Betsy's fear of Russ and his threatening behavior described in the mysterious letter. She looked at the judge and said, "We ask that you listen to Betsy's voice and find him guilty."

Joel Schwartz thought that Askey had avoided wild tales of secret game-night co-conspirators this time, but her second closing argument still was based only on theories and suppositions unproven by a single piece of evidence or a line of valid testimony. Pam Hupp's attempt to frame Russ Faria, aided by police incompetence or worse, had failed, and no spin by the prosecutor in a closing argument could manufacture guilt that wasn't there.

Schwartz began his closing argument by saying it had been difficult to decide what to say because the State had produced no evidence to prove how or when Russ could have killed Betsy. "I don't know how we got here," he said. "So I thought about it, and what we got here by is speculation—mere unadulterated speculation."

He contrasted the prosecution's lack of evidence with the overwhelming evidence from the defense—videos, store receipts, cell phone records, and testimony by the four game-night players—all proving Russ was nowhere near his home or Betsy between five o'clock and nine thirty-five at night. First responders who checked Betsy's body estimated she had been dead two to three hours, which would have put her time of death between seven and eight o'clock at night while Russ was still at Corbin's house.

Schwartz turned to his prime suspect, attacking Pam Hupp's transparent, evolving lies and deceptive conduct that the police not only willingly accepted and excused, but also encouraged and even coached. Detective Harney helped create a story for Pam so she could incriminate Russ by saying she had seen him and another man in a car outside the house. She recently claimed she and Betsy had been lovers—an absurd allegation she had never made before in almost four years. But that salacious fiction gave Pam an explanation for her equally unsupported accusation that Russ had shoved her against a wall and threatened to kill her—just two weeks before Betsy was killed.

The evidence proved Pam Hupp had spent the day of the murder trying to control Betsy's movements to get her home alone that evening while Russ was gone. She ignored Betsy's clear instructions not to come to the chemo session. She made an inconvenient trip to Betsy's mother's to ensure she could take Betsy home, another lengthy drive for someone who claimed she didn't drive at night and was terrible at directions. Pam called her husband from Betsy's at 7:04 p.m. and then called Betsy's phone at 7:27 p.m.—a call that cell phone towers located near or even at Betsy's home. During that same time period, Betsy failed to answer calls she had promised to answer from her daughter from 7:21 to 7:30 p.m.

"Something made Betsy break that promise," Schwartz said.

There was another factor that brought everyone to this place on this day. "I would submit to the court that, if Russ Faria did not call in and say, 'I think my wife killed herself,' we wouldn't be here today. That's what caused them to jump to a conclusion." But the defense had proven all of the factors that explained why Russ—in shock and "not in his right mind"—was justified in jumping to the suicide conclusion.

What about that ominous letter? It was saved on the laptop on December 22, 2011, when Betsy's profile was open on the laptop between 11:50 a.m. and 12:05 p.m., when Pam was with Betsy at her tennis club—and on a day when the laptop was connected to a network called "The Club." The letter was the only document on the laptop with an unidentified author. It was written using Word '97 software, but Betsy's laptop only had Word 2003. Schwartz told the judge he was certain the content was copied and pasted from another document created on a different computer and transferred to Betsy's, probably in fifteen minutes while Betsy played tennis and Pam had her laptop.

Schwartz respectfully suggested Bobbi Wann was mistaken when she testified Betsy had discussed Russ holding a pillow over her face and her plan to replace Russ as her beneficiary while at the chemo session. Bobbi never mentioned those things until she had two years of discussions with Pam Hupp and Betsy's family.

What about the physical evidence? Sergeant Pirtle's recollection of water droplets in the shower was suspect, coming just before this trial and providing the only support for Askey's theory that Russ took a shower after killing Betsy. Pirtle's recollection was thin on details and even the judge asked him questions to try to get more information. And if Russ had taken a shower, wouldn't there have been plenty of other evidence—wet shower walls, a wet tub, wet towels, trace evidence in drains and pipes?

What about the bloody slippers? Even the State's expert testified that the stains appeared to result from the slippers being swiped in blood. There were no bloody footprints anywhere and no spots where blood had been stepped in. An untrained police officer said the slippers appeared to have made the pattern in the blood on the switch plate, but there were two different patterns.

Schwartz thought the examination of the suspected dog paw print on Betsy's pants was inconclusive, and he wasn't sure what it would mean even if it had been left by the dog. There weren't any other bloody paw prints anywhere and no blood was found on the dog.

All of the experts said it would be impossible for Betsy's killer not to have her blood on them—and there was no blood on Russ or his clothes.

As Schwartz recalled there was no blood found in the kitchen or dining room—despite widespread use of Bluestar luminol to test the floor, cabinets, drains, mops, and other surfaces—he began a pointed attack on the police investigation. Detective Mike Merkel had testi-fied that photos taken of the Bluestar tests showed "absolutely noth-ing" because of a camera malfunction. But he had admitted that was false after Schwartz produced the photos. "These pictures simply didn't show what he wanted them to show. . . . And there's no doubt about it—he perjured himself," Schwartz said.

Sergeant Ryan McCarrick had encouraged Pam Hupp to fund a trust for Betsy's daughters before the first trial to make the case against Russ look better. It wouldn't look good if she didn't open a trust, he noted, because she was the last one to see Betsy alive, had just been named Betsy's beneficiary, and had collected the $150,000 in insurance without giving it to the girls, as Pam first said Betsy had wanted. Pam did as the police asked; just days before the first trial, she opened a trust in the girls' names with $100,000. But that was just more deceit. Just weeks after Russ was convicted, she revoked the trust and withdrew all but $300.

Schwartz also pointed to the vast difference in the ways the police treated Pam and other witnesses. McCarrick testified the police made no effort to confirm her account of her activities the night of the murder, when she arrived home, or what condition she was in. No detective could say where she was at any time that night. They didn't even try to track her locations through cell towers. The police interview with her husband—while she sat next to him—was so am-ateurish and worthless that Schwartz called it a joke. The police didn't confirm what she was wearing and waited hours before seizing the clothes, only she said she had worn.

Schwartz rhetorically asked the judge if he didn't find it interest-ing that the State didn't call the person at the center of this entire case to testify, now that the defense could really cross-examine her. Pam Hupp had told contradictory, ever-changing, and often absurd stories about everything—putting herself at the center of Betsy's murder. But the cops and prosecutor never considered her a suspect.

Schwartz closed with a couple of stunning facts and a plea to ac-quit Russ Faria.

"Russ Faria was the beneficiary for over ten years—that's over three thousand six hundred fifty days. Pam Hupp was the beneficiary for four—and that's all. She was the last one with her, and nobody can account for her whereabouts, and she lied about everything that we know about it.

"Judge, the State has not proven much of a *possibility* that Russ could have done it, much less a *probability*—not even close to proof beyond a reasonable doubt. Thank you."

Askey began her rebuttal argument by answering Schwartz's question about why Pam Hupp hadn't testified.

"Judge, I'm not going to talk much about Pam Hupp because there hasn't been any evidence about Pam Hupp. Pam Hupp has been here and available to be called by the defense. They are the ones that have put on their dog-and-pony show about Pam Hupp for the last few years. We didn't call her because we didn't have to. If they wanted to call her, they could."

But she did address the beneficiary issue by asking if it made sense for Pam to kill Betsy to collect the insurance money without even knowing if Betsy had mailed the change form to the insurance company. There would be no motive for her to kill Betsy when she was already dying of cancer. But it did make sense for Russ to kill Betsy if he knew she was planning to remove him as beneficiary.

It also made no sense, Askey argued, for Pam Hupp to write a letter incriminating Russ Faria and then hide it on a computer so well that it took almost four years for police to find it.

Detective Mike Merkel did not lie about the photos of the Bluestar tests. He meant only that they showed "absolutely nothing" in terms of the luminescence. Officer Pirtle did not lie about the water droplets in the shower. If he was lying, wouldn't he have made up more details—"a whole lot better story"? Two other detectives weren't wrong when they quoted the gamers as saying they played a game before watching movies, and changed their stories after their first interviews. "I have no idea—maybe they were too stoned to remember," she said.

But the State had proven Russ was a liar. He lied about lying down in front of Betsy's body, because he did not have blood on his clothes. He lied when he told police he did not have an affair.

The nature of Betsy's murder—fifty-five stab and slash wounds, some shockingly deep and damaging—were signs of rage, passion, and greed. They required an extreme amount of force and exertion—like a man of Russ's physique could deliver. His conduct after he found Betsy's body was suspicious, rotating between calm and hysterical, and then sitting in a police car smoking cigarettes and laughing.

"Judge, I ask you to please help us finally get justice for Betsy Faria and her family by finding the defendant guilty."

And then the second trial of Russ Faria was over. The judge called the lunch break and said he would reconvene court sometime later that afternoon. Everyone knew he meant he would return his verdict then.

Joel Schwartz looked intensely into Russ Faria's face and nodded; Russ nodded back. They knew they had taken their best shot and it was all in Judge Ohmer's hands now.

Russ remained optimistic Ohmer would recognize the absurdity of the charges and the total lack of evidence against him. He wanted to be confident that he was close to being cleared of the murder of the wife he had loved deeply, if imperfectly. But the courts in Lincoln County had convicted him once before and he knew it surely could happen again. If it did, Russ feared, he would never get another chance to win his freedom.

There was one more bitter exchange between the prosecution and the defense before the judge could return his verdict. Schwartz was talking to Russ as he smoked a cigarette in the courthouse parking lot when Nate Swanson called to relay a take-it-now-or-leave-it offer for a plea bargain from Leah Askey. Schwartz felt a rush of dread. He thought it was possible Askey would offer to let Russ plead guilty of involuntary manslaughter and be sentenced to time served. That would be a difficult offer to refuse, Schwartz thought, because there would be no more jail time even if Russ had to plead guilty to a crime he did not commit.

But then Swanson disclosed Askey's offer: If Russ would plead guilty of second-degree murder, she would recommend a sentence of "soft life"—meaning Russ would be eligible for parole. Schwartz was relieved that Askey's ridiculous offer showed just how far out of tune Askey was with the state of the case.

When Schwartz told Russ about the offer, Russ's anger and frustration from the last four years erupted in his response: "She could give me a parking ticket and I'd tell her to stick it up her ass." Schwartz relayed Russ's perfect response verbatim to Swanson to transmit back to Askey. Swanson said later that he told Askey that Russ wouldn't even plead guilty to a parking ticket now—but he left out the exact location Russ suggested Askey could deposit the offer.

CHAPTER FIFTY-TWO

Judge Steven Ohmer's call for court to reconvene at 3:45 p.m. came sooner than almost anyone expected. Joel Schwartz told Russ Faria it was impossible to know how to read a quick verdict from an experienced judge like Ohmer. If a jury ready to convict a defendant of murder deliberates an average of four to five hours, what could it mean that the judge had been out for three hours?

Pam Hupp was not in the courtroom now, as she had been during closing arguments. Schwartz would learn later that she had already left the courthouse by a side door reserved for employees.

After everyone was seated in the courtroom, the judge swept onto the bench with a business-like demeanor and a quick greeting of "Good afternoon, folks." He was pleased there had been no incidents in the courtroom during the trial and he didn't expect any now, but he made it clear anyone creating a disturbance supporting or opposing his verdict would be escorted out. He asked the defendant to stand; Russ Faria, Joel Schwartz, and Nate Swanson rose quickly behind the defense table.

"There's no question that this was a brutal murder," the judge began solemnly, "and I'm sorry the family, or any of us, have to witness such horror."

He explained that a defendant is presumed innocent and the State has the burden of proving guilt beyond reasonable doubt. He added, "The charges here of murder in the first degree and armed criminal action are totally appropriate for the facts and circumstances of this case."

Russ was concentrating on the judge's every word and he suddenly feared that last comment might not be a good omen.

"There are two separate theories submitted to this court by the parties. First, the State surmises that the defendant killed Betsy in a fit of passion and rage. Next, the defendant surmises that Pam Hupp conspired to kill Betsy and set up the defendant to take the fall."

The judge looked over the courtroom and then read from the paper in front of him: "'The investigation into the facts and theories of this case by law enforcement is rather disturbing and, frankly, raises more questions than answers.'"

Joel Schwartz didn't hear another word the judge said over the next sixty seconds. He now knew exactly what the judge was about to say and what the verdict would be.

Russ was encouraged by the judge's blunt criticism of the cops and their investigation, but none of that included the exact two words he ached to hear.

"Inconsistencies and/or lies do not equate to murder where the hard facts do not support the conclusion, but rather support speculation, innuendo, and supposition only. Unfortunately, the hard facts alone are insufficient to give a clear resolution to this messy case," the judge continued.

"A reasonable doubt is a doubt based upon reason and common sense after careful and impartial consideration of all of the evidence in this case. Proof beyond a reasonable doubt means proof that leaves you firmly convinced of the defendant's guilt. The law does not require proof that overcomes every possible doubt. If the fact finder is not firmly convinced of the defendant's guilt, the court must give him the benefit of the doubt," Judge Ohmer read.

"Consequently, as to Count I, murder in the first degree, the court finds the defendant, Russell Scott Faria"—Russ sucked in a quick breath that made his chest quiver and he could feel his heart pounding all the way up to his throat as the judge completed his verdict—"not guilty."

Russ legs went weak and he feared he would collapse until he felt Nate Swanson's arms around him, holding him up. Schwartz turned and smiled into Russ's face, took his arm, and said almost too softly to hear, "It's over."

Russ vaguely heard his family and friends behind him trying to stifle their happy cries; he didn't hear the shocked gasps from Betsy's family on the other side of the courtroom.

Russ was savoring those two words he had waited so long to hear, and he was about to hear them again as the judge continued. "As to Count II, armed criminal action, the court finds the defendant, Russell Scott Faria, not guilty. The court further orders the defendant discharged in this cause. The court stands adjourned."

Schwartz hadn't cast a glance toward Leah Askey until he noticed she had packed up and was leaving the courtroom.

Russ turned and rushed back to his mother's arms—without any interference from a deputy sheriff this time—and was immediately surrounded by his father, his sister, Mary Anderson, and other relatives and friends. Amid the hugs, kisses, and tears, Russ began to realize that, for the first time in almost four years, he was about to walk out of the courthouse into complete and total freedom without the threat of prison or the cloud of guilt hanging over his head.

Betsy's family and friends left the courthouse quickly and drove away without speaking to anyone. Celebrating outside the courthouse front door, many of Russ's supporters pulled on purple T-shirts they had made especially for this outcome. Under his picture was printed: RUSSELL FARIA—INNOCENT. Some of his friends cracked open a bottle and began drinking toasts to freedom for Faria.

Leah Askey later issued a simple statement. "While I believe in our justice system, I disagree with this verdict. My job is to seek justice for our victims and present evidence in the best way I can. My condolences go out to Betsy Faria's family."

Russ and Schwartz made short and simple comments to the media. Asked how he felt, the beaming Russ said, "Relief. Glad it's over—finally."

Schwartz couldn't begin to express what he was feeling. It had taken almost four years, but he had kept his promise to an innocent man. This was the kind of case, and Russ Faria was the kind of person, Schwartz had gone into the law to defend.

Through a smile he tried to restrain, Schwartz told reporters,

"We're happy that justice has finally begun to prevail. I still hope for justice for Betsy and her family."

That wasn't a casual remark. After Anderson chauffeured Russ away from the courthouse and to a celebration with family and friends at a restaurant, Schwartz made a phone call to Richard Callahan, the U.S. Attorney for the St. Louis District in Eastern Missouri, to ask him to conduct a comprehensive review of all aspects of the Faria case, including the suspicious death of Pam Hupp's mother. Callahan said he thought the facts warranted at least some conversations with the judge, the Missouri Attorney General's Office, and the local prosecutor.

Schwartz urged Callahan to follow through aggressively. If Pam Hupp didn't face justice—if Pam Hupp wasn't stopped—Schwartz warned, "Someone else is going to die."

CHAPTER FIFTY-THREE

Russ Faria was suddenly a free man faced with the challenge of rebuilding a life shattered by the loss of his wife to a violent murder, and almost four years in prison for a crime he didn't commit. Living again with his parents in O'Fallon, he took a few weeks through the holidays and into early 2016 to rest and begin to readjust to life outside of a prison cell. He soon collected on two of Betsy's life insurance policies that had been frozen while the court battles raged. He bought a mobile home and began to renovate it. He eventually would go to work for a friend who ran a motorcycle service shop, doing work he really enjoyed. It was a good way to start restoring at least a semblance of normalcy as he looked for a new direction for his life.

He cultivated a friendship with Ryan Ferguson, another man wrongly convicted of murder in Missouri, and joined Ryan in efforts on behalf of the Missouri chapter of the Innocence Project, the organization that works for the exoneration of people wrongly convicted. Ryan spent eleven years in prison for a murder he did not commit, winning his release in November 2013, just before Russ entered the same Missouri prison where Ryan had been held. (Today, Russ continues to make regular speaking appearances around the state to raise funds for the organization and advocate for the exoneration and release of its innocent clients.)

Russ's search for justice in his own case and especially in Betsy's murder continued, while Pam Hupp was hardly slipping quietly into obscurity.

In January 2016, the suit by Leah and Mariah Day to recover the $150,000 from their mother's insurance from Pam Hupp went to trial before St. Charles County Circuit Judge Ted House. David Butsch—the Days' attorney who provided that vital tip to Joel Schwartz about Pam and her trust fund—argued that Pam committed constructive fraud and benefited from unjust enrichment—two civil law concepts seldom heard around the edges of a murder case. His theory was that Pam accepted the role as beneficiary to Betsy's insurance money under an agreement with Betsy to give the money to the Days when they were older—a promise Pam personally repeated to the Days, Betsy's family and friends, and the police.

Instead of doing that, she commingled the money with personal funds of hers and her husband's and used it to invest in real estate and pay for a new house. Pam Hupp's attorneys argued there was no binding agreement requiring her to give any of the money to the Days, and she was free to do with the money as she pleased.

With FOX 2's cameras capturing the trial, Pam Hupp quickly became the sensational star witness with a predictable blizzard of contradictory answers and nonsensical explanations. Called as a hostile witness by the Days' attorneys, she said she didn't remember telling the police that Betsy wanted her to give the money to the Days, and if she did, she only meant she would consider giving them some money if their behavior improved. When asked if she deposited the money in her personal account with her other funds, she replied, "I did. It was my money."

Pam admitted she lied to Betsy's sister that she had given away the money. Asked if she lied to anyone else about the money, she said, "Anybody that would bug me and bug me and bug me and bug me."

Did she have memory problems?

Yes and no; whatever she said sounded like the truth to her then, but she sometimes learned later it was not.

And there was that sexual-affair stuff to discuss. She said she hadn't told the police or Leah Askey before Russ Faria's first trial that she and Betsy had had a sexual relationship because she had not talked to Askey or those other detectives until Russ's second trial was approaching.

The most memorable moment came as one of the Days' attorneys asked Pam a question that confused her. As the attorney pressed for an answer, she began waving her left arm around as she protested loudly, "Whoa, whoa, whoa, whoa, whoa, whoa, whoa!" When the attorney pressed again, she gave him another round of "Whoa, whoa, whoa!" The attorney asked Judge House for help and he instructed her to just say she didn't understand the question.

Pam was such a terrible witness that even her lawyer refused to vouch for her in closing arguments. "I'm not going to argue about her credibility," he said to the judge. "She's not a credible witness. But that's not the issue. The issue is what the intent was of Miss Faria."

Her performance convinced David Butsch that he was correct to judge her as a manipulative psychopath and unashamed, unrestrained liar. He thought she believed she could manipulate any situation until she was in control, and that her gibberish about whether she had a memory problem would absolve her of any need to give a specific and truthful answer.

As Pam left the courthouse after the final day of testimony, she noticed the camera crew from *Dateline NBC* filming her departure with her husband, Mark. As she crossed the street, Pam's face lit up as she smiled and said directly into the camera, "Say hi to Cathy." The unexpected and audacious greeting to Cathy Singer, the *Dateline* producer on all of the Russ Faria episodes, would become the dramatic opening of yet another *Dateline* on the Faria and Hupp case. Anchor Lester Holt opened the show by describing how Pam Hupp had surprisingly made *Dateline* a named player in the case.

(Keith Morrison had already delivered a personal message to Joel Schwartz. Morrison recalled Schwartz telling him after he collected the interviews for the first episode that he would be back for more after Russ won a new trial. Morrison told Schwartz that he often hears that from defense attorneys, but this was the first case in which it had actually happened.)

A month after the trial, Judge House returned a verdict allowing

Pam Hupp to keep Betsy's insurance money. He said there was not enough evidence to determine to a legal certainty what Betsy intended for her to do with the money. Betsy could have specified that on the form when she made Pam the beneficiary, but she didn't.

"Betsy left it up to Pam Hupp," Judge House said. And since the form was a legal change to Pam Hupp as beneficiary, she was entitled to keep the money.

Butsch was surprised and disappointed. He filed a detailed appeal, but the appellate court upheld Judge House's verdict. Butsch said Leah and Mariah Day were disappointed, but accepted the decision graciously. They were sweet young women who had been pulled into a vortex of accusations, court actions, conflicting emotions about the man they had considered a father figure, and a host of adults telling them what they should do. Butsch thought they were weathering that storm pretty well.

Joel Schwartz understood the legal reasons for the verdict, but it nonetheless was disturbing and frustrating. Pam Hupp continued to slither out of every attempt to hold her responsible for her greedy and homicidal conduct that seemed determined to destroy Betsy, her husband, her daughters, and even Pam's own mother—so far.

Although Judge House rejected efforts by Pam Hupp's attorneys to make Russ Faria a party in the Days' suit, Russ and Schwartz decided to take their own run at recovering the insurance money. Schwartz filed a suit against State Farm Insurance in St. Charles County Circuit Court in April 2016—less than two months after Judge House's decision—attacking the validity of the change in beneficiaries. Schwartz alleged the beneficiary form was incomplete, was not received by State Farm until after Betsy's death, and State Farm's investigation before paying the $150,000 to Pam Hupp was inadequate. Eight months later, State Farm would settle the suit out of court for an undisclosed sum.

But that suit paled in comparison to a massive eighty-two-page suit Schwartz and another leading attorney in the St. Louis region, Bevis Schock, worked together to file in U.S. District Court in St. Louis in July 2016 against Lincoln County Prosecuting Attorney Leah Askey, and Sheriff's Detectives Ryan McCarrick, Mike Merkel, and

Patrick Harney. (McCarrick, by then, had become an officer for the nearby Florissant Police Department.) On the first page alone, the suit charged that Askey and the detectives "fabricated evidence, ignored exonerating evidence, and failed to investigate the obvious suspect" as part of a conspiracy to wrongly convict Russ Faria. Their actions deprived Russ of his civil rights and his liberty without due process in violation of the Fourth and Fourteenth Amendments.

In 532 paragraphs, the suit documented all of the facts of Betsy's murder, Russ's alibi, and the police investigation, and described each and every act of misconduct by Askey—such as prohibiting DNA testing of a pair of gloves or the dog's feet for blood—and by the detectives—such as coaching witnesses, conducting what Schwartz believed was a fake polygraph on Russ to coerce a confession, and plotting to mischaracterize the lack of blood found by luminol tests in the Farias' kitchen and dining room. The suit listed the evidence that should have made Pam Hupp a suspect, while explaining in detail how Askey and the detectives bungled the investigation or, worse yet, intentionally misdirected and shaped it to support their conclusion that Russ Faria murdered his wife.

The suit charged that the evidence failed to establish even a probable cause for arresting and trying Russ, but Askey and the detectives "conspired together" to convict Russ of a crime he did not commit. Their conspiracy put Russ Faria through an unimaginable four years in prison; caused emotional distress, which included terror, stress, fear, anxiety, humiliation, embarrassment, and disgrace; caused the loss of reputation in the community, and the loss of trust in law enforcement.

Russ and Schwartz knew the resolution of that suit could be years down the road. Still, they had no idea what was about to happen just weeks after they filed the federal suit. No one could have imagined.

CHAPTER FIFTY-FOUR

12:06 p.m., Tuesday, August 16, 2016—O'Fallon, Missouri

"Nine-one-one. What's your emergency?"

"Hey! Hello? There's someone busted in my house! Help!"

The woman's voice was loud and excited, but seemed oddly flat for someone reporting a live break-in at her house.

As the dispatcher for the O'Fallon 911 system asked for the woman's address, the woman said again, "Hey! Help! Help!" And then a muffled, garbled man's voice could be heard saying something that seemed to end with "what we did to your wife."

The woman yelled, "No, I'm not getting in the car with you! No! Get away! Get out! Get out! Get out!"

After what sounded like someone pounding on a wall several times, the dispatcher asked again for the address. The caller said in an oddly soft voice, "No, no," before saying louder, "No!" Over the next fifteen seconds, the caller said, "Help! . . . Help! . . . Help!"

The dispatcher continued to try to get the woman to respond. "Ma'am, can you hear me?"

Seconds later, there are the staccato sounds of five gunshots in rapid succession.

After seven seconds of silence, the woman again said, "Help! Help! . . . Help!"

The dispatcher continued to ask the woman's address, until she finally responded, "Hello! Hello! . . . I just shot an intruder in my house."

The woman gave an address on Little Brave Drive and said she didn't know the man she had just shot, but he was still in the house. She yelled, "I'm going outside. I'm going outside. . . . Hurry, hurry, hurry. He tried to get me in my car and I ran into my house. . . . I'm in the garage."

"Are there any weapons in the home?"

"Yes, there's a gun on my bed. I shot him!"

"There's a gun on your bed and you shot him?" the dispatcher asked with a new sense of urgency.

"Yes, he tried to get in my bedroom after me and I shot him. . . . Hurry! . . . Where are they? Where are they?"

"They're on the way, ma'am. . . . Are you injured?"

"No, he didn't get to me. He didn't get me."

Almost four minutes into the call, the dispatcher asked, "What's your name?"

"My name is Pam."

The dispatcher didn't ask for a last name.

At four minutes and twenty-five seconds into the call, the woman said an officer was pulling up in front of her house and she ended the call.

Captain John Neske arrived first at the ranch house and saw a blond woman, in a blue-and-white-striped blouse, blue-and-white-striped capri pants, and athletic shoes, pacing in the driveway while holding a yellow Labrador dog on a leash. The driver's door was open on a dark gray SUV in the driveway and the overhead door to the two-car garage was open. The excited woman was almost yelling that she had just shot a man, who was still lying in a hallway just inside the door from the garage into the house. She had dropped the gun she used on the bed in her bedroom.

Neske and a patrol officer went through the door from the garage into the hallway and found a tall young man lying on his back directly inside the doorway, clearly dead from several gunshot wounds in the chest. He was dressed in a gray tank top, blue workout-style shorts, and running shoes; a ball cap lay nearby. Neske went through the doorway to the bedroom on the right and found a five-shot black Ruger .38-caliber pistol on the bed. All five rounds had been fired.

The excited, emotional woman in the driveway told the police her name was Pam Hupp.

And, as anyone familiar with the Faria case would expect, Pam Hupp had quite a story to tell. She said she had been about to back out of her driveway when a silver car with two men screeched to a stop across the end of the driveway and the man, now lying dead in her hallway, raced over and jumped into the passenger seat of her car. The driver of the other car squealed the tires pulling away. The man in her car called her "bitch" and pushed a knife to her throat as he yelled that she was going to drive him to her bank to "get Russ's money." He was difficult to understand, almost as if he was drunk, but she didn't smell alcohol.

She screamed for him to get out of her car and then hit his arm, knocking the knife out of his hand. She jumped out of the car and fled through the garage and into the house, with the man in fast pursuit. She tried three times to call 911 on her cell phone before she heard the dispatcher answer. She was unable to lock the door from the garage or hold it closed against the man's efforts to push it open. Still on the phone with 911, she fled into her bedroom just to the right of the door from the garage and tried to close the bedroom door. She knew it was difficult to lock, so she quickly retrieved the pistol from her nightstand and turned to face the door just as it flew open.

With the man now standing in her bedroom doorway, she began to advance toward him as she fired the pistol. She kept firing until she heard it clicking on discharged rounds. At first, the man had just stood there looking at her as she shot him, until he finally fell backward into the hallway. She dropped the gun on the bed, ran into the hall to retrieve her dog, and then fled outside into the driveway.

The police asked Pam Hupp several times if she knew a "Russ" whose money her attacker believed she had in the bank.

"I don't know anyone named Russ," Pam Hupp said repeatedly. "I don't know what he was talking about."

CHAPTER FIFTY-FIVE

Detective Kevin Mountain looked across the small table in O'Fallon Police Department Interview Room #1 and tried to digest Pam Hupp's account of shooting this unidentified man she said tried to pull off a violent kidnapping in a quiet neighborhood at noon on a sunny, summer Tuesday. She was shedding a few tears, but seemed remarkably composed for an average housewife in Middle America who had just pumped five rounds point-blank into the chest of a man outside her bedroom door. She said she didn't want the interview to be recorded on video because she always ended up on the TV news. The lead detective explained that recording interviews was standard procedure.

Pam told Mountain and Detective Sergeant Matt Wolf the same story she told police in her driveway, adding more details as the detectives asked questions. Yes, she now realized that the "Russ" in her attacker's wild ramblings had to be, of course, Russ Faria, and the money in her bank had to be, of course, the $150,000 she received as beneficiary to Betsy Faria's insurance. She provided this description of the driver of the kidnapper's car: dark hair, which resembled a buzz cut; dark skin, like a Hispanic complexion. Mountain would later realize she was offering a description that could match Russ Faria. .

While her story, at first, did not seem totally impossible, Mountain soon began assembling a growing list of discrepancies and evidence that made her account less and less believable. She demonstrated holding the pistol with both hands as she shot the intruder, but said she was still on the phone with the 911 dispatcher as she fired the gun. So, how was she holding the phone and using both hands to shoot the pistol at the same time?

Mountain also was certain most people in the life-or-death situation she described would retreat from the attacker, not advance on him as she was shooting. Mountain found it interesting that she said she bought the pistol for protection after being harassed and getting death threats during the Betsy Faria case.

Mountain later listened several times to her 911 call. He didn't buy it. Her reactions and responses just weren't right for a woman under attack by an armed kidnapper forcing his way into her home. The more he listened to it, the more it seemed staged, almost scripted.

Investigators at her house were quickly making intriguing discoveries. The dead man had no identification on him, but his pants pocket contained a ziplock plastic bag inside another plastic bag holding a ballpoint pen and a barely legible note scrawled on white notepad paper that appeared to be detailed, grotesque instructions for kidnapping, robbing—and murdering—Pam Hupp in a strikingly familiar manner.

Get Hupp in car in garage, part of the note read. *Take to bank. Get Russ money. Should be 100 to 150,000. Take Hupp back to house. Get rid of her. Make look like Russ wife. Make sure knife is sticking out of neck.*

That was one of the most chilling things Kevin Mountain had ever read.

But there was more. In the same plastic bag were nine crisp, new $100 bills. Did that suggest the dead man was a not-so-successful hired assassin? The answer soon appeared when police found an envelope containing $500 in cash in Pam's dresser drawer—three $100 bills and four $50 bills. One of the $100 bills bore a serial number ending with 712B. Five of the $100 bills in the man's pocket bore consecutive serial numbers ending in 713B through 717B. What were the chances that two strangers who came together in such a fatal meeting would have in their possession $100 bills with consecutive serial numbers? Why would Pam Hupp and the dead guy share $100 bills?

That was just the beginning. The knife she said she knocked out of the man's hand in her car was found not on the floor or in the backseat, but suspended, blade down, by the handle in the small space between the passenger seat and the console—the same position as several knives in her kitchen: blades down and suspended by the handles in the small space between the counter and the stove.

None of her neighbors, including some who had been outside in their yards or driveways, had seen anything suspicious, although some had heard several loud bangs. No one had seen an older-model, silver sedan, which she described as delivering the prospective kidnapper.

Pam submitted to a request for a DNA sample and surrendered her cell phone. Mark Hupp brought his wife some clothes so the police could test what she was wearing during the shooting. Mountain thought Pam was becoming increasingly eager to leave as the interview went on throughout the afternoon. And although she had agreed to submit fingerprints from her and her husband, they left the police station at five o'clock in the evening—after four hours of interrogation—without doing that.

His name was Louis Royse Gumpenberger and it was 9 p.m. when Mountain was notified that the dead man had been identified through his fingerprints. They were in the database from a few minor scrapes with police in 2003 and 2004, including a DWI and a third-degree domestic assault. He also had a couple of court entries involving child support issues in 2005 and 2006. More digging by Mountain soon revealed his father was deceased and his brother was a guest of the Missouri Department of Corrections.

The search through records soon led Detective Matt Myers and Sergeant Matt Wolf to a woman who knew him and could provide an address for his mother in St. Charles. When the detectives knocked on her door the morning after the shooting, Margaret Burch told them she had just returned from filing a missing persons report on her son with the St. Charles City Police Department. Myers had the sad duty of informing her that her son had been shot to death by a woman who said he forced his way into her home in O'Fallon.

Margaret burst into tears and sobbed, "Not Louis. Not my Louis."

And then Margaret Burch destroyed the very core of Pam Hupp's account of a violent attack by Louis Gumpenberger. A traumatic brain injury in a car crash in 2005 left Margaret's now–thirty-three-year-old son operating on the mental level of a twelve-year-old and with physical limitations that made it difficult for him to talk or walk any distance—and he was unable to run at all. He couldn't drive a car or use a computer. He was friendly and gullible, and other people sometimes took advantage of him. She was the legal guardian for him, as well as his eleven-year-old son. She had noticed her son was gone from the apartment about 9:30 a.m. the day before. He hadn't left her a note, as he always did, but he had left behind the cargo shorts he always wore, his wallet, and his ever-present cigarettes.

The police talked to his doctors and confirmed his mental and physical limitations. Several people who knew him said he was an affable, kind young man with obvious physical and mental limits who never showed any violent tendencies. Not only were they confident he could not physically commit the acts claimed by Pam Hupp, but they also were sure he would never even think of doing such things.

So, how did Louis Gumpenberger end up dead in Pam Hupp's hallway? As the police tracked her movements by mapping her cell phone activity, they placed her in the parking lot of his apartment building for four minutes between 11:25 and 11:29 a.m., barely forty minutes before the shooting. The phone then showed movement until it reached the area near the entrance to her subdivision at 11:41 a.m. After ten minutes at that location, the phone moved to near or at her home from 11:54 a.m. until her 911 call at 12:06 p.m.

All of that suggested she had driven to his apartment complex, picked him up, driven to her home, and shot him to death in a hallway—all in about forty minutes. But why?

While Mountain and the detectives were trying to sort that out at 5:30 p.m., Wednesday, the day after the shooting, the St. Charles police called with a report that would—in the most common cliché—blow the case wide open. The police had received a call on August

10, six days before the shooting, from a woman named Carol McAfee, who reported that she was on her porch with her dog in a mobile home park—coincidentally, the same park where Mike Corbin lived—when a blond woman in a dark gray SUV drove by and waved, turned around, and then pulled up to the end of her driveway.

Carol approached the car and asked, in her characteristically straightforward tone, "Can I help you?"

The woman smiled and asked, "Do you babysit?"

Carol, a substitute teacher, maintained her natural bluntness and responded to what she thought was a ridiculous question with a sharp "No, I don't babysit."

The woman then asked, "Do you know what a sound bite is?"

Carol shot back, "Yeah, I know what a sound bite is. I'm not stupid."

The woman said she was a producer for *Dateline* and offered Carol $1,000 to help reenact a 911 call for the show. "It'll be in cash under the table—no paper trail to Uncle Sam," the woman added with a grin.

The alarm bells were sounding in Carol's normally suspicious mind already, but she was curious. What could this woman in blue jeans and a hospital scrubs-type blouse be up to? She said she might be able to help and the woman responded, "Oh, if you do, you can't bring your keys, your wallet, your cell phone, or any cigarettes. The producers hate clutter."

Carol took her dog into the house, but also slipped a pocketknife up the sleeve of her hoodie, put a steak knife in her hoodie pocket, punched 911 into her cell phone without placing the call, and put the phone in her pocket. She got into the woman's SUV and asked where they were going to record this sound bite.

The woman said she had rented a house behind some shops in nearby Lake St. Louis. Carol couldn't think of anyplace that fit that description as the woman said, "My name is Cathy and I'm from Chicago." More red flags. The woman's SUV bore Missouri license plates and there was no indication it was a rental. As the woman drove through the mobile home park—carefully observing the fifteen-mile-per-hour speed limit, which everyone else ignored, and turning the wrong direction to leave the park—Carol decided it was time to pull the plug on whatever this woman was planning.

Pointing out that she was barefoot, as was usual, Carol told the woman she needed to go back home to get shoes and lock up the house. The woman drove back to her house, where Carol told the woman she wouldn't be able to help now, because her son needed a ride home from work. The woman started to get out of the car as she was asking if Carol could help if she came back in an hour. But for the first time, she noticed the security cameras mounted on the corners of the home.

The woman quickly slid back into the car and said, "Oh, you have security cameras?"

Carol ended the entire charade by saying, "Yes, and I have a knife in my pocket and I'm calling 911." She turned and went into the house as the woman immediately drove away. Carol McAfee quickly posted a warning on the neighborhood's online bulletin board about a suspicious woman driving a gray SUV trying to pick up people, and then she called the police to tell them what had happened.

With that amazing information, Detectives Kevin Mountain and Scott Pierce called Carol McAfee and, without telling her why, arranged to pick her up at home and drive her to the O'Fallon police station. Still not answering her repeated questions about what was happening, they took her into an interview room to get a hand-written statement about her contact with the woman in the SUV a week ago. And then they showed her a lineup of six photographs. Carol positively identified the third photo as the woman who had offered her $1,000 to enact a 911 call for *Dateline*.

It was a photo of Pam Hupp.

It now seemed obvious that she had auditioned Carol McAfee for the role of the dead kidnapper, and only Carol's suspicious nature had saved her life. Pam had been forced to find a different victim—Louis Gumpenberger—for her psychotic plot to frame Russ Faria in yet another killing connected to Betsy's murder. Mountain and the detectives concluded that, now that Russ's acquittal in Betsy's murder had refocused suspicion on Pam, she hoped to deflect that suspicion by framing Russ again in a new and seemingly related murder.

The police would learn later that she had been trolling the area for at least a week looking for someone to fill the role of victim in her newest murder production. She tried to unsuccessfully recruit at least two other men—one at a service station and one she approached as he was cutting grass in the mobile home park.

The police immediately reviewed the video from Carol McAfee's security cameras. When the SUV pulled in the driveway to bring her home, the camera on the corner of the front porch captured the license plate on the front of the car. The police traced the number to H2 Partners LLC at Pam Hupp's home address. State records showed Pam and Mark Hupp each were 50 percent owners of H2 Partners.

The police realized that Carol McAfee had become a key witness in Pam Hupp's murderous saga, and that might have put her in danger. Although she tried to resist, the police posted a twenty-four-hour security detail outside of her house for the next several days.

The police were quickly filling in more details of Pam Hupp's plan. An extensive search for surveillance and security cameras on homes and businesses along the route between Louis Gumpenberger's apartment and Pam Hupp's home produced a fuzzy, grainy—and almost haunting—image of what appeared to be her car driving toward her home with someone who definitely resembled Louis in the front passenger seat.

The note in his pocket included instructions to leave the money in a wood pile at an address that turned out to be the home of Russ Faria's parents. A neighbor's surveillance camera documented her car passing back and forth in front of the home on August 10, just nineteen minutes before Pam contacted Carol McAfee.

Detective Russ McDermott searched online for the source of the santoku knife, with the five-inch blade, made by Royal Norfolk Cutlery, which Pam said Louis had used. He located that exact model for sale at Dollar Tree stores. The manager of the nearest store documented the sale of three of the knives in the last month. Pam's cell phone records put her at or near the store seven times between August 2 and August 16, including two times the morning of the shooting. One of her stops at the store was on August 8, the same day a receipt produced by the manager showed a cash sale for $8.64, which included one of the knives and six other items. When detectives checked the photos from her house, they found five of the items on the receipt on the shelves in her linen closet: ziplock plastic bags, like the ones in Louis Gumpenberger's pocket, a gel air freshener, cotton balls, and two different flavors of Crest toothpaste. At the store, some of those items were within reach of the ballpoint pens and notepaper, like the ones in Louis's pocket.

And then there was the opinion by the handwriting expert, who compared Pam Hupp's handwritten phrases from one note to the other. His conclusion? She wrote the note in Louis Gumpenberger's pocket.

Russ Faria didn't know what to think when he heard that Pam Hupp had shot a man in her home after he tried to make her take him to the bank to get "Russ's money." The story made no sense. He had never heard of Louis Gumpenberger and didn't recognize his photo appearing on the TV news and in the newspapers.

Joel Schwartz was flabbergasted when Russ called to tell him about the shooting. He wasn't surprised that Pam Hupp had killed again—he had warned U.S. Attorney Callahan and others that more people would die if she wasn't stopped. But he was shocked that she had committed a calculated, cold-blooded murder that she would never be able to pin on someone else.

Russ wasn't surprised or offended when the O'Fallon police called and asked him to come to the police station for an interview. Despite his disastrous experience with a similar invitation almost five years ago, he tried to assure himself the O'Fallon police would recognize he had nothing to do with what he was sure was Pam Hupp's third murder—Betsy Faria, Shirley Neumann, and now Louis Gumpenberger.

Detective Kevin Mountain and the police knew the mention of Russ Faria's name in this sordid killing required an official determination of whether he was involved or was an innocent man being framed, again, by Pam Hupp. While Schwartz was out of town, Russ was accompanied to the police station by one of Schwartz's partners, John Rogers. Once there, Russ eagerly accounted for his activ-

ities the day of the shooting. He was in the shower when his father
called him from work to tell him about the shooting, after a friend
had told his father. Russ said his mother and sister could verify that
he was at home with them at the time Pam said the silver sedan delivered the kidnapper to her driveway. Russ provided handwriting
exemplars using his right and left hands to reproduce phrases from
the note in Louis Gumpenberger's pocket. He agreed to let police
take a buccal swab inside his mouth for a DNA sample and take his
fingerprints. He turned over his cell phone for examination.

Russ and Schwartz were confident the police knew what had
really happened, and Russ would be in the clear. Their optimism
was justified. The police quickly concluded there was absolutely no
link between Russ Faria and Louis Gumpenberger, or his death.

CHAPTER FIFTY-SIX

St. Charles County Prosecuting Attorney Tim Lohmar had been in constant contact with the O'Fallon police since minutes after Pam Hupp pulled the trigger on Louis Gumpenberger. Lohmar certainly recognized her from what he remembered as a salacious controversy between Russ Faria's first and second trials in neighboring Lincoln County. After listening to her 911 call, Lohmar knew this was not simply a suburban housewife shooting a man breaking into her house. This was something no one in St. Charles County had ever seen before. And the forty-three-year-old Lohmar was no rookie.

Lohmar had been prosecuting attorney for almost four years after being appointed to fill a vacancy in 2013 and then winning election in 2014. Before that, he had served two years as an associate circuit judge and had been in private practice. His late father had been a circuit judge in the county for twenty-five years.

Pam Hupp was being interrogated at the police station on August 16 when Lohmar arrived to listen to the 911 tape. By the time Lohmar met with detectives again, late on August 17, after much of the damning evidence was found, and Carol McAfee had told her story, the detectives had concluded this was a cold-blooded, premeditated murder by Pam Hupp—and Lohmar agreed. He was impressed with the fantastic investigation by the O'Fallon police that was building a strong case against her quickly.

By the next Monday, August 22, Lohmar had decided to charge

Pam Hupp with first-degree murder and armed criminal action—co-incidentally, the same charges that were filed against Russ Faria—and to arrest her the next day, exactly a week after the shooting. Police were careful to keep the decision quiet while they made plans for the arrest and set up surveillance on her home, in case she tried to leave before the arrest.

That was exactly what happened. Just before 11 a.m. on Tuesday, August 23, Pam Hupp backed her dark gray GMC Acadia out of the garage and started to drive away. When the surveillance team reported her departure, Detective Lieutenant Mike Grawitch—who had developed and was directing the plan for the arrest—ordered patrol officers to stop and arrest her. Sergeants Jodi Weber and Brian Buchanan pulled her over about a block from her home and told her she was under arrest. They asked her to step out of her car and turn around to be handcuffed, which she did without comment.

Wearing an orange T-shirt and denim capri pants, with fashionably torn knees, she was placed in the front seat of an unmarked police car. As Detective Matt Myers approached the open car door, she finally asked why she was being arrested. He explained she was under arrest for the murder of Louis Gumpenberger. She offered no response or reaction. But she soon noticed that a TV crew had arrived and was filming her.

"There's a camera," she said quietly as she leaned forward to hide her face below the dashboard. "I don't want to be on camera."

She seemed calm as Myers took her into an interview room at the police station to begin an interrogation. She said she understood the Miranda rights he read to her and she signed the form with a pen. She was willing to answer some questions, but would like her lawyers to be called. Myers left the room to find her lawyers' phone number, but soon noticed on the surveillance camera that she was standing by the door.

He went to the door and she said, "I have to pee."

Myers asked Officer Holly Garza to escort her to the bathroom, and as they walked down the hall, she told Garza quietly, "I have diarrhea." Garza stood outside the unlocked door while she was inside. Garza asked twice through the door if she was OK, and the suspect said each time, "I'm almost done." Garza finally heard a faucet turn on, but did not hear the toilet flush. She knocked loudly twice on the door, but got no response.

As Garza opened the door, she was shocked to see blood on the floor and blood spatter on the wall. Pushing the door open farther, she saw Pam Hupp on her knees, leaning forward with her face touching the bloody floor in front of the sink. Garza radioed for medical assistance, called down the hall for help, and was immediately joined by Sergeant Jeffrey Cook and Detective Myers.

They pulled Pam out of the small bathroom and laid her on the hallway floor, where they could see she was bleeding from her wrists and neck and her blouse was saturated in blood. Myers took a bloody disposable ballpoint pen from her right hand as the officers began using paper towels to try to staunch the bleeding from a series of small, circular wounds to both wrists and both sides of the neck, where she had stabbed herself repeatedly with the pen. Myers saw what appeared to be the metal tip from the pen still protruding from the left side of her neck. As medics began treating her injuries, Myers saw the tip of the pen fall from her neck to the floor.

Pam's eyes were closed, but she seemed to be conscious. She answered "Yeah" when Myers asked if she could hear him. Her first full comment was that she didn't want anyone to get in trouble because she stole the pen. In an ambulance on the way to the hospital, medics asked why she did it, and she responded, "I don't know why. I was scared." She didn't respond when asked if she was attempting suicide, but she said later that she did not want to die.

Pam underwent surgery at St. Louis University Hospital to ensure she had not inflicted significant damage to her neck and wrists and to repair the mostly superficial wounds. An O'Fallon police officer was posted outside her room for the two days she was in the hospital before she was released and transferred to the St. Charles County Jail. At Prosecuting Attorney Tim Lohmar's request, a judge ordered her held on a $2 million cash-only bond.

Even before the ambulance hauled her away from the police department, Detective Myers reviewed the surveillance video from the minutes she was alone in the interview room. He watched her nonchalantly slide her water bottle next to the pen she had used to sign the Miranda form. She then casually moved her right hand to cover the pen and slid it back to the edge of the table in front of her. She palmed it in her right hand and reached behind her back to slip the pen into the back of her pants.

It wasn't as smooth as David Copperfield's sleight of hand, but it was effective enough.

The news of Pam Hupp's arrest and bizarre self-inflicted injuries exploded across the region—the latest developments in the too-strange-to-be-fiction saga reaching back almost five years to Betsy Faria's murder. But it was her mug shot from booking at the St. Charles County Jail on August 25 that quickly became an instant classic in the region's visual history of crime and punishment. With her blond hair wildly unkempt from her days in the hospital, she stared into the camera with an odd look on her face—perhaps a cross between a smirk and a frown. But the two thickly padded bandages flanking the sides of her neck took the image to the absurd. Some of the more cynical observers began to refer to the mug shot as Pam Hupp's "maxi-pad shot."

Russ Faria and Joel Schwartz told the media during the frenzy of coverage after Pam Hupp's arrest exactly what many others were thinking. If Lincoln County police and Prosecuting Attorney Leah Askey had done their jobs correctly and competently—jobs that Schwartz said any fifth grader could have done—they would have charged Pam Hupp with Betsy Faria's murder, and she never would have been free to kill Louis Gumpenberger. That was a harsh accusation against the authorities, but Russ and Schwartz knew it was the unvarnished truth.

Askey issued a surprising statement the day after Pam Hupp's arrest, saying Lincoln County officials had been cooperating for months with the U.S. Attorney's Office in St. Louis in a review of Betsy Faria's murder. Askey said her office would defer to the federal prosecutor "for guidance and direction on any further investigative efforts." U.S. Attorney Richard Callahan in St. Louis confirmed the review, but had no other comment.

*   *   *

Just three hours after Pam Hupp was arrested on August 23, detectives executed a search warrant at the home of her twenty-nine-year-old son, Travis Hupp, not far from his parents' home. The only notable discovery was a bank folder with a deposit slip recording a deposit of $122,574.84 into his account and a plastic bag containing a handwritten note dated and notarized on August 19 that read: *H2 Partners LLC is giving Travis Victor Hupp a loan in the amount of $122,574.84. Interest to be paid at the rate of $5.00 a year.* The note was signed by Pam and Mark Hupp, the owners of H2 Partners. Travis told police his mother had come to his home the morning of August 20 and had given him the endorsed check she wanted him to deposit in his account in case the courts froze her bank accounts, as they did in 2014 when Betsy Faria's daughters sued her over the insurance money. Travis said he thought he was just doing a favor for his parents and he found nothing unusual about it.

On August 25, Detective Scott Pierce contacted Mark Hupp to ask him to provide fingerprints, a DNA sample, and handwriting exemplars. Pierce reported Mark said he would talk to his attorneys and let the police know what they decided. Then he made this comment: "There is a, uh, as you well know, a bigger picture to all this. And I am not going to, uh, succumb to being implied that I was in, anywhere else. I don't know how else to say it. I'm not going to come right out and say it, but I, you know. Let's just say Russ Faria's friends never gave samples, so I don't think I'm going to give samples."

Pierce reported that he never heard from Mark Hupp again.

The police would search two plastic trash bags they found in Pam's car that they believed to be the ones they saw Pam and Mark Hupp carrying to the car the night after the shooting when they were on their way to an overnight stay with relatives. Along with seven shirts and blouses and two pairs of flip-flop sandals, the bags contained a copy of Betsy Faria's death certificate; a federal tax 1099 miscellaneous form (with Betsy listed as recipient); transcripts of Pam Hupp's testimony in Russ Faria's first trial, and one of her interviews with police; bank statements for the Hupps; five manila folders with various records for Hupp's mother, Shirley Neumann, and a brother-in-law; a yellow sticky note with bank account numbers, and one with Hupp's mother's name; and, without explanation or details, what a detective described as a "note from [an] individual who had [an] affair with Mark."

Trying to tie up another loose end in the investigation led to a somewhat sardonic discovery by the police. They had photographed, but not seized, the cash they found in Pam Hupp's dresser drawer the day of the shooting, including the $100 bill that was sequential to the $100 bills in Louis Gumpenberger's pocket. They hoped to find that bill again after they obtained a search warrant for the Hupp house on September 1.

No one was home when police arrived, and they tried repeatedly to contact Mark or his attorneys so someone could unlock the door. When no one responded, the police took the only option left. They literally knocked down the front door. They had to cover the doorway with a sheet of plywood when they left.

But they couldn't find the $100 bill or the envelope that had contained it and other cash. They did find, however, a small safe. They took the safe to the police department while they got the combination and a key from Pam Hupp's attorneys. When they opened the safe, they found only one surprising item—a tube of K-Y Intense gel, a sexual lubricant and stimulant.

The cops thought the suggestive message to them from the Hupps was obvious.

Prosecuting Attorney Tim Lohmar delivered a more grave message to Pam Hupp a few months after her arrest. He announced he would seek the death penalty if she was convicted of Louis Royse Gumpenberger's murder. In his court filing invoking the death penalty, he cited as grounds the statutory aggravating factor: *[The] murder in the first degree was outrageously or wantonly vile, horrible or inhuman in that it involved depravity of mind.* Supporting that conclusion, Lohmar said choosing Louis as her victim "was random and without regard to the victim's identity." He maintained that she had "exhibited a callous disregard for the sanctity of all human life." He acknowledged the death penalty was a rare and "extraordinary remedy," but he said her crime qualified as "one of the worst of the worst."

No one had faced the death penalty in St. Charles County for at least a decade. Bonnie Brown Heady, the last woman executed in Missouri, went to the gas chamber in 1953 on federal convictions for participating in the kidnapping and killing of six-year-old Bobby Greenlease Jr. His abduction and murder had drawn national headlines. The last execution in Missouri had been in January 2017, after nearly nineteen years of appeals and delays.

CHAPTER FIFTY-SEVEN

While the murder case against Pam Hupp was slogging through pre-trial motions and routine delays, the Betsy Faria murder case came back to haunt Prosecuting Attorney Leah Askey and Circuit Judge Christina Kunza Mennemeyer in the Lincoln County elections in 2018.

Mike Wood—the young assistant prosecutor who was so appalled at Askey's closing argument in Russ Faria's first trial in 2013 that he resigned from her office—declared his candidacy for prosecuting attorney as a Republican and made Askey's performance in the Faria case a major issue. Askey—who had dropped her ex-husband's last name and was going by Leah Wommack Chaney, using her maiden name and her current husband's last name—then changed her political party. Although she had been elected twice as a Democrat, she switched to the Republican Party before the Missouri primary elections in August 2018 and forced a primary battle with Wood. Lincoln County was heavily Republican and Chaney may have decided she had a better chance in the Republican primary against Wood than she would as a Democrat against Wood in the general election in November.

Meanwhile, Circuit Judge Christina Mennemeyer was battling her own issues. In January 2017, she drew a six-month, unpaid suspension—recommended by the Missouri Commission on Retirement, Removal and Discipline, and unanimously imposed by Missouri Supreme Court justices. She decided not to oppose the suspension based on allegations that included mishandling cases as a private attorney and as a sitting judge. None of the allegations involved the Faria case. But the supreme court found that, among her errors or misconduct, she intentionally delayed the cases of eight people for sixty to seventy-nine days in a dispute with the county's public defenders—some who were repeatedly filing motions to remove her from their cases. The delays resulted in those defendants staying in jail longer while awaiting trial or disposition of their cases.

She had won the Republican primary in 2012 and pulled off a close, unexpected victory in the general election over a popular Democrat associate judge who nearly everyone thought would win. But when she ran again in the Republican primary in August 2018—after her suspension—she placed third in a three-way race with just 21 percent of the vote. The Republican who won, Patrick Flynn, made Mennemeyer's suspension a major issue in the campaign, but acknowledged many voters wrongly assumed her suspension had something to do with the Faria case. Flynn defeated the Democratic candidate for the judgeship in the general election in November 2018.

Republican voters deciding between Wood and Chaney (Askey) faced no such confusion over her role in the Faria case. Wood called Chaney's performance inept and at the top of the list of her many mistakes and poor performance. She defended her prosecution of Russ Faria and said it was unfair to judge her record over eight years as prosecuting attorney by that one case.

After a bitter campaign, Wood took nearly three-quarters of the Republican vote in the primary, inflicting a stunning defeat on Chaney. No Democrat sought the prosecuting attorney's office in the general election, leaving Wood to take the office unopposed in November. Chaney returned to private practice.

CHAPTER FIFTY-EIGHT

Pam Hupp had been in the St. Charles County Jail for almost three years by the time her trial was scheduled for June 2019. She had regular phone calls with her husband, but very few visitors. Jail officials told Prosecuting Attorney Tim Lohmar that she told other prisoners in the women's wing she was being held on traffic charges. At sixty-one, she was significantly older than most of the other prisoners and seemed to take a "mother hen" role, listening to their stories and talking to them about their cases and their lives. But Lohmar also was told she continued to be manipulative, sometimes trying to pit prisoners and even guards against each other. Lohmar thought she still was driven to exert as much control over others as she could, given she now lived in a world mostly beyond her control.

Her team of attorneys—led by well-known criminal defense attorneys Brad Kessler and Nicholas Williams—was fighting hard for her in the courtroom, aware that the death penalty hung over her head. They had convinced Circuit Judge Jon A. Cunningham that jurors from St. Charles County had been exposed to too much publicity to give her a fair trial. The judge decided jurors would be chosen from Platte County, north of Kansas City, some 250 miles away, and brought to his courtroom in St. Charles for the trial. He agreed with defense attorneys that there would be no mention in the trial of her mother's death. But he rejected their effort to prohibit evidence about Betsy Faria's murder, Russ Faria's trial, or her involvement in those cases. Cunningham said a certain amount of background about the Faria case was necessary for jurors to understand the case against Pam Hupp and the references in the note in Louis Gumpenberger's pocket to "Russ's money" and to make Pam's death look similar to Betsy's, including leaving a knife sticking out of her neck.

In early spring 2019, Lohmar proposed a plea bargain to Pam's attorneys. If she would plead guilty of first-degree murder, he would drop his demand for the death penalty in favor of a life sentence without parole. He thought avoiding a trial, the protracted and expensive death sentence process, and years and years of appeals and delays would be the best solution for everyone, while still securing justice for Louis Gumpenberger and his family. Louis's mother agreed.

For weeks, it seemed to Lohmar that the defense attorneys were struggling to convince their reluctant client to take the deal. She finally agreed, if she could enter what is known as an Alford plea. She wouldn't have to admit she committed the murder, but would agree the prosecution had enough evidence to convict her in a trial.

The crowd that turned out to see Pam Hupp plead guilty on June 19, 2019, was so large that the hearing had to be moved to a bigger courtroom. Even that space was packed with a hundred spectators, including two rows of O'Fallon police and other law enforcement officials. Russ Faria was there, along with members of his family and friends, and Joel Schwartz and Nate Swanson. Louis Gumpenberger's mother, Margaret Burch, was there. The media were there en masse. When a sheriff's deputy asked if there was any of Pam Hupp's family in the courtroom, there was absolute silence.

Few of those crowded together on the benches were prepared to see the Pam Hupp who was escorted into the room by sheriff's deputies. Gone was the plump bleached blonde with the short, puffy hairdo. The woman seated at the defense table in the dark blue jacket and light blue blouse was slim to the point of appearing gaunt. Her hair was mostly a dull gray and hung straight almost to her shoulders. The chubby face that had been in the news so often over the last eight years was now so thin and drawn as to be barely recognizable.

Judge Cunningham called Pam Hupp to the witness stand to confirm she was voluntarily pleading guilty. After one of Lohmar's assistants summarized the facts in the murder of Louis Gumpenberger, Judge Cunningham asked her how she pleaded to the count of murder in the first degree under the terms of an Alford plea.

She paused for seconds that seemed like hours to Lohmar and others who feared she might change her mind again. She finally said softly, "Guilty." The judge accepted her plea and set sentencing for August 12.

Tim Lohmar called a press conference immediately after the hearing. He praised the "brilliant" investigation by the O'Fallon police and discussed much of what he called "overwhelming" evidence. He played her 911 call, stopping just before the sounds of the five gunshots. He said he agreed to accept an Alford plea because the result was the same—she was guilty—and he doubted she had the courage to admit her guilt straight out. He said her attempt to frame Louis Gumpenberger as a kidnapper and killer sent by Russ Faria was "sloppy."

"It just doesn't make sense," he said. "It sounds like something a middle-school kid would come up with to write a crime story."

He said Pam Hupp was now linked to three separate deaths—Betsy Faria, Shirley Neumann, and Louis Gumpenberger—and he was gratified that "she will never spend another day of her life outside a prison cell."

And Lohmar made it clear that Russ Faria had nothing to do with this unhinged kidnapping-robbery-murder plot that Pam Hupp had tried to pin on him to deflect suspicion away from herself in Betsy's murder.

Russ told reporters he was relieved she had pleaded guilty to the Gumpenberger murder, but was disappointed she had never confessed to killing Betsy.

In Lincoln County, one county to the west of St. Charles, Prosecuting Attorney Mike Wood announced he was officially reopening the investigation into the murder of Betsy Faria. He said seven boxes of evidence had already been retrieved from storage and detectives were meeting with a new team from the Major Case Squad. He was convinced Betsy's murder could be solved.

* * *

It seemed almost anticlimactic when everyone reassembled August 12, 2019, for Judge Cunningham to sentence Pam Hupp. This time, the gaunt and gray woman was brought into court in an orange jail uniform with her hands shackled to a belt around her waist. And though the occasion seemed to call for a certain solemnity, she could be seen giggling and joking with her defense team before the hearing started.

But her smile soon faded. Sitting in the first row in the courtroom, close to Pam Hupp, was the woman who played such an important role in her capture and imprisonment—Carol McAfee. Unknown to anyone except their closest family and friends, Carol and Russ had fallen in love and would soon move in together. Carol had vowed to spend every day for the rest of her life making Russ smile. But she had a different message that day for Pam.

Carol leaned forward and got Pam's attention before saying, "I want you to know I'm the one who put you here, bitch." Pam's attorneys complained to a deputy sheriff, who told Carol that she would have to move. She refused and sat there for the rest of the hearing.

Louis Gumpenberger's half sister, Krystal Conn, delivered a tearful victim impact statement that riveted the courtroom as she called Pam Hupp a serial killer and monster who had taken an innocent man away from his children, his mother, his family, and his friends. Describing her as a coward, Krystal said it was clear to her that Pam Hupp had murdered three people—"a friend, her mother, and my brother." Krystal said she hoped she lived long enough to see the prisoner's death, but would strive to forget about her "as she sits lonely and alone in her jail cell."

When the judge asked if the defendant had anything to say before he imposed the sentence, Pam Hupp—stone-faced and appearing pale under the low lights in the courtroom—made no statement.

The judge said only that Louis Gumpenberger "was an innocent person whose life did not deserve to be extinguished by you" before imposing the sentence already set under her plea agreement—life in prison without parole. A concurrent thirty-year sentence for armed criminal action was little more than a formality.

                                    *   *   *

"Where does it live—evil?" Keith Morrison's unmistakable voice asked as a new season of *Dateline* opened on NBC on September 27, 2019, with a two-hour episode called, "The Thing About Pam." Host Lester Holt introduced the show as "a new chapter in our most twisted mystery ever. At the heart of it, a woman as cagey as they come." But calling Pam Hupp "cagey" didn't seem to reach deep enough into depravity for Morrison as he continued his opening: "This story is about the evil that smiles and helps and sympathizes—that worms its hidden way into unsuspecting minds—and kills. This is about such a woman as we have never seen. And, though we followed her for years, we had no idea, until now. The story we can finally tell."

The premiere was screened in a theater in New York City in an exclusive event with Russ Faria and Joel Schwartz in attendance as special guests.

The first hour of the show told the full story of Betsy's murder and Russ Faria's prosecution, all in Pam Hupp's shadow. And when the second hour began, Lester Holt promised "a stunning new twist in tonight's *Dateline* as someone tries to impersonate—us . . . a dark new scheme about to come to light." Now the story focused on Pam Hupp's search for a new murder victim while pretending to be a *Dateline* producer and her merciless killing of Louis Gumpenberger.

"The Thing About Pam" was the fifth *Dateline* episode on the Faria/Hupp case. The only shows to draw higher rating were those on O.J. Simpson and JonBenét Ramsey. Shortly after the fifth episode was shown, *Dateline* posted a six-part podcast also called "The Thing About Pam." The month it debuted, it was the highest-rated podcast in the country.

And *Dateline* still wasn't finished with Pam Hupp. NBC announced in May 2020 that the podcast would be the basis of a six-part scripted TV series and later added that the cast would include Academy Award winner Renée Zellweger playing Pam, Josh Duhamel as Schwartz, Judy Greer as Chaney, and Katy Mixon as Betsy.

Pam Hupp tried to withdraw her guilty plea in September 2020. She filed a handwritten petition asking for the plea to be dismissed, claiming that her defense attorneys pressured her into accepting the plea agreement as they kept her in the dark about her case. She blamed a prison lockdown because of the COVID-19 pandemic for missing the February 2020 deadline to file such a petition, even though the prison was not locked down until months after the deadline. She never mentioned the facts in the case or Louis Gumpenberger. Judge Cunningham denied the petition in February 2021.

Pam Hupp was a single woman by then. While she sat in prison, the husband who seemed to stay faithfully by her side through all of the chaos between 2011 and 2019 filed for a divorce in St. Charles County Circuit Court on October 12, 2020. Mark A. Hupp's divorce petition said he and his wife of twenty-six years had been separated since her arrest in August 2016, adding: *There remains no reasonable likelihood that the marriage of the parties can be preserved and, therefore, the marriage is irretrievably broken.* The divorce was listed as uncontested and a judgment of dissolution of marriage was entered exactly a month later, on November 12, 2020.

Although the court files show the divorce was uncontested, an insider source said Pam was furious because she and Mark had agreed before she went to jail that there would be no divorce. And not only was there a divorce, but the source said there had been a quick remarriage for Mark just weeks after the divorce was final. Neighbors said in 2021 that he was still living in the house where his ex-wife gunned down Louis Gumpenberger.

There had been more court action against Pam Hupp even before the divorce. In July 2020, a judge in St. Charles Circuit Court ordered her to pay $3 million in damages to Margaret Burch in a wrongful-death suit over the murder of Louis Gumpenberger. Margaret's attorney acknowledged that the jailed inmate had no money, but he said the judge's decision would prevent Pam from ever profiting from her story through books or movies. The award would be a collectable debt on any income Pam Hupp would ever receive.

Russ Faria, however, did collect on his federal suit over the investigation and prosecution that put him in prison for almost four years. A judge dismissed former prosecuting attorney Leah Wommack Chaney and Lincoln County as parties to the suit in 2019, citing their sovereign immunity for acts committed as part of their official duties. But the insurance company representing Detectives Ryan McCarrick, Mike Merkel, and Patrick Harney agreed in March 2020 to pay Russ the policy limits of the officers' coverage—just over $2 million. As usual in such settlements, the detectives did not admit any wrongdoing and all of the parties were prohibited from discussing the details.

Joel Schwartz and the two attorneys who worked with him on the suit were gratified to get at least that measure of justice for Russ Faria. Schwartz told the media that the money obviously couldn't repay Russ for the loss of his wife or nearly four years in prison. But even without an official finding of wrongdoing by the onetime prosecuting attorney Leah Askey and the detectives, the result was recognition of the wrongs he had suffered.

Russ Faria made similar comments to the media, especially noting that there was still no resolution of Betsy's murder. But he hoped that, even though the detectives did not admit wrongdoing, the settlement would be seen as vindicating him completely while condemning the cops' actions and behavior.

CHAPTER FIFTY-NINE

By the time Pam Hupp went to prison for murdering Louis Gumpenberger and was widely assumed to have killed Betsy Faria and her own mother, there was a long list of descriptions and explanations for the horrifying things she had done and the mind-boggling things she had said. She's a psychopath, some opined. A serial killer. A monster. She's crazy. Or she's simply evil.

But how could any of that be true about a woman whose childhood and many years as a seemingly average wife and mother in Middle America offered no obvious clues to the kind of shocking behavior that seems to have begun when she was fifty-three years old? Had something happened that changed her so drastically? Was there a trigger?

Could Pam Hupp's turn down the path that left three people dead and led her to the rest of her life in a prison cell be traced to a single event in November 2009?

Pamela Marie Neumann was born in October 1958, the third of four children in a middle-class family in the St. Louis suburb of Dellwood. Her father was a lineman for Union Electric and her mother was an elementary-school teacher. A family insider said few people knew both of the Neumanns were functioning alcoholics who could be verbally and occasionally physically abusive. As Pam grew up in that environment, she developed a rebellious streak that could make her outspoken and confrontational—something of a "loose cannon," as one source said. No boundaries and no filter. She rejected any effort to tell her what to do, even by her parents, and would sometimes do the exact opposite of what she had been told.

Despite all of that, she was described as a happy kid who could be goofy and fun-loving, always up for a challenge with a willingness to try anything once. She was the one who would ride her bicycle across busy Chambers Road without waiting for a break in the traffic and then berate friends who were more careful. She was a good athlete, excelling as a shortstop on the softball team at Riverview Senior High School, where she also participated in gymnastics and was on the pom-pom squad—a cheerleader. Smart, but easily bored, she hated school. Her father called her "Catfish"—all mouth and no brains.

She began dating a boy when they were juniors and they were still seeing each other after they graduated in 1977. They found out in August she was pregnant and got married the next month. Their daughter was born in March 1978. Her husband had a soccer scholarship to Washington University in St. Louis, but soon discovered it was impossible to travel with the team when he had a wife and baby at home. He quit school and went to work as a carpenter. Pam also started classes at the University of Missouri-St. Louis, but had to drop out. The young couple was broke, there was some conflict, and the marriage fell apart.

By the time what has been described as an ugly divorce was final in July 1983, Pam had already begun seeing another man, Mark Alan Hupp, who was spending that year as a catcher for the minor league baseball team affiliated with the Texas Rangers before he became a carpenter. They married in November 1983, four months after her divorce was final. The Hupps moved to Florida and Pam not only got a degree in computer science from a college in Naples, but they also had a son in 1987. Pam began working at State Farm Insurance while they were in Florida and that continued when they returned to St. Louis in 2001. On her first day of a job at an insurance office that year, she met Betsy Faria, who was already working there.

Although there were no accounts of any violent behavior, sources said Pam Hupp could be difficult and even vindictive in her personal relationships. There were reports that she hated her mother, Shirley Neumann, and avoided contact with her as much as possible, even after her father died in 2000. And there was this shocking story: When her married daughter told her she was going to bid on a house in foreclosure, Pam said the house was too expensive for her. Pam then bid $1,000 more than she knew her daughter would offer, winning the house and later selling it for a profit.

Joel Schwartz's investigator uncovered reports that she had been fired from two insurance jobs over allegations of forging documents. Conflict with other employees allegedly resulted in her car being "keyed." There were no details or confirmation of any of those reported problems at work, but they suggested she was willing to slide into criminal conduct if it suited her purposes.

But it was an event in November 2009 that may have changed Pam Hupp and the lives of people in her orbit forever. She was working in a UnitedHealthcare office and carrying a stack of files when she stumbled over a box on the floor and fell headfirst into a file cabinet. She suffered head and back injuries that would require surgery and substantial physical care and rehabilitation; relatives said it was brain damage that resulted in drastic personality changes. While she was in the hospital, they said, she suffered depression, anxiety, confusion, pain, fear, and significant memory deficit. She became delusional. She began to tell paranoid stories about a man who would sneak into her room at night and stare at her. He planned to kill her, she said, and she had saved a drinking straw to jam into his eye if he attacked her.

Her conduct continued to be so erratic that her family sent a letter in August 2010 to the rehabilitation center to complain that her recent care had been ineffective. Her physical problems had not improved as quickly as the family had hoped, and balance issues had resulted in repeated falls. Despite doctor's orders not to drive, she had been driving to physical therapy appointments and had car crashes. The letter alleged that she had been "over medicated," listing ten prescriptions, including the antianxiety medicine Valium, antidepressant Effexor, and pain relievers, including oxycodone and hydrocodone. The list also included zolpidem, classified as a sedative hypnotic and sold as Ambien. One website said: *[Zolpidem users] got out of bed and drove their cars, prepared and ate food, had sex, made phone calls, sleepwalked, or were involved in other activities while not fully awake. After they woke up, these people were unable to remember what they had done.*

The family's letter expressed great concern about the effects of her brain injury: *We, as a family, have noticed that her mental status has gone from bad to worse. . . . Her everyday confusion and inappropriate actions are very stressful and the family was brought to a breaking point.*

One source said Pam had become delusional and paranoid, imagining that some relatives were planning to kill her, that other people were following her and spying on her, and, eventually, that Russ Faria's friends were going to kill her. A source said Pam was suspected of poisoning some of the family members' dogs with antifreeze because she felt they were not being cared for properly. She threw away her own computer after Betsy Faria was murdered, a source said, because people were writing mean things to her. She also was suspected of odd behavior by some of her neighbors. After she shot Louis Gumpenberger, one of Pam's neighbors told police she "had been told by other neighbors the female resident at 1260 Little Brave Drive, Pamela Hupp, had supposedly been going around to neighbors' residences peering into windows late at night, as well as spraying weed killer on other people's lawns."

A family insider had always suspected that Pam Hupp's brain injury was responsible for the inexplicable and ultimately violent turn in her behavior and the outrageous comments she had made to police, lawyers, and others. The source couldn't understand why her defense attorneys did not try to make her mental condition an issue in court before she pleaded guilty to the Gumpenberger murder. Defense attorney Nicholas Williams had no comment about that.

But Joel Schwartz never believed Pam actually had a significant brain injury. Convoluted statements and bizarre actions that could be argued as behaviors resulting from brain damage, he saw as manipulative lies and illegal conduct springing from a purely criminal mind. He thought brain damage would have manifested in more ways than Pam displayed. She never even offered a definitive diagnosis of any health or brain injuries; it changed from her back to her neck to a drop foot to her leg to her head. She seemed to use the fall in 2009 as a crutch, Schwartz thought, perhaps as an excuse for her supposed memory lapses and contradictions.

Plus, despite her complaints, there was news video of her running away from a TV camera, exhibiting no apparent physical impediments. Schwartz saw no reason to give Pam Hupp any legal cover with a defense of diminished mental capacity or mental incompetence, let alone insanity.

Joel Schwartz and Nate Swanson have their own thoughts about what might have happened that night at the Faria house and they attribute it to a murderous conspiracy led by a truly criminal mind. Pam Hupp clearly made every effort to be with Betsy at her house while Russ was at game night. It is likely, Schwartz believes, that Pam either had help attacking Betsy or, perhaps, she had someone else kill Betsy at her direction. Pam's job would have been to get Betsy home alone and get the dog chained up outside so the killer could enter the house. Swanson is less sure she had any assistance. But they both believe many of her lies had a grain of truth and could provide clues. Pam may have really seen someone in a car outside the house when she and Betsy arrived—perhaps the actual killer or killers. The story about Russ holding a pillow over Betsy's face could mean that was part of the effort to subdue and kill Betsy. It was unfortunate that no pathologist checked her nose, mouth, or airways for threads or particles a pillow night have left behind. It was equally unfortunate that there was no effort to search Pam's car or other vehicles she had access to or to find out exactly what she had been wearing that night. The lack of a complete investigation of Pam as a suspect played right into her hands.

Schwartz was certain of this, however. Pam Hupp killed two people for her own financial gain and killed a third simply for self-preservation—and tried twice to put an innocent man in prison for her crimes. She didn't deserve an excuse for mental health or any other reason. She deserved to be locked up for good.

CHAPTER SIXTY

July 12, 2021—nine and a half years
after Betsy Faria's murder

The facts in the murder of Betsy Faria were recited again in a new document filed in Lincoln County Circuit Court on July 12, 2021, by the sheriff's office. But this time, the conclusions drawn from those facts—and a new six-month investigation into Betsy's death—were vastly different than those from 2011 and 2012. First, the document said, it was "clear" that Russell Faria was "not involved in his wife's death." And second, the facts established probable cause "to charge" Pamela Hupp with the "first-degree murder of Betsy Faria."

And that is exactly what Prosecuting Attorney Mike Wood did. He charged Pam Hupp with first-degree murder and armed criminal action and announced at a news conference that day that he would seek the death penalty against her.

"I do not take lightly the decision to pursue the death penalty, but this case stands alone in its heinousness and depravity, such that it shocks the conscience," he said. "After a complete and comprehensive review and investigation, I came to the conclusion that, beyond a reasonable doubt, Pamela Hupp killed Betsy Faria—and I believe her motivation was simple—for greed. . . . We have a person who not only murdered her friend, [but] then mutilated the body, staged the scene, testified against an innocent man, and then, once he was acquitted, went and murdered someone in St. Charles County to prevent herself from being considered as a suspect. . . . I can't pick a case that was more depraved than that."

But Pam Hupp was not Wood's only target that day. He also announced he and Sheriff Richard "Rick" Harrell were opening an investigation into possible criminal misconduct by the police and prosecutors who conducted the first investigation that led to murder charges against Russ Faria, two trials, and his imprisonment for almost four years. He didn't mention any names in the announcement, but clearly directed his criticisms at former prosecuting attorney Leah Askey Chaney and former detectives Ryan McCarrick, Mike Merkel, Patrick Harney, and possibly others.

Wood said the new investigation that led to charges against Pam Hupp had "largely corroborated" the allegations in the federal suit filed by Joel Schwartz that accused the police and prosecutors of a conspiracy to violate Russ's civil rights. And Wood said the investigation also uncovered statements by three separate and independent sources that they "were asked to lie on the witness stand by the prosecutor in that case." He also said that, after Russ was acquitted, the previous sheriff's department prepared an order for the destruction of all of the evidence that, fortunately, was not carried out. Wood said he had the St. Charles police keep the evidence to protect it.

Wood blasted the original investigation as a case of "confirmation bias" and said the police and prosecutors were clearly uninterested in investigating any lead that did not confirm their theory.

"This was one of the poorest examples of investigative work that I, as well as my team, have ever encountered—driven largely by ego, working toward an agenda rather than truth," Wood said. "It's clear to me that investigators made up their minds early into Betsy's death and that they never once considered Pamela Hupp as a suspect, despite overwhelming evidence. . . . That investigation was mismanaged from the beginning."

He said the prosecutors and police "doubled down" on their misguided and perhaps corrupt efforts to convict Russ Faria after his first conviction was overturned and he won a new trial. He said they were concerned about their own exposure to civil damages, as evidenced by the $2 million-plus settlement in Russ's federal suit against the police officers.

Wood said he was obligated as county prosecutor not only to get justice for Betsy Faria by prosecuting Pam Hupp as her killer, but also to show county residents that no one is above the law—"not prosecutors, not police officers."

Wood called the facts pointing to Pam Hupp as Betsy Faria's killer "quite simply indisputable" and said they constructed "an extremely compelling circumstantial murder case, one that is very difficult to deny—yet prosecutors and investigators denied it all the same. Sadly, all of these facts were available to prosecutors at the beginning, even while Betsy's husband was twice prosecuted for her death."

He also disclosed that the new investigation indicated the pattern in the blood on the bedroom switch plate resulted from the killer wearing Betsy's socks on their hands while handling the knife and other evidence, staging the murder scene, and then touching the light switch. The five-page probable-cause statement said: *The blood stains [sic] on the socks resemble impressions of fingers and not toes.* Investigators also concluded the blood on Betsy's right heel appeared to have been left there when the killer held her foot to put the bloody sock back on.

Just days before Wood announced the charges against her, Pam Hupp denied everything—killing Betsy Faria and even the murder of Louis Gumpenberger—when investigators interviewed her in prison for more than four hours. Sources said they were convinced she would stand trial on the new charges—even risking the death penalty—rather than enter a guilty plea as she did in the Gumpenberger murder. (In fact, she entered a plea of not guilty to the charges and never uttered a word when she made her first appearance in court on July 27, 2021. Wearing orange prison scrubs, glasses, and a COVID-19 face mask, she never looked at the crowd in the courtroom that included some of Russ Faria's family, as well as one of Betsy's daughters and one of her sisters.)

Russ Faria was sitting just feet away from Mike Wood when he announced the charges and internal investigation on July 12, 2021, which gave Russ his first new hope for justice for Betsy. He had doubted that he would ever see this day and was grateful to Wood and the new investigative team for their efforts. He vowed to take the witness stand against Pam Hupp when she was tried for Betsy's murder. And despite general opposition to capital punishment, he said he supported Wood's decision to seek the death penalty for Pam Hupp. He also said he hoped Wood would be able to deliver an appropriate measure of justice to the prosecutor and the police who, he believed, conducted an incompetent and corrupt investigation that so wrongly targeted him and protected Pam Hupp.

Russ was joined at Wood's announcement by Carol McAfee, Mary Anderson, his sister, Rachel, and his brother, Josh. And as he stood before the reporters and cameras again, Russ took from his pocket a small urn of Betsy's ashes so everyone would know she was there to receive justice that day as well.

Joel Schwartz and Nate Swanson were there, too, as Mike Wood confirmed everything they had been saying since they began defending Russ and examining the facts and evidence. They couldn't have predicted the outrageous court battles and tragic events they would face over those ten years. But as they stood again in a courtroom in Lincoln County, they knew that justice for Betsy and Russ Faria finally was within sight.

Clearly stung by Wood's allegations of incompetence and perhaps actual wrongdoing in the Faria case, Leah Askey Chaney broke her self-imposed silence two days after his news conference to defend herself and her conduct in the case. In an interview with the Christine Byers, the excellent crime reporter for KSDK, the NBC affiliate in St. Louis, Chaney denied that she did anything improper, unethical, or illegal while prosecuting Russ Faria through two trials. She never withheld evidence or told any witness to lie, she insisted while accusing Wood of character assassination and attacking her for his own political agenda. She said the only evidence presented to her from the investigation into Betsy's murder implicated Russ and her prosecution of him was appropriate. She had found no substantive evidence that Pam Hupp could be the killer.

Chaney said she had been the target of a relentless, unfair, and inaccurate social media campaign that she could not ethically answer while Russ's case was pending or before she was dismissed as a defendant in the federal suit Russ filed against her and the police officers. Being subjected to constant criticism was difficult to endure and it affected every part of her life. She said she regretted ever running for prosecuting attorney and the worst thing that ever happened to her was winning the conviction against Russ in the first trial.

Schwartz rejected Chaney's claims that her prosecution of Russ was fair and appropriate. And he found a moral victory against Chaney in her regrets about running for prosecuting attorney and winning the conviction against Russ. He found those regrets from an elected prosecuting attorney remarkable admissions of a job badly done.

Russ Faria laughs easily these days. He still has a ready sense of humor. He enjoys working at the motorcycle service shop, where he has been for a couple of years now. He is financially secure and wise enough not to spend money on a big house he doesn't want or need or any of the other material things that would be tempting to some. He saves his money for travel to the many places he always has wanted to visit.

And he has someone he is happy to share his life with now. When he talks about Carol McAfee, his voice softens, his eyes glisten, and he says how happy they make each other. And Carol understands the special place in his heart where he keeps his memories of Betsy. He will always love and miss and mourn Betsy. As Carol suggested, Russ keeps the urn with Betsy's ashes on the headboard of his bed. But he knows Betsy would want him to live his best life, and that is his goal every day now.

He has avoided bitterness, though God knows he has every reason to be. He did find new hope and satisfying righteousness in the murder charges in Betsy's death filed against Pam Hupp in July 2021. He is grateful for Prosecuting Attorney Mike Wood's dedication and drive to get justice for Betsy and everyone else in the case. He hopes Wood's continuing investigation will lead to official acknowledgment and punishment for the prosecutor and the cops whose misconduct he believes far exceeded incompetence. Russ still acknowledges anger at former judge Christina Kunza Mennemeyer for her role in the injustice inflicted on him.

But he keeps all of that mostly locked away and remembers some good advice he heard once: The best revenge is to live well. He likes to think about those who tried to destroy him catching his occasional appearance on TV, where they have to see his "smiling mug."

Russ can't find the words to express his gratitude and love for his parents, Richard and Luci; his sister and brother, Rachel and Josh; his cousin, Mary Anderson; and all of the family and friends whose active support and love carried him through those bad years.

He is eternally grateful to Joel Schwartz and Nate Swanson for their unfailing belief in him and his innocence, and their tireless, masterful efforts to get justice for him and Betsy.

He credits the relentless news coverage by Chris Hayes of FOX 2 with bringing the truth to the people. That goes as well for Robert Patrick of the *St. Louis Post-Dispatch* and for *Dateline*—especially reporter Keith Morrison and producer Cathy Singer—and its incomparable ability to capture the truth, as well as the drama, in the evil that can visit some people's lives.

Russ knows some of Betsy's family and others still want to believe he is guilty, and he regrets that they can't accept his innocence.

His time in prison is a distant memory. He doesn't remember dreams, but he is sometimes aware when he wakes up that he has had a bad one. He can feel it in his guts. And Carol McAfee always knows when he is in the midst of a bad one. She sometimes will even talk to him while he is asleep to try to help him get past it.

Russ focuses on his Christian faith and believes there is a reason he went through hell for so many years. His religious mother taught him that as he was growing up, and he still believes it. He remembers her saying that bad things can happen to anyone, and they can make you bitter or better.

Russ Faria chooses to be better.

Authors' Note

Nearly all of the dialogue and conversation among sources in this book are taken verbatim from court transcripts, deposition transcripts, and video and/or audio recordings of police or attorney interviews. The remaining dialogue and conversations are presented as closely to verbatim as participants could provide.

Acknowledgments

Telling this incredible story in depth and in truth would not have been possible without the gracious assistance of a great many people. That especially applies, of course, to Russ Faria, whose strength and courage made this story worth telling as a cautionary tale that drives deep into the heart of the American justice system. Russ's grace and power under some of the worst circumstances anyone can imagine are the foundation on which this book is built and on which it stands. And his unfailing confidence in coauthor Joel Schwartz as his defense attorney through all of the setbacks and challenges was a humbling, touching, and inspiring honor.

At the top of the list of those the authors must thank is Mary Anderson, whose ferocity in defense of Russ Faria is matched only by her dedication to getting justice for everyone involved in this case—on both sides of the law.

Special recognition must go to Carol McAfee, the woman whose exceptional courage helped find a major piece of the Pam Hupp murder puzzle and who now completes a special picture of the life of Russ Faria.

We also want to give special thanks to the other half of the legal defense team—Nathan Swanson—whose expert lawyering was supported by an encyclopedic memory of the facts and fictions in the case—and who is equipped with a remarkably valuable and famously off-beat sense of humor.

Joel Schwartz affectionately acknowledges the special and invaluable support from his wife, Mary Ann Schwartz, an accomplished criminal defense attorney in her own right, who provided an incomparable sounding board and offered valuable suggestions on how to deal with the specific challenges of judicial ineptitude and police corruption that threatened the pursuit of justice in this case.

The list of people and organizations that generously lent their assistance and expertise is long and impressive. The authors are indebted to the man who pushed for justice for Betsy Faria after ten long years, Lincoln County prosecuting attorney Mike Wood, as well as the current Lincoln County Sheriff's Office and Sheriff Richard "Rick" Harrell. Our thanks and appreciation also go to the O'Fallon Police Department and especially Detective Kevin Mountain for his tireless assistance and guidance; the St. Charles County Sheriff's Department and the St. Charles City Police Department; the St. Louis County Police Department; the Metropolitan Major Case Squad of Greater St. Louis; and attorneys David Butsch and Andrew Beeny. Special thanks also go to St. Charles County prosecuting attorney Tim Lohmar.

Our gratitude also goes to investigative reporter Chris Hayes of FOX 2 in St. Louis, whose recognition of raw injustice drove his relentless pursuit of the facts that could have stayed hidden without his ability to get the story and get it on the air. He is joined in uncovering and reporting that story by Robert Patrick of the *St. Louis Post-Dispatch*. And special gratitude and appreciation go to Cathy Singer, the unrelenting producer of *Dateline*, and the incomparable reporter and storyteller, Keith Morrison.

There are others who contributed valuable information and insight who prefer to remain unnamed. The authors recognize a deep debt of gratitude to them as well.

And finally, the authors extend their thanks and gratitude to our excellent editor, Michaela Hamilton, and her team at Kensington Publishing for their work in turning our manuscript into the book you hold in your hands. We appreciate their continuing efforts to bring this story to life and to readers.

About the Authors

CHARLES BOSWORTH JR. is a *New York Times* and Amazon bestselling author of six true-crime books, with millions of books in print, as ebooks, and audiobooks. He developed an expertise in writing about crime and the courts in twenty-seven years as a daily newspaper reporter, including twenty years with the *St. Louis Post-Dispatch*. He also has reported for the *New York Times* and the *Chicago Tribune*. He spent years in corporate communications with a number of global companies and a leading St. Louis law firm, and as a vice president for one of the world's leading PR and communications agencies. He lives in Southwestern Illinois in the metro St. Louis area.

JOEL J. SCHWARTZ has spent thirty years as a criminal defense lawyer in the St. Louis region as a principal in Rosenblum, Schwartz & Fry, one of the area's leading law firms. He has handled nearly every type of criminal case in state and federal circuit courts and appellate courts in Missouri, Illinois, Michigan, and Iowa, and has represented clients in California, Colorado, Texas, Arizona, and Nebraska. His recognized expertise in criminal law also has led him to serve as a lecturer at legal educational |institutions and a legal commentator for a number of news organizations. He earned his law degree from the University of Texas School of Law. He has been selected to the annual Super Lawyers list seven times in recent years, is a member of the Top 100 Trial Lawyers for the American Trial Lawyers Association, and is a lifetime member of the National Association of Criminal Defense Lawyers. He lives in the metro St. Louis area.